YOU, ON PAPER
EXPERT HELP ON HOW TO WRITE A RESUME

Greg Fall

Also the author of *Job Search Rescue: 101 Strategies on How to Get Unstuck*

Core Choices Publishing

You, On Paper: Expert Help on How to Write a Resume

Copyright © 2014 by Greg Fall

All rights reserved. Without prior written permission of the author, absolutely no part of this book may be copied, reproduced, stored electronically in a database or retrieval system, recorded, transmitted, or distributed in form via any means.

The publisher and author, while using best efforts, make no representations or warrantees as to the accuracy or thoroughness of this book and disclaim any implied warrantees. No warrantee may be created by sales agents. The counsel and advice contained in this book may not apply or be suitable to your situation. Neither the publisher nor the author shall be liable for any profit, loss, or commercial damages whether incidental, consequential, or other.

All resumes and other supporting materials have either been created by the author or have been freely allowed by others. All names utilized in this book on the sample resumes and other documents or in the context of illustrating learning points have been manufactured by the author and do not represent actual individuals. All illustrations, stories, and examples in the book are the creation of the author from many thousands of observations over 15+ years of career work and, again, do not specifically represent actual individuals.

Core Choices Publishing

ISBN 978-0-9960988-0-9

Fall, Greg
    You, on paper: expert help on how to write a resume / Greg Fall
    Includes index
    ISBN: 978-0-9960988-0-9
    1. Authorship. 2. Resume Writing. 3. Job Hunting.

Sincere appreciation…

For the thousands of clients who have been my teachers.

For each job seeker who just wants to get past all the hiring fuss and get down to work, growing professionally and adding value to their next employer.

For each person who contributed to the effort of getting this book in the hands of those who need it – whether by contributing sample resumes and other material, offering your perspectives, or getting the word out.

For Katy Harkleroad, a talented proofreader, editor, and artist, who increased the usability of my jungly writing.

For David Lee, a trusted colleague and friend, who provided encouragement and guidance in getting my ideas to those who will most benefit.

For all the teachers who inspired confidence and built my competence, including Karen, Mike, Will, Zark, and Jack.

For the family, friends, and colleagues who gave me support and unconditional positive regard during the writing process, including Gretchen, Bill, Amy, Carl, Lilly, Cynthia, Roy, Joy, Earl, Alice, Willy, Seymour, Sandy, Jim, John, Rhys, Coach Bru, and Mike.

For dad, an unparalleled worker and manager, who gave me a strong foundation in the world of work.

And, most of all…

For mom, my greatest teacher and mentor, who still guides me to help others, to be positive and empathetic, to forgive easily, to be grateful, and to live in the light.

Table of Contents

Preface ... ix
Suggestions for Book Use ... xii

Part 1: Organize

Chapter 1: You, On Paper ... 3

Resume Phobia ... 8
Authenticity and Credibility ... 11
"You" in the Resume ... 13

Chapter 2: Self-Assessment ... 15

Professional Values ... 17
Strengths ... 18
Successes and Failures ... 19
Personality-Related Behaviors ... 20
Transferrable Skills ... 24
Technical Abilities and Skills ... 28
Career Transition Goals ... 32

Chapter 3: Professional Branding ... 39

Branding FAQ ... 41
You Already Have a Brand ... 45
Professional Branding Exercise ... 49
Alternative Approaches to Define Your Brand ... 54
Consistency is Critical to Credibility ... 57

Part 2: Write

Chapter 4: Resume Rules ... 63

Top Resume Truths ... 65
Top Resume Myths ... 67
No-Nos ... 71
Formatting and Organizing Guidelines ... 73
Top Writing Priorities ... 76

Chapter 5: Writing by Section ... 81

Writing by Section ... 83
Information Bank ... 85

Chapter 6:	**Writing: Heading**	**87**
Chapter 7:	**Writing: Profile**	**93**
	Adding a Title	*97*
Chapter 8:	**Writing: Technical Skills**	**103**
	Including a Technical Skills Section	*104*
Chapter 9:	**Writing: Experience**	**109**
	How Far Back Should You Go?	*110*
	Company Title	*111*
	Position or Job Title	*112*
	Company or Position Descriptions	*115*
Chapter 10:	**Writing: Bullets**	**119**
	Review of Sample Bullets	*121*
	Uncovering Accomplishments	*124*
	Action Verbs	*128*
	Guerilla Tactics for Writing Bullets	*130*
Chapter 11:	**Writing: Education**	**133**
	Abbreviating the Type of Degree	*136*
	Partially Completed Degrees	*139*
	GPA	*141*
Chapter 12:	**Writing: Extra Sections**	**147**
	Training	*148*
	Military Service	*152*
	Community or Volunteer Activities	*154*
	Combining Sections	*156*
Chapter 13:	**Gaps in Employment**	**161**
	Years Matter, Months Don't	*162*
	Gap Fillers	*165*
Chapter 14:	**Other Considerations**	**169**
	Employment Agencies	*170*
	Hard Skills	*171*
	If You Are Really Stuck	*173*
	Hiring a Resume Writer	*175*

Chapter 15: The "One Resume" — 181

Core Strengths = Brand Differentiators — 182
Pareto's Rule — 184
2 to 3 Core Strengths vs. 15+ Total Strengths — 185
Priority: Technical Skills — 187
What are YOUR Core Strengths? — 191

Chapter 16: Resume Supplements — 195

Portfolio — 199
Physical Work Samples — 200
Web-based Work Samples — 201
Letters of Reference — 202
Reference List — 205
"Targeted Reference List" Format — 208
Timing is Everything — 212

Part 3: Customize

Chapter 17: Customizing — 219

Results — 222
Skills — 223
Fit — 224
Research, Research, Research — 225
ATS/Applicant Tracking System — 229
Analyzing Job Advertisements — 230
Choosing Key Words and Phrases — 234

Chapter 18: "Core Hiring Motives" — 239

Identifying Core Hiring Motives — 240
Customizing Your "Core Strengths" — 243
Adding Core Hiring Motives from Scratch — 249
Uncovering "Hidden" Core Hiring Motives — 252

Chapter 19: Cover Letters — 257

The "Email Cover Letter" — 259
T-Style Cover Letter — 261
Bullet Style Cover Letter — 262
"News Article Cover Letter" — 263

Part 4: Market

Chapter 20: Using Your Resume — 271
- Alternative Resume Delivery Methods — 278
- When Not to Use a Resume — 280
- Business Cards — 284

Chapter 21: LinkedIn and Recruiters — 289
- Get the Word Out — 291
- Top 10 LinkedIn Startup Tips — 295
- Search Firms/Recruiters and Staffing Firms — 297

Chapter 22: Online Search — 305
- Employers Will Check You Out Online — 307
- Finding Job Openings — 308

Chapter 23: Power Networking — 313
- Daily Networking Goal — 316
- Organization/Tracking of Contacts — 319
- Networking Email with Resume Attached — 322
- What an Elevator Pitch Is and Is Not — 324
- Collaborating with Competitors — 329

Chapter 24: Interview Success — 335
- Five-Minute Phone Screen — 338
- In-Person Interview — 340
- Pre-Employment Testing — 344
- The Three Types of Questions — 348
- Core Hiring Motives — 351
- Turbo-Charge Your Examples — 353

Chapter 25: Confident Negotiating — 359
- Pre-Negotiations — 360
- 1-2-3 Negotiating — 361
- Post-Negotiations — 368

Appendix: Sample Resumes — 371

Selected Sources — 417

Index — 421

Preface

A resume will not get you a job.

A resume will not necessarily get you an interview.

So, "why do I need a resume, let alone one that I will spend hours upon hours creating?" you might ask. Good question.

You need an expertly crafted resume in your job search toolbox as a foundation to your efforts in executing what I maintain are the only 2 functions which matter in today's job search. To …

Get Noticed

and

Close the Deal

It has been my contention, for years now, that the fundamental changes in the employment marketplace which plague job seekers today were born not so much out of the Great Recession as they were out of the recession of 2001-2003 when the tech boom of the 1990s finally ended.

The *good* jobs have been scarce ever since.

By the time the NASDAQ tanked in March of 2000, the seeds of change had already been sowed. In the decade that followed, BIG changes happened to give employers much of the hiring power, which they may retain for years and years to come.

Among the many market changes that accelerated in the new millennium:

- globalization
- digital hiring processes
- rise in the number of college graduates (v. living-wage jobs)
- companies' focus on cost cutting and short-term profitability

Therefore, with a few exceptions related to changing technologies or suddenly booming industries, the supply side of the employment equation may not be moving much for many years into the future. In terms of the demand side, every year there are additional millions of well-educated and experienced candidates who are working more than one job just to pay the mortgage or their college loans – they are hungry and they are your competition.

Bottom line #1: With the increasing amount of digital "noise" in the networking and job search marketplace, the ease of companies to quickly search for and attract a strong pool of candidates, a limited supply of good opportunities, and competition from more well-educated and skilled professionals … you must **get noticed** by the hiring company. *You must make better resume choices to get noticed.*

Bottom line #2: After you get noticed by the hiring company and have navigated your way through the interview process, you will end up as one of 2 or 3 finalists. Each finalist offers the potential of an excellent fit with the company's requirements … you must **close the deal** to get the offer. *Your resume must be aligned with your interviewing strategy.*

You used to be able to get noticed and close the deal by scoring a grade of B+ or A- on your networking, resume, interviewing, and other job search fundamentals. But we are in an era of job seeker grade inflation.

You will need to score an A or A+ to get noticed and close the deal.

Therefore, while resumes do not hold all the power they once did, a compelling, "A" quality resume is critical to your job search campaign.

It has always been true:

There are no 2nd chances when it comes to 1st impressions.

The choices you make and the time you invest in resume writing and other job search activities are directly related to your chances of success. There are no "quick fixes."

This book offers you perspective from one accomplished resume writer and career coach. There are many ways to write a resume and there are many other resume experts. There are also pretenders who will just "pretty" up your resume without adding value. I encourage you to avail yourself of multiple expert resources for your situation.

This book is a guide: take what is useful to you and discard the rest.

Throughout the process, *remain true to yourself/be authentic*. Resumes are marketing tools intended to grab a reader's interest and hold it long enough for them to take a second look. At no time should a resume misrepresent you as a candidate or mischaracterize you as a person – companies want to hire real people to solve real problems.

Honor yourself by taking action – all you can do is to try your best. Try, stumble, and learn…but keep trying! Writing a resume is a unique, individualized process: own it and commit to excellence.

Kind Regards and Best Wishes,

Greg

Suggestions for Book Use

What this book "is" and "is not"

What should you expect?

This book focuses on helping you understand how to craft a high quality resume in order to maximize your chances of getting noticed and to prepare you for a productive, targeted interview in the private sector. You will need to combine your resume with active networking and other job search activities to secure an interview. While this book does contain some useful tips on networking, interviewing, negotiating, and other areas, it is not intended to be a comprehensive guide to those areas.

Although I do touch on a couple of other specialty hiring processes and their corresponding resume requirements, this book is not focused on helping you develop a specialized resume such as a CV or Federal resume. You will need to access specialty resources for those efforts.

My Direct, Conversational Writing Style

My style of writing might be described as detailed, direct, conversational, and sometimes a bit provocative. Please know that my sincere wish is to positively impact your employment situation. The book's hard-hitting undertone is meant to get your attention and challenge you to produce only a top quality product, for the external world can be quite unforgiving.

Whether you like my writing style or not, please know that I keep this perspective in the forefront of my thinking at all times: *No one can walk in your shoes.* However, reading this book might allow me to offer some assistance in your journey.

Resume and Job Search Tips

Throughout the book, there are a few boxes containing two types of recommendations or tips.

They look like this:

> **Resume Tip**
> Tactical tips offering specific advice for taking action related to your resume. These are intended to highlight important steps for you to take in order to maximize the resume's effectiveness.

> **Job Search Tip**
> Concepts and specific counsel about a wide variety of career transition and job search subjects. They may be either strategic or tactical in nature; you might find your own unique ways of relating to and using them!

Hands-on, How-to Guide

This book is intended to be a very detailed "how-to" volume.

There are a few exercises in the book for you to complete, especially when it comes to self-assessment of various skills and abilities. There are also calls-to-action, in which I strongly suggest you move forward with specific tasks after or during reading a section. Utilize this book in whatever way is most useful to you and keep it on a nearby shelf for quick reference during your career transition process.

Sample Resume Resources

Given the high number of available books and web resources that offer examples of different styles of resumes, this book instead focuses on writing and using your resume. Although nearly 30 resume samples can be found in the appendix and also throughout the book, I would recommend investing in a resume sample book for additional style and formatting ideas.

You might look for a companion book that relates to a specific area of interest. Wendy Enlow and Louise Kursmark offer such sample books—I often refer to their *Expert Resumes for Military to Civilian Transitions* book when I teach TAPs (Transition Assistance Program) classes for retiring and separating members of the US military.

Federal Resume Resources

This book will help you write a private sector resume. Federal resumes are different. A 2 page private sector resume would have to be reformatted and might be expanded into 3-5+ pages for a Federal position! I suggest you acquire a companion book for more information.

Kathryn Troutman, who has written *Ten Steps to a Federal Job* and *Federal Resume Guidebook*, is one of the foremost experts on writing Federal Resumes and I often recommend her materials to clients, as well.

Your Choice …

You will only succeed if you make decisions and take action. As stated, some of my favorite additional resources are referred to and listed in the back of this book. Just know that once you have all the data on a subject, the key is to: *make and act on your own choices*.

You are accountable to you.

Scan First, Read Key Parts, Refer Back

This is not a novel. Although there is a certain benefit to understanding the often-interrelated concepts, you are encouraged to use it as a reference book—*use the parts which make sense to your particular situation.*

To that end, I would recommend …

1. **Scan First**: Take an hour or two and scan the book, noting those parts that might be especially useful. You might fold over the corners of pages, use a highlighter, write up a one-page sheet of important points, place sticky-notes on pages, or even rip out pages to tape on your bulletin board if you wish! Hint: instead of ripping out pages, simply use your phone to take a picture of key pages, email to yourself, and print for quick reference!

2. **Read Key Parts**: If you already have your brand identified, skip the branding section! If you don't like my take on the "One Resume," use the pages for kindling! Following your scan and identification of the key parts most useful for your particular situation, invest some time in reading and outlining for greater understanding. It will pay off later when you're tired of the whole writing process and run the risk forgetting critical information.

3. **Refer Back**: Keep the book (or what's left of it!) handy as you go about your writing. Since I have included some foundational stuff in these pages, many of the tips and concepts will have some value for years to come so keep the book in a safe place for future revisions and use.

4. **Ask for Help**: There are times when we all need help. Don't be afraid to ask for it. Choose to reach out and enlist the support of others, whether you need feedback, don't understand a concept, want someone to bounce ideas off of, just need a supportive hug, or want an "accountability buddy" to help keep you on track.

Part 1: Organize

Chapter 1

You, On Paper

> *"You never get a second chance to make a first impression."*
> — Oscar Wilde

7 seconds.

That is how long it takes a hiring manager to form an opinion about your resume...*if* he or she actually decides to look at your resume. Your resume will then either be placed in the circular file or in another pile for further consideration.

You have no margin for error.

But, you do have a choice of how your resume is going to look.

Companies today have constant access to tens of millions of potential candidates through resume databases. Yet, very few resumes are well written and present a clear and compelling message. Here is your chance to stand out from the crowd. Consider the "Before" and "After" examples on the next few pages.

"Before"

Sara S. Sample, CPA

23 Laramore St., Apt. 1, Anytown, VA
000-000-0000, ssample@qqqemail.com

<u>Chief Financial Officer</u>

Objective

Senior CFO seeking top accounting management position or lead accountant for smaller, growing firm. Experienced in cost accounting and computer systems, with record of improving efficiencies and bottom line profitability, as well as cash flow. Responsible for risk management initiatives. Strengths:

Budgeting/Forecasting	Hyperion	Vendor Mgmt.	Conversions
G/L and Reconciliation	Team Leadership	Monthly Reports	Research
Cash Management	Cost Accounting	JD Edwards	Audits
IPO Experience	Contracts	International Tax	Bank Relationships

Experience

January, 2012 – June, 2014 CFO at *NBG Company*
- Involved with saving company significant funds on cost conversion. **Recognized by President** for leading all employees in effort
- Strong support for senior management team with IPO spin off
- **Re-wrote company protocol** for bidding on contracts, reducing bottlenecks
- **Traveled to Mexico** twice for 3 days and then 2 days to set up books for Mexican subsidiary, including all international taxes

May, 2004 – January, 2012 Controller / Accounting Manager at *NBG Company*
- Responsible for finances for 3 divisions' operating plans, annual forecasting and reporting, and daily flash reporting. Focused on **improving operating income** by a substantial amount over a two year period through primarily costing efforts
- Won Division's coveted **Excellence in Management Award**, including trip to US Virgin Islands, by **increasing cash flow**
- Supported purchasing in leading negotiations for improved cost savings

November, 1999 – February, 2004 Cost Accountant at *XDV Company*
- Identified costs for raw material and personnel, making recommendations which **saved the company at least $5,000 per month**
- Research into market fluctuations impacting net margins of existing lines and potential impact on NPI. Served on 7 person project committee to **analyze market problems and create recommendations**, with specific attention to new products

Education

CCV College – Bachelor of Science in Business Administration, 3.2 GPA, Anytown, IL, 1992-1995
BCQ Community College – Associates in Accounting, 3.5 GPA, Anytown, IL, 1989-1991
CPA in Virginia (originally passed exam in Illinois)

Community Activities

Membership Directorship of the AICPA, DC and Treasurer of the NVREDC, Virginia
Wednesday Night Toasters Club Chairperson, BNG Church, Anytown, VA
Soccer Travel League Coordinating Parent, U12 Boys, 2009-2011, Anycounty, VA
(Set up league schedule for 38 teams and officiated at 2 road games per week over 5 months)

References Available Upon Request

"After"

SARA S. SAMPLE, CPA
23 LARAMORE STREET
ANYTOWN, VA 00000

000.000.0000
SSAMPLE@QQQEMAIL.COM
WWW.LINKEDIN/IN/SSAMPLE

Leadership of both finance and accounting functions with background in manufacturing and public accounting. Proven problem solving and analytical abilities. Expertise in Excel, JD Edwards, Hyperion, and other software tools. Team approach prioritizes integration across departments and maximizes impact of cost control. Direct style balanced by compassion, humility, and fairness. Core strengths:

BUDGETING/FORECASTING
Delivers accurate forecasts and budgets based on customized systems that analyze organization-wide data and align with market events. Financial statement preparation and reporting integrated with up-to-date forecasting to allow for monthly review by senior management and stakeholders.

COST ACCOUNTING
Develops close working relationships at all levels to leverage expertise in cost control and reporting. Automates systems and analyzes data to realize savings and improve accountability.

CASH MANAGEMENT
Leads creation of detailed, automatic revenue and expense tracking systems as foundation to effective cash management, even in difficult situations. Maintains credit and vendor relationships in tight cash flow situations while incorporating "no risk" cost reduction strategies.

EXPERIENCE

NBG COMPANY, Anytown, VA   2004 - 2014

CFO
Delivered financial leadership and hands-on management at $28M private manufacturer of Z-tubes.

- Led conversion to new cost system with improved accountabilities, resulting in $5K quarterly savings and improved profitability on major account sales of $100K+. Involved employees to create ownership of changes and develop positive cross-functional working relationships.
- Led negotiation of new carrier contracts, saving $128K over 2-year period.
- Directed preparation of all related financial documents and met regulatory requirements for $8M spin off with IPO. Created deferred compensation and incentive plans for executive team.
- Determined market valuation of spin-off to 95% accuracy, ensuring integrity of business plan.
- Spearheaded re-write of organization's protocol for bidding on multi-million dollar contracts, resulting in smoother process and 30% increase in number of bids submitted each month.
- Organized all financial systems for Mexican subsidiary, completing tax returns for 1st year and incorporating transfer pricing model. Teamed with Mexican peers for smooth implementation.

Controller / Accounting Manager
Managed finances for 3 divisions totaling $21M in revenue. Responsible for leadership of process improvements, operating plans, forecasts, reporting functions, financial statements, and daily flash reporting.

- Improved DSC's growth in operating income from 5.3% in 2005 to 9.2% in 2007 by updating standard cost system, analyzing trends, and recommending efficiency strategies.
- Enhanced cash flow by $800K average per quarter by consolidating and renegotiating long-term debt, contracting out facility services, and implementing automatic tracking systems for revenue and expenses. Changes afforded senior management increased flexibility.
- Led renegotiation of 3 primary vendor relationships, without sacrificing "loyalty factor," to average of 5% or $215K annual savings. Developed team approach to vendor management.

SARA S. SAMPLE, CPA

XDV COMPANY, Anytown, MD 1999 - 2004
Cost Accountant
Managed cost functions for $51M manufacturer of lab cabinets used in immaculate atmospheres.

- Identified actual production costs for both material and labor, correlating recommendations for savings with monthly output targets. Recommendations implemented saved between $5K and $8K per month over 3- year period.

- Reduced scrap by 86%, utilizing lean concepts, for average $28K+ in annual savings. Initiated idea of "efficiency committees" for each department, which eventually led to consolidation of lines and outsourcing of non-essential functions, resulting in additional savings.

- Researched and reported on market fluctuations impacting net margins of existing lines and potential impact on NPI efforts. Served on 7-person cross-functional team to develop strategies for addressing problems.

HGR, BMN, AND ASSOCIATES, CPAs, Anytown, MD 1996 - 1999
Senior Accountant
Led audits and reviews of 49 profit and not-for-profit entities with revenues of up to $15M. Prepared work papers, financial statements, and tax returns. Completed 240+ individual tax returns per year.

VVN CORPORATION, Anytown, IL 1995 - 1996
Junior Accountant
Maintained G/L, prepared monthly financials, projected cash flow, and reconciled bank statements.

EDUCATION

BS Business Administration, CCV College, Anytown, IL

AS Accounting, BCQ Community College, Anytown, IL

CERTIFICATION

Certified Public Accountant, License #000000000, Virginia

PROFESSIONAL AFFILIATIONS

Membership Director, Greater DC Chapter of the AICPA, 2010-2014

Member, Confederation of International Tax Practitioners, 2009-2014

Treasurer, Northern Virginia Regional Economic Development Group, 2009-2013

Quality...They Will Know It When They See It

Could you tell the quality difference? If not, no worries. There are many finer points. That's why you bought this book! I'll help you get there.

Of course, there are many different ways to format and write a resume. Even accomplished professional resume writers, while agreeing on many foundational tenets, have their own preferences. I have mine. Rest assured, we will thoroughly examine the specifics. We will refer back to the examples on the previous pages to assist with your learning. For now, though, here are just a few of the important advantages the "After" resume offers:

- It is well organized and professional looking, yet doesn't pigeonhole the candidate into being considered for only CFO jobs.
- The candidate's name is subdued so that it does not compete with important content.
- There are just three core strengths clearly stated up front, with some detail following should the reader care to know more. The "Before" version lists 16 strengths … can you remember all those?
- Bullets begin with deliberately selected action verbs and tie into accomplishments and numbers/quantification when possible.
- Two-page length conveys experience/substance. Other resumes may require only one page, but not this candidate's.
- There is balance between the three core strengths that stand out during a quick first scan and the well-developed, content-rich bullets to inform an interested reader on a second read (Note that the left and right margins would allow more "white space" in full size version; on these I chose not to reduce the font size further).
- Focus is on experience, with no "Community Activities" section, "References available upon request" or other distractions.

Did this quick "Before-and-After" start to challenge some of your pre-conceived notions about resumes? Do I have your attention?

Resume Phobia

Scared yet?

You are not alone.

Why are the majority of my clients initially apprehensive or even downright terrified of writing their resume? The reasons vary.

Here are a few of them that I've heard:

> "I find it intimidating. I can create a dynamite presentation for c-suite executives but when it comes to touting my own horn in print, I just freeze."

> "Forget about it. No way I'm gonna create a piece of junk for others to laugh at. No way. I never needed one anyway—I'm just an equipment operator."

> "It's intimidating. I don't know where to begin and, even if I did, I refuse to embellish my experience to get hired. Plus, I didn't even finish my degree."

> "It is embarrassing that I'm a CPA who can't write."

While I have seen a few exceptions to the rule over the past 15 years, most of us need an effective resume as part of the networking and application process. It's time to confront your fear by marshaling resources and putting pen to paper. If you don't choose to confront your resume anxiety, you will instead confront a harsh market reality:

Without a best-in-class resume, all your hard work at networking and applying for jobs is likely to go unnoticed.

Whether you create it yourself or engage an accomplished resume writer to help with your process, you cannot afford to present anything less than your best on paper.

Overcoming Resume Phobia

To overcome any fears you may have about writing a resume, you must choose to *identify* and *address* your barriers. How you do this is up to you, but this must be 1st on the getting-organized agenda.

Here are a few questions you might ask yourself to help the process along when you come up against a barrier:

- Why can't I get started? Why can't I continue? What do I fear?
- What could I do differently? How could I think differently?
- What if I chose to be right-minded/positive instead of negative?
- If I fail, what will that look like and how will I respond? Will I bounce back somehow? If so, what have I to fear?
- Are others "feeding into" my anxiety?
- Is my frustration healthy for me? For my family?
- Could I go to the library or another place to help myself focus?
- Do I celebrate my successes? Even if it just writing a few lines?
- What are resources for both resume writing and dealing with anxiety? Do I hire a resume writer (hint: if they are any good, you will still be writing a lot yourself … we'll discuss how you might explore this option in a later chapter).
- When I am anxious about other things in life, how do I prevail/overcome barriers? Could I borrow a lesson from those times?

Identify Barriers

Choose to identify barriers early. Whether fears, physical limitations, time constraints, or other obstacles, simply being honest in identifying barriers will diminish their power.

Tools, Time, and Space

Part of getting organized is having the right tools and the right space. Try to think of all the ways to make your life easier such as:

Raw Material: Have your writing ammunition together in one place. Collect items such as: old resumes, performance reviews, letters of recommendation, personality or other test results, and training lists.

Scheduled Time: You don't have to follow it strictly, but you need to block off some time slots in the calendar.

Scheduled Time Off: The breaks need to be frequent. Get up and walk around at least five out of every 30 minutes or 10 out of every 60 minutes— your brain will thank you...and the result will be a much better product.

MS Word (or equivalent): I don't get kick-backs from Bill Gates but his program is the one you want. Too expensive? Try Apache open office— available on www.sourceforge.net. With nearly one million downloads a week, it might be the next best thing.

Portable Office: A backpack loaded with manila folders, pens, paper, highlighters, sticky notes, healthy snacks, packet of tissues, bottle of water, etc. should do the trick. The house may work most days but you need to be ready to transition easily to the beach or to the library for a change of scenery...and fewer distractions!

Team You: You will need friends who will put up with you venting your frustrations, and a few others who can help proofread or provide honest critique.

Family/Roommate Expectations: These folks need to know and respect your requirements for quiet and alone time—be clear with them.

Your Expectations: Expect your best effort. Nothing more and nothing less. Some days your best effort will yield glorious results. Some days your best effort will yield crap. Get over it. Just focus on effort. And get to it...you are going to do just fine!

Web Access: Whether looking for a better online Thesaurus, resume samples, or lists of action verbs, you need easy access to the web.

Authenticity <u>and</u> Credibility

Arguably, this is the most important concept in resume writing and in job search.

We have to spend some time with this one, now and in later chapters.

All too often, these two concepts are found opposing one another, as in:

Authenticity vs. Credibility

Indeed, you will naturally be pulled in one direction or the other. But here, need for balance has to prevail…you must have <u>both authenticity AND credibility</u> for the resume to be compelling and work correctly. So, what exactly do each of these mean? Well, here are my thoughts:

Authentic = the inner self; *being true to yourself*; "personal" you; how you naturally behave; who you prefer to be at home.

Credible = the outer self; *believable to others*; "professional" you; how you might intentionally behave in a work setting.

Do you see the dilemma?

Many candidates think they must shelve their authenticity and go 100% with credibility—just sell, sell, sell. They may get hired, but after a couple weeks on the job—when their authentic self emerges—the hiring manager who made the job offer will scratch his or her head and ask: "Who is this person?" And the feeling will be mutual. Those candidates will either return to job searching or be less effective in their work.

On the other hand, if you just let it all hang out and behave the way you do around friends, you may never interview or receive an offer.

Employers want you to be BOTH authentic and credible.

> ### *Credibility AND Authenticity*
> You must be both <u>authentic</u> AND <u>credible</u> in the resume and in your job search activities to become a final candidate.

The resume has to both market you AND present the real you. While a resume will always be more geared to boosting your credibility, the resume's words must fit with you as a person.

So, how do you put your authentic self in a resume?

<u>Think about *how* you prefer to perform your work when others around you are supportive of your authentic self.</u>

It is that easy.

Let's examine the "After" resume from just a few pages ago.

Assuming this candidate is being honest about *how* he/she naturally goes about his/her work, we can look in the first paragraph. It says: "Direct style balanced by compassion, humility, and fairness." Additionally, two themes of *how* the candidate practices his/her professional craft seem to dominate the first page:

Leadership: Derivations of the word "lead" appear nine times on the first page. "Leadership" is the first word in the opening profile paragraph, "led" begins three of the nine bullets, and it also appears in both italicized overviews for the CFO and Controller positions.

Team Orientation: On the first page, the reader is presented with: "team approach integrates efforts," "develops close working relationships at all levels," "involved employees to create ownership," "teamed with Mexican peers," and "developed team approach."

> **Put "You" in the Resume**
>
> Choose to present the authentic you. Just make sure you do so in the context of the work environment. Choosing to be real will make you a more compelling candidate.

Although we are focused on the resume, many of you may wonder how this authenticity thing plays out in an interview. Because this is an über-important concept for job searches I'll go on just a brief detour…

While the resume is about *marketing*, the interview is about *selling*.

Therefore, when you hear the advice "just be yourself," it <u>does not mean</u> you should be completely relaxed, casual, wear your flip-flops, or tell them about crazy Aunt Eunice (we all have one). It <u>does mean</u> you should be professional and assertive but also personable, you should not try to over-sell or over-convince, you should ask questions that are truly important to you, and you should speak honestly about *how* you will be able to take away their pain (or prevent it from happening) in your unique way.

Talk about who you are as a person, *how* you prefer to go about your work, what your values are, what positive personality characteristics you hold, *how* you develop effective working relationships with others, and why you think you will fit in the position and with the organization.

In resume writing, interviewing, and in all aspects of the job search process, it is important to be in the mindset of conveying *who* you really are and *how* you go about adding value when you are working. Even if two candidates have exactly the same skill sets, each candidate will have their own distinct ways of applying those same skill sets.

<u>Don't be afraid to stand out for who you really are.</u>

Chapter 2

Self-Assessment

"know thyself"
        - Inscribed in the Forecourt at the Temple of Apollo at Delphi

Bummer. Just when you were ready to write.

Instead, you have to stop and take an inventory of your values, strengths, notable successes, notable failures, personality-related behaviors, transferrable skills, technical abilities and skills, and career transition goals. You may choose to take additional assessments, such as an MBTI, DISC, or EQi. But, at a minimum, complete this inventory, which spans both the internal, authentic self and the external, credible self. Please do it now. Do you really have to? Yup. You really have to.

In the next chapter we'll move on to branding. But, in order to tease out the essence of your brand, you need to first identify the many aspects of the brand's foundation via self-assessment. Onward!

The Importance of Periodic Self-Assessment

You may have held similar core beliefs and personality traits over the past 30 years. But you have undergone many other changes related to your professional life. Like it or not, the digital age has forced us to adapt.

Even if you have held a similar position for 20 – 30+ years, there would probably be significant changes in your skill set, your abilities, perhaps even in how you approach the job. For instance, a design engineer trained in the 70s and 80s might have been using a slide rule back then. In the 90s and 2000s, the slide rule was replaced by 2-D CADD computer programs. Finally, 2-D was replaced by 3-D or solid modeling software. If the design engineer highlights their slide rule experience on the resume it would be game over. Not only does no one care about obsolete skills, but highlighting these skills will make the job seeker seem outdated as well. Today, that design engineer will be highlighting up-to-date software skills in order to get noticed. But there's more…

Over time, the design engineer's soft skill set has had to shift and develop as well. As their employers have become more team oriented and matrixed, so too has the design engineer had to develop their skills around teamwork, wearing multiple hats, and reporting cross-functionally. The design engineer probably behaves the same or similar at home as they always have. But their working style and strengths have evolved with the market in order for them to remain effective in their job.

Without conducting a quick self-assessment now and then, you would be stuck focusing on the outdated you. It would be like trying to sell a flip phone to someone looking for the newest iPhone. You may love flip phones, but unless you update what you're selling, you won't find a buyer in the iPhone market.

Professional Values

Values, unlike morals, may shift over time, depending on your needs. Knowing your work values—that is, what is important to you in your job—will increase your chances for both cultural fit and job satisfaction.

Take a moment and list your top 3 work values using the list below (or come up with your own if not on the list).

Top Work Value: _____

Top Work Value: _____

Top Work Value: _____

Independence	Supervision	Optimism
Teamwork	Entrepreneurism	Originality
Competitiveness	Community Support	Perfection
Routine	Part-Time Work	Sincerity
Integrity and Honesty	Achievement	Accuracy
Focus on Quality	Promotion	Discipline
Fast-Paced Environment	Expert Knowledge	Calmness
Salary/Pay	Learning New Skills	Growth
Health Benefits	Organization	Charity
Flexible Hours	Creativity	Completion
Job Security	Family	Humor
Recognition	Kindness	Courage
Helping Others	Respect	Adventure
Teaching/Training	Change	Determination
Decision Authority	Global Impact	Local Impact
Power or Influence	Challenges	Awards
Physical Work	Friendship	Balance
Professionalism	Problem Solving	Focus on goals

Strengths

Strengths can relate to personality/attitudes, specific skills, and abilities. They can be both natural and learned/developed. Strengths are critical to demonstrate on a resume.

Take a moment and list your top 3 strengths using the list below (or come up with your own if not on the list).

Top Strength: _____

Top Strength: _____

Top Strength: _____

Organization	Good Under Pressure	Reliability
Planned	Crisis Management	Confidence
Leadership	Problem Solving	Quick Learning
Management	Flexibility	Can-do Attitude
Supervision	Versatility	Compassion
Coordination	Technical Expertise	Solving for the Root
Project Management	Visionary	Languages
Idea Generation	Listening	Procedural Knowledge
Follow-through	Executive Presence	Positive Energy
Relationship Building	Mentoring	Critical Thinking
Marketing	Coaching	Emotional Intelligence
Selling	Training	Meeting Deadlines
Writing	Consulting	Leading Change
Ethical	Road Warrior	Global Thinking
Process Improvement	Results-Focused	Public Speaking
Prioritizing	Influencing	Presenting
Analyzing	Research	Following Directions
Resolving Conflict	Customer Orientation	Resiliency

Notable Career Successes and Failures

Identifying notable successes and failures will help you hone in on your strengths and your limitations. After jotting down a couple words to describe each, notice WHY you chose these (Was a success notable because others recognized it or because it was a personal accomplishment? Was a failure notable because it was on a large scale or maybe because you were never able to fix it?). What does each choice tell you? What can you learn here? Are there clues about which skills and abilities to highlight on the resume and which limitations to omit?

Notable Success #1

Notable Success #2

Notable Failure #1

Notable Failure #2

Personality-Related Behaviors

Our personality preferences are largely set by the time we reach 18-22 years old. There are many areas of preference, which are often referred to as dichotomies or opposites in various personality inventories. For instance: some individuals are more social while others are more private, some individuals are more planned while others like to live life as it comes, and some individuals are more cerebral while others are more oriented toward their feeling side. There are no right or wrong personality preferences, but there can be distinct differences between individuals as well as seeming inconsistencies within the same person.

For each individual, some preferences may be stronger and others more moderate. A very strong preference allows greater strength in that area, along with the opposing weakness. For example, a very outgoing person might be a strong public speaker but may also struggle with being a good listener. A more moderate preference means the strength will not be as pronounced, but neither will the weakness. Again, there is no correct level of strength for a preference – it just is what it is.

If you wish to go beyond the inventory on the next several pages and take a more in-depth personality assessment for greater self-examination, I would recommend you consider these: MBTI Step II (Myers-Briggs Step 2), DISC, and Strong (RIASEC). If administered by a qualified professional, each might cost you in the $125-175 range. Of course, there are a multitude of free versions online, but most are not that accurate. However, if you want to just get a sense of these by taking a free version of each, the website www.123test.com has them available under different titles. In addition, <u>one of the best books on **choosing a career to fit your personality**</u> is *Do What You Are* by Paul Tieger and Barbara Barron.

For our purposes, the following pages will examine personality in the workplace, as manifested by preferred behaviors.

Personality-Related Behaviors Inventory

When completing the inventory, please consider how you would prefer to be MOST of the time when at work. The inventory is comprised of 30 word/word group choices. **Step I**: Please hand-write your personality preferences in the box to the right of each word pairing. **Step II**: When you have made all 32 choices, scan down the hand-written list. Choose 14 of these words/word groups that BEST describe you when at work. Write the 14 final words/word groups in the boxes below, *adding any other positive words that strongly describe you at work.*

Step I (write your choice for each word pair on the line to the right)

Self-directed	v.	Compliant	
Individual Contributor	v.	Team Oriented	
Gets Results	v.	Concentrates on Processes	
Meets Deadlines	v.	Completes Tasks Early	
Lead	v.	Manage	
Analytical	v.	Compassionate	
Customer Oriented	v.	Product/Service Oriented	
Trusted	v.	Skilled	
Task Focused	v.	People Focused	
Detailed	v.	Conceptual	

Eager to Learn	v.	Steady Contributor	
Reliable	v.	Energetic	
Considerate	v.	Fair	
Competitive	v.	Collaborative	
Accomplished	v.	Expert	
Proven Work Ethic	v.	Seeks Growth Opportunities	
Takes Personal Responsibility	v.	Confident in Abilities	
Positive Attitude	v.	Consistent Performer	
Direct Communicator	v.	Proven Listener	
Fast Paced	v.	Quality Driven	
Takes Initiative	v.	Eager to do Assigned Work	
Motivated	v.	Dependable	
Engaged	v.	Committed	
Versatile	v.	Specializes	
Promotes Change	v.	Focuses on Efficiency	
Accommodates	v.	Compromises	
Flexible	v.	Organized	

Easy-going	v.	Professional	
Asks Questions	v.	Follows Directions	
Supports Efforts	v.	Coordinates Efforts	
Improves Processes	v.	Highly Productive	
Builds Trust Relationships	v.	Recognized for Expertise	

Step II (write the 14 best words from the 30 choices you made in Step I)

Transferrable Skills

Transferrable skills are skills that can be used in another job, whether it is a similar job or a very different one. They can be used on your resume in several ways: as action verbs to begin bullets, as keywords, and to describe your 2–3 core strengths (which we will discuss in a later chapter).

It is often useful to think of categories of transferrable skills. On the following pages, choose two categories to which you can most relate. Next, choose up to three transferrable skills from each of these two categories. Then, scan all categories and choose up to four additional skills. Finally, *write your choices on the lines below.* Don't feel constrained by the lists; it is OK to come up with your own!

Category # 1 Transferrable Skill: _____

Category # 1 Transferrable Skill: _____

Category # 1 Transferrable Skill: _____

Category # 2 Transferrable Skill: _____

Category # 2 Transferrable Skill: _____

Category # 2 Transferrable Skill: _____

Additional Transferrable Skill: _____

Additional Transferrable Skill: _____

Additional Transferrable Skill: _____

Additional Transferrable Skill: _____

Partial Lists of Transferrable Skills Arranged By Category

PHYSICAL/MECHANICAL	**RESEARCH/ANALYTICAL**	**OFFICE/BUSINESS**
Operate	Research	Manage
Control	Write	Coordinate
Drive	Investigate	Organize
Fabricate	Assess	Manage Projects
Test	Report	Meet Deadlines
Inspect	Process	Create Spreadsheets
Calibrate	Collect	Prepare Reports
Maintain	Classify	Calculate
Assemble	Catalog	Audit
Manufacture	Survey	Improve Processes
Make	Examine	Create Documents
Create	Study	Manage Budget
Construct	Interpret	Analyze/Control Costs
Build	Observe	Deliver Presentations
Overhaul	Monitor	Input Data
Install	Analyze	Direct
Engineer	Question	Plan
Review	Customer Oriented	Supervise
Produce	Scrutinize	Hire
Improvise	Sort	Administer
Repair/Fix	Probe	Delegate/Assign
Set up	Explore	Establish
Troubleshoot	Find	Reorganize
Clean	Search	Collaborate

Partial Lists of Transferrable Skills Arranged By Category

CREATE/DESIGN	**SALES/COMMUNICATION**	**HELPING/FACILITATING**
Create	Market	Help
Design	Sell	Facilitate
Develop Ideas	Negotiate	Train
Invent	Present	Serve Customers
Construct	Persuade	Teach
Craft	Influence	Coach
Imagine	Listen	Empathize
Compose	Edit	Mentor
Write	Communicate	Prepare
Experiment	Question	Enable
Adapt	Convince	Assist
Conceive	Author	Clarify
Test	Retail	Explain
Customize	Wholesale	Demonstrate
Formulate	Contract	Diagnose
Utilize Software	Discuss	Administer Treatment
Utilize Tools	Mediate	Counsel
Integrate	Inspire	Recommend
Brainstorm	Encourage	Explain
Illustrate	Guide	Promote Safety
Arrange	Motivate	Respect
Integrate	Speak	Show Compassion
Design for Manufacture	Promote	Advocate
Originate	Adapt	Instruct

Partial Lists of Transferrable Skills Arranged By Category

LEAD AND MANAGE	**PROBLEM SOLVING**	**TECHNOLOGY/TOOLS**
Lead	Research	Utilize
Inspire	Identify	Train
Develop a Vision	Access Resources	Apply
Establish Goals	Solve	Configure
Develop Ownership	Work in Teams	Troubleshoot
Analyze and Take Risks	Create Systems	Maintain
Generate Ideas	Test Theories	Convert
Manage Conflict	Cross-Functional Work	Synchronize
Develop Trust	Implement	Help Others
Demonstrate Values	Question	Impact Productivity
Act as Servant-Leader	Present Findings	Fix
Manage Situations	Utilize Tools	Diagnose
Encourage Teamwork	Gather Data	Research
Manage	Evaluate	Team with Others
Supervise	Analyze	Manage Projects
Coordinate	Define	Repair
Forecast	Review	Test
Develop Action Plans	Diagnose Problem	Interpret to Laymen
Execute	Appraise	Coach
Direct	Assess	Purchase
Control Costs	Calculate	Manage Security
Reorganize	Prove	Improve Usability
Develop High Potentials	Promote Dialog	Attain Expertise
Coach and Mentor	Consider Alternatives	Plan

Technical Abilities and Skills

This may be a very long list or a very short one. The key here is to understand the meaning of the term "technical" and to indicate which of these abilities and skills are significant to your job search (i.e. employers are seeking them) and how strong you are in each area.

Everyone has technical abilities and skills. A store clerk runs the cash register and balances their drawer. A machine operator runs a particular piece of production equipment. A human resource generalist may use both HRIS and ATS/applicant tracking systems. An IT professional may utilize 10-30 different software programs. Other examples might relate to: six sigma, SEO, project management, webinars, Access, Excel macros, or technical writing.

So, on the next page, please make a list of your technical skills and abilities. Rank each one's importance in today's market (3 = gotta have it, 2 = maybe helpful, or 1 = less necessary) and rank your competency level (3 = expertise, 2 = proficiency, 1 = knowledgeable). You can come up with your own ranking system, but you need to know how prominent each should be on the resume.

But first, take a break.

If you keep pounding away for too long, quality will suffer!

Master the 5 Minute Break

<u>Take short, regular walk or stretch breaks.</u> They are critical to focus and quality. A rule of thumb? Take a 3—5 minute break every 30 minutes. Choose to put in 3—5+ quality hours today with 30—45 minutes of total break time (instead of working for 2 hours straight with no breaks and then crashing).

Technical Skills and Abilities List

Technical Skill or Ability	Market Importance	Level of Competency

That's it for many of you on this section.

But, for you IT gurus, engineers, and technicians, take out an additional pad of paper and keep writing because your technical skills and abilities are even more important to the hiring managers!

Special Sauce

Everyone is special. But some of you have the special sauce—an uncommon, distinctive, or notable skill—that may be important to list on the resume. I have jotted down a few categories here to help you along, but feel free to make up your own. <u>Dig deep and put everything down</u>. Sometimes only current skills/experiences/certifications/etc. are relevant but, depending on where you target your resume, you just might need to reach a bit further back in time if a specific opportunity pops up. It's good to have the "special sauce" list already written!

Foreign Languages (include level of proficiency)

International Experience (while stationed abroad or in the US)

Patents

Publications (include relevant and significant blogging)

Military Service

Licenses and Certifications

Professional Affiliations (include any positions held)

Conferences, Trade Shows, and Meetings

External Training (include length in hours or days and who delivered)

In-House Training (training at the company)

Awards (must include effort or accomplishment leading to award)

Career Transition Goals

Notice that the title of this section is NOT "Career Goals."

Certainly, it is important to know your longer-term career goals, but we need to develop a resume to market you now, not in 10 years. With few exceptions, the "objective" part of the resume died years ago, so we need a general idea of where you want to be headed in order to make sure the resume is of interest to that market segment.

Later, you will modify the completed resume to target specific jobs.

When determining your career transition goals, be specific and <u>weight your priorities in order of importance</u>.

For example: if you currently live in Miami and want to move to Houston, then you might assign "relocation" a top weighting of 3, while "compensation" might be weighted a bit lower at 2 and "working hours" might be weighted even lower still at 1. After you are successful in your relocation to Houston, you can then bump up "compensation" and "working hours" in priority.

If you give them all a rating of 3 right now, you will not have good inputs to guide your decision-making and job search tactics.

The intent here is to help you focus.

Step 1: Assign a weight of 0 to 3 to each "Potential Priority" on the next two pages (3=top priority, 2 = medium priority, 1 = lower priority, and 0 = not a priority). *Add additional areas if needed.*

Step 2: When you have finished weighting, reflect on all your 3 level priorities and pick only the top 4 as your very TOP priority goals, listing them in the boxes on this page.

Step 1

POTENTIAL PRIORITY *Possible Career Transition/Job Search Goal*	IMPORTANCE *0 – 3 Weighting*
Compensation (Salary or Hourly Wage)	
Health Benefits	
Flexible Hours	
Relocation	

Commute	
Working From Home	
Traveling	
Updating or Learning New Skills	
Total Career Change	
Working in a Team	
Working Independently	
Being Recognized as a Technical Expert	
Supervising, Managing, or Leading	
Supportive Co-Workers	
Recognition	
Opportunity for Advancement	
Size of Company	
Bonus or Deferred Compensation Potential	
Job Security *(arguably, this may not exist anymore)*	
Support for Taking Initiative	
Leading or Participating in Change	

Entrepreneurial Environment	
Structured Environment	
Using Current Skills or Education	
Family Oriented Culture	
Market-Leading Organization or Products	
Specific Industry (list which one)	
Other:	
Other:	
Other:	
Other:	
Other:	

Step 2

Top Priority Goal	Top Priority Goal
Top Priority Goal	Top Priority Goal

Self-Assessment Summary Page

Take most or all of the results from the previous sections and type them onto a single self-assessment summary page.

This will be especially useful in the upcoming chapter on branding, when we will want to examine your: top 3 work values, top 3 strengths, top 14 personality-related behaviors, and 10 top transferrable skills.

It will also serve as a reference tool when writing the resume bullets, preferably the accomplishment ones.

In addition, when writing the resume, you will have all this information ready in one easy-to-access location.

Finally, viewing the totality of information together, you might:

- Notice additional strengths which are absent.
- Examine the relative strength of each word.
- Identify any words which really don't belong.
- Identify which words you can and can't back up.
- Notice similar and dissimilar words.
- Recognize which words may be grouped together.

You might also present the information to a trusted colleague or friend to get their take.

Another person may offer additional observations that could result in greater clarity when you are making meaning out of the data. Perhaps they could suggest additional descriptors or appropriately challenge some of the descriptors you have selected.

And, during the self-assessment process, don't try to be the lone ranger.

If you try to go solo through the various parts of career transition, you'll likely miss many opportunities.

Remember to ...

> **Involve Others in the Process**
>
> Make your own resume-writing choices. But, seek occasional counsel of trusted friends and colleagues several times in the process to make better choices. They will help keep you honest about yourself and help you remember strengths and accomplishments that you might have overlooked.

Chapter 3

Professional Branding

"Your brand is what people say about you when you're not in the room."

- Jeff Bezos

Brand matters.

Question: If you had to pick up some food for a company networking event with senior managers, would you choose known brands or would you take a chance on unknown, less expensive no-brand alternatives?

Question: If you had to staff a very important project team, would you choose co-workers who have a reputation for getting results and have specialty expertise or would you take a chance on lesser known people?

Question: If your family was in a crisis situation out at sea and needed to be rescued, would you be more likely to entrust the mission to the United States Coast Guard or to a private charter service?

<u>Branding is simply messaging related to trust and value</u>.

Defining your brand on the resume makes it *easier* for a reader to quickly assess your value. Remember, a first resume scan lasts only seven seconds (or less).

Choosing to define your brand = choosing to *get noticed*.

But isn't there an easier alternative?

Not really.

Not unless you want to try your luck at standing out from a crowd of other no-brand candidates. Such a crowd may be comprised of highly accomplished and desirable professionals...but if none of them gets noticed, does it really matter?

Hey, the world has definitely changed. You don't have to like it but it is a reality that any candidate without a compelling professional brand message is at a distinct disadvantage in today's marketplace. The choice is yours.

I have seen the difference with hundreds of my clients:

Candidates who convey a well-thought-out brand appear more confident, valuable, and trustworthy. **They generate more interest.**

Candidates who don't have a well-thought-out brand appear unsure and scattered, of less value, and less trustworthy. **They generate less interest.**

Protect Your Brand

Professional brands are built over a lifetime but are destroyed in minutes. Have you Googled your name lately? Protect your brand by making good personal and professional choices.

By the way, if you want to dig a bit deeper than this book, I suggest starting with one of the first calls to recognize the importance of branding for individuals. It even pre-dated the digital age!

In 1997, Tom Peters wrote an article for *Fast Company* magazine entitled: "The Brand Called You."

That was over 15 years ago, so…we have no time to lose!

Versatile

Once you define your brand, it will be useful way beyond the resume.

Are you familiar with the concept of a 30–60 second "elevator" or marketing pitch? It is foundational to networking. And, even though I have my own issues with its traditional delivery (I never advocate just blurting it out, but instead favor using its components in a more natural, two-way conversation), I completely agree that you need a powerful, succinct brand message to convey your professional value.

How about that LinkedIn profile? Again, you will need to anchor it with your brand message. Business cards? Once more, you will need a succinct, compelling way to convey what value you have to offer. Of course, given digital media we could go on and on: Google+, Vimeo, Twitter, Quora…your brand can work for you 24/7!

Branding FAQ

Do you still have questions? I don't blame you. This is pretty involved and important stuff. And don't feel bad—before working with me, most of my clients had never heard of professional branding before either.

To help you get a handle on this professional branding thing, following are answers to some common FAQs I have been asked over the years…

How succinct does my brand message have to be?

No more than a couple sentences or ten seconds if verbalized (remember, it will need to be contained within a 30–60 second "elevator" or marketing pitch).

Is a brand message like a motto or tagline?

It can be—sometimes I use a tagline on a resume—but it doesn't have to be. I like to anchor a brand with two or three of what I call "core strengths" or brand differentiators.

That's few enough for someone else to remember and most of us only have two to three core strengths anyway. It also leaves you more room to maneuver than a tagline.

If I do consider a creating a motto or tagline, what do you consider to be effective? Can you give me some examples?

Well, almost every company or product has a brand tagline so let's take a look at a few of them. Can you identify the organizations behind these? Do they describe the essence of the brand? Are they effective? Do they differentiate it?

"Just do it." "I'm lovin' it." "Explore. Discover. Understand." "I think. Therefore, I am." "The World On Time." "Human energy."

Why can't I have more than two or three core strengths/brand differentiators?

The way the human brain works, more differentiators translate into less clarity and credibility.

If you want your message to be remembered, you need to keep it short and focused. Don't agree?

Ask yourself this question: "Do the people I most respect really have more than two to three core strengths or differentiators that are responsible for their success?"

Can personal qualities, values, or personality traits be brand differentiators?

Absolutely.

There might be debate as to which personal qualities were responsible for the success of these people, but consider:

George Washington: courage, perseverance, unselfishness

Ronald Reagan: communication, delegation, peace through strength

Mohandas Gandhi: non-violent disobedience, truth, compassion

So, name a very few words you would use to describe these people:

Mother Theresa? Albert Einstein? Jack Welch? Your last boss? You?

What do you mean when you say "a brand message has to be consistent?" Does this relate to how it is utilized?

Yes.

If it isn't consistently used across all communication platforms, it will not be effective and will instead be viewed as disjointed, inauthentic, and poorly constructed.

You should be using the same succinct brand message in your resume, cover letters, emails, verbal conversations, and social media (e.g. LinkedIn) profiles.

Doesn't a brand message pigeon-hole or limit me in my search?

Only in the sense that it helps keep you and others honest about considering only those positions and organizations that will be a good fit.

Also, sometimes a person's two to three brand differentiators are rather disparate and, as such, actually paint a picture of versatility.

All that having been said, we will discuss their potential customization later on.

What factors do I need to keep in mind as I identify my two to three core strengths/brand differentiators?

How about your values, strengths, notable successes, notable failures (to stay away from), personality-related behaviors, transferrable skills, technical abilities and skills, and special sauce? Do these ring a bell? You may choose to use other inputs, but your homework from Chapter 2 has probably yielded almost all the material you will need.

Please provide examples of core strengths/brand differentiators, some of which might demonstrate combinations of words.

Customer Service Excellence	Compassionate Caregiving
Creative and Graphic Design	Mergers and Acquisitions
Commitment and Professionalism	Technical Team Collaboration
Cross-Generational Mentoring	Values-Centered Leadership
E-Commerce Project Management	Accounting and Budgeting
Process Improvement Planning	Heavy Equipment Operation
Organized and Systems Focused	Commercial Loan Processing
Strategic Planning Facilitation	IT Architecture Management
Help Desk Support	Security and Law Enforcement
Builds Trust Relationships	PC Board Quality Inspection
Advanced Excel and SPSS	Research and Proposal Writing
Machine Maintenance and Repair	Warehousing/Inventory Management
Motivates Key Contributors	Appreciates Alternative Viewpoints
Artistic Expertise	Regression Analysis and Graphing
Resolves Customer Conflicts	Crisis Management at Sea
Major Gifts Fundraising	Vendor Relationship Management
Capital Equipment Sales	International Negotiations
Repositions Strategic Assets	Consultative Leadership
Transfer Pricing	Major Account Sales Conversion
Electronics Troubleshooting	Versatile Marketing Support
Reduces Operating Costs	Investigates Ethical Concerns

Is my professional brand related to my past accomplishments, my present value, or my future potential?

> An effective brand exists only in the present, a.k.a. what you have to offer an employer right now. So, your future potential seldom relates but your past accomplishments do relate if they match up with your current capabilities. If the technology has changed or your skills are not updated in that area, however, then the accomplishments would only relate as connected to soft skills such as teamwork, leadership, project management, or communication…

There. Did the FAQ section boost your understanding of professional branding? There are many ways to go about it, but let's review some important concepts about creating your professional brand.

You Already Have a Brand

Your brand is not something you are trying to become. That would be inauthentic and misleading.

Your brand is within you right now!

Whether you were aware of it or not, you have developed your brand identity through years of work or a combination of school and work. No doubt you are proud of what you stand for and what you have accomplished; you are already known for certain traits, accomplishments, and areas of expertise.

Since you already have a brand, now you just need to take stock of what that brand is and how to communicate it succinctly and powerfully. Consider your self-perceptions, consider how others perceive you, consider how the market will perceive you, and consider how your brand aligns with the market. Above all, be honest with yourself. And take note—you get one opportunity to define your brand; once it is defined it must not change too much.

Aligning with the Market

This does not have to be difficult. All I am driving at here is that you must consider two market-related factors when defining your brand:

1) Do you use <u>language</u> that the market understands?

2) Will the market be <u>interested</u> in the value you are offering?

Why are these important and how would you go about making sure you are considering each of these factors? It's not that difficult, but let's briefly explore each.

Market Language: Simply make sure the market understands what you mean. Of course, you will need to know the market language, which can be accomplished by arranging a few informational interviews, networking, and reading professional/technical blogs. You might even review the LinkedIn profiles of others who have similar professional backgrounds. Then, just apply what you have learned to creating the wording of your brand statement. For example:

> If you are an individual contributor and much of your expertise and experience relates to being involved with, coordinating, and following through with/completing projects, you might be referring to your work as "**project coordination**." Unfortunately, the market probably views your activities as "**project management.**" Make the change to the latter in your professional brand and then use words like "coordination, follow through, and completed" as a more detailed description of "project management."

It is completely up to you when, in your branding and resume writing process, you choose to align your brand with market language. Just make sure you don't forget…or the market will remind you…with its silence!

Market Interest: While sometimes this is common sense (the design engineer or drafter is not going to be highlighting their slide rule experience but instead their 3-D and solid modeling technical competencies), testing the waters might not be a bad idea. Certainly, you can also do your online research as with determining market language. However, there are few substitutes for networking with potential hiring authorities and recruiters to ascertain what is hot and what is not. An example:

> Let's say 10 years ago you made a significant career change. Due to employability and work-life balance factors, you left your career track as a manufacturing supervisor or manager and became trained in IT/network engineering. While "supervision" and/or "management" might be core strengths of yours, if you are applying for IT/network engineer individual contributor positions (and aren't trying to become a supervisor in that area), you would want to leave out the "supervision" or "management" terms in your brand statement.

> Of course, they might still appear on your resume from prior to 10 years ago and certain aspects of that experience might be relevant (think "teamwork," "process improvement," "coaching employees," "fast-paced environment," etc.) but when the market wants to hire an IT/network engineer, it is largely focused that person's up-to-date technical abilities. Anything else is a potential distractor from promoting your brand.

Remember that while you need to remain authentic, you need to engender a high level of credibility with potential hiring authorities.

It is good that you are proud of all your victories, skills, and personality traits, but you are only going to get paid for certain ones.

Zero in on what matters to the employment market when you are defining your brand.

Back Up Your Brand

Since branding is related to trust and value, it is imperative that you are able to back up your brand statement. Otherwise, it really won't be a compelling brand at all. You have several options to accomplish this.

Results: Your achievements or accomplishments are one of the strongest ways to back up your brand. Employers always hire with the intent that you will be realizing specific results. So they will be looking at your past results to predict your future performance. While results may not always appear within the brand statement itself, your resume's bulleted statements are the perfect place to give specificity to the past results you have achieved.

Technical Expertise: Particularly for individual contributor and specialist positions, your level of technical skill and ability may be exactly what an employer is looking for and, therefore, a way to back up your brand. Whether they involve how to manipulate certain software programs, how to run a LH-6511 fluoropolymer extruder, or how to administer prescription medications, your technical expertise may be found in very close proximity to your brand statement and, on the resume, possibly on the top half of the first page. And some certifications, like Microsoft Certified Architect or Adult-Gerontology Primary Care Nurse Practitioner, may even become the core of your professional brand!

Education: Whether you have just finished a degree and are 22 years old, you have just completed re-training as part of a career change, or you have gone back to school to complete an advanced degree, recent education may become the way to back up your brand. As a rule of thumb, if your degree relates to the positions you are applying for and was completed in the last 18 months (or you are about to be awarded it in the next 6 months), then it is catapulted to near the top of the resume. Whether we like it or not, more and more frequently a specific degree or training is required in order to be considered for many positions.

Professional Branding Exercise

Hopefully, the last few pages have really tuned you on to this whole branding thing. You may have an idea of what anchors your present professional brand or even have already jotted down a draft brand statement. In any event, here is an exercise that is very likely to start giving you some clarity about your own brand and how to describe it.

This exercise involves a review of the results from most of the previous self-assessment sections.

So, if you have not already done so, **please create a one page self-assessment summary** with a minimum of the results from the values, strengths, personality-related behaviors, and transferrable skills sections. Also include any other important pieces of information from the other sections and that might be useful in identifying your brand.

You will then examine the various words, in total, to identify any patterns of similar or relating words. Group related words together and identify each of the groups using a system that makes sense to you (you might choose several different color highlighters, for example). Then, consider how each of the word groups relate to your professional brand. Hint: often times, the group itself represents one of your two to three core strengths. A few examples:

The words "create, design, develop" suggest a core strength.

The words "teach, instruct, facilitate" suggest a core strength.

The words "manage, supervise, coordinate" suggest a core strength.

The following two pages offer a before and after exemplar of this exercise. Sid Sample has been an operations manager at a traditional manufacturing facility and has previous background spanning lean manufacturing, program management, and quality control, with formal training as an engineer.

BEFORE: Sid Sample's Assessment Summary

Top Values
Teamwork
Problem Solving
Leadership *(Sid added this one in on his own – you can do the same!)*

Top Strengths
Builds Relationships
Leads Change
Process Improvement

Top Personality-Related Behaviors

Self-Directed	Proven Listener
Team Oriented	Builds Trust Relationships
Lead	Initiative
Conceptual	Quality-Driven
People Focused	Confident in Abilities
Collaborative	Improves Processes
Analytical	Accomplished

Transferrable Skills

Category 1: Lead and Manage	*Category 2: Problem Solving*
Lead	Cross-Functional Work
Engender Trust	Promote Dialog
Control Costs	Analyze

4 Additional Transferrable Skills

Coach	Act as Servant-Leader
Develops Ideas	Creates Systems

Potentially Important Items from Other Sections

High (level 3) competency with: Excel/Macros, Lean Manufacturing, and Statistical Analysis.

Notable Success #1: Created and spearheaded senior manager's group and system which led to improvements in manager's behavior.

Notable Success #2: Delivered world-wide product upgrade on six continents; on-time and within budget.

AFTER: Sid Sample's Assessment Summary

Word Group #1
Leadership
Leads Change
Self-Directed
Lead
Initiative
Lead
Act as Servant-Leader
Engenders Trust *(on two lists)*
Notable Success #1 *(on two lists)*
Notable Success #2

Word Group #2
Teamwork
Builds Relationships
Team Oriented
People Focused
Collaborative
Proven Listener
Builds Trust Relationships
Engenders Trust *(on two lists)*
Cross-Functional Work
Promote Dialog
Coach
Notable Success #1 *(on two lists)*

Word Group #3
Process Improvement
Analytical
Improves Processes
Develops Ideas
Creates Systems
Problem Solving
Lean Manufacturing
Statistical Analysis
Excel Macros

Additional Words
Conceptual
Confident in Abilities
Accomplished
Quality Driven

"After" Assessment Summary At-A-Glance:

- Clearly three distinct groupings of words
- Groupings could relate to three potential brand "core strengths:"
    - Word Group #1: **Leadership**
    - Word Group #2: **People**
    - Word Group #3: **Systems/Process Change/Engineering**
- Notable Success #1 is found in two groups
- Each Notable Success could also be an accomplishment bullet
- All words could also be used throughout resume
- Interesting lack of the word "manage" — might explore further

Identifying Two to Three Core Strengths

As you may notice from the previous before-and-after example, sometimes, just by creating groups of word from a self-assessment, your core strengths become readily apparent. Other times, it takes a bit more digging or looking at additional components of your background or career. Occasionally, there exists an outlier so powerful that, by itself, it becomes a core strength *(example: think of the recent college grad with a Political Science degree who has also taken advanced Excel training and perhaps a statistics course or two – their ability to crunch numbers may stand apart as a core strength and actually lead the brand such that they are attractive for some entry level numbers positions such as underwriter, credit analyst, or financial analyst)*. Often, additional input is needed from external sources—to keep you honest, add additional perspective, and add additional data. Remember the resume tip I previously mentioned: Involve Others in the Process.

Ask Others for Help

This is exactly what Sid Sample did. And it paid off. What seemed like a clear-cut statement of his three strengths from the grouping exercise became even clearer once he involved others in the process.

First, Sid spoke with a select group of his peers, bosses, subordinates, vendors, and others who knew his work first-hand. They told him that, although he was one of the warmest, most considerate, and engaging people they had ever worked with (high praise), first and foremost he was known as someone who consistently delivered results. Sid needed to temper his own self-perception with this slightly different perception that others had of him. To them, Sid delivered on *improvements to KPIs (key performance indicators)* ... even when no one thought there was any room for improvement. Of course, Sid accomplished all this through very loyal and committed teams but, nonetheless, he was the leader and always laser focused on results.

Second, Sid spoke with several headhunters, HR/human resources managers, and potential hiring managers. Their input validated the response of the first group Sid had asked and added two more considerations:

1. At Sid's senior manager level, the market was interested in candidates who could lead *change*; impacting both productivity and a positive work environment. Of course, Sid had this in spades throughout his career but he had not thought to really promote himself as an agent and leader of change.

2. In these days of shrinking budgets, companies were looking for senior leaders who could balance cost control with increasing revenues, specifically when *launching new products*. Fortunately, Sid also had this experience, both recently as well as earlier in his career when he had been a program manager.

After considering all inputs (and knowing he would be customizing the brand toward specific opportunities anyway), Sid decided to go with:

Sid's Brand Statement / Tagline

Operations leadership at the intersection of ideas, people, and systems.

Sid's Core Brand Strengths (and mini-taglines)

Leads Strategic Change — Maximizes human potential to realize sustainable change.

Achieves KPIs — Realizes creative and collaborative solutions.

Develops New Products — Connects marketing and process improvements to maximize profitability.

Sid kept his authentic and strong people focus in the tagline and in defining core strengths. And, he also <u>aligned his self-assessment/self-perception with other's observations and with what the market wanted.</u>

Alternative Approaches to Define Your Brand

Did the professional branding exercise not resonate with you? Want another method for determining your professional brand? Here are a few other methods I have utilized with clients, described in terms of the key questions you need to answer:

Customer Centric Method

<u>What</u> is the problem you are known for solving (your value)?
<u>How</u> do you solve it / your unique way of working at it (your process)?
<u>Who</u> does your problem solving benefit or impact (your customer)?

Market Advantage Method

What is the <u>unique advantage</u> that you have in the marketplace (whether related to skills, personality, attitude, or another factor)?

Standing-Out-From-The-Crowd Method

What sets you apart from the crowd; what <u>differentiates</u> you?

Who-What-How Method

<u>Who</u> are you as a professional?
<u>How</u> do others view you?
<u>What</u> do you do?
<u>How</u> do you do it?
<u>What</u> are the results?
<u>Who</u> do your actions benefit?

Additionally, there are many resources on the web and in print for helping you define your professional brand. Tip: other folks may refer to defining your "personal brand"…it's the same thing. Dan Schwabel, author of *Me 2.0*, is one of the top branding gurus I will often refer clients to for a more in-depth take on branding.

Does Your Professional Brand Pass the Tests?

Test #1

Does your professional brand succinctly and powerfully describe an authentic value proposition which is backed up by your accomplishments, experiences, and/or skills?

Test #2

Does it meet all of these requirements?

Core: it represents your core strengths and is authentically "you."
Concise: it is succinct; you can remember it easily.
Clear: it is easily understood.
Confident: it is clearly and strongly stated, without apology.
Connects: it connects to what the market wants.
Compelling: it conveys value; it interests others.
Consistent: it will be used consistently across all communication venues.

Test #3

Does it meet the trust and value test?

Value: it clearly states the value proposition you are offering.
Trust: it is backed up by real results and the observation of others.

Test #4

Does it meet the get-you-noticed test?

Question: *Does it grab the reader's interest so that they want to know more?*

Road Test Your Brand

Run your professional brand statement, core strengths, and other branding words past your team of trusted friends and advisors. While you may have already been asking them for input during the process of defining your brand, it is a prudent choice to get their input on the final product, after conducting one or more of the previous self-tests and prior to introducing your brand in your resume.

Integrating Your Brand into the Resume

We'll get to this in later chapters but to get you thinking in the right direction, you might...

- Place your brand statement or elements of your brand—such as tagline, core strengths, descriptor words—near the top of the resume's first page, perhaps in the profile/summary paragraph or shortly thereafter.

- Remember that you need to back up your brand by showing the results you were able to achieve or the skills you used, so... write accomplishment bullets which are brand aligned.

- Review your entire resume—both in a quick scan and in a longer more detailed look—to see if your brand message stands out.

- Tailor your brand statement and core strengths/brand differentiators to the particular position. Just be careful that you are maintaining the integrity and authenticity of your brand by not straying too far.

Utilizing Your Professional Brand

We have been focused on developing your brand as a key part of resume development. However, the wise use of your brand is critical to its power. Think of this analogy: A scientist makes a globally significant discovery, only to have a fatal heart attack in the moment following, leaving behind no notes or other indicators of her breakthrough. Once defined, you must use your brand, and use it wisely. The alternative? <u>The marketplace just might incorrectly define your brand for you.</u>

We aren't going to dive into all the ways in which you might apply your brand across multiple digital and non-digital venues, but we are going to conclude this branding section by taking a look at one of the most often messed-up aspects of branding: consistency.

Consistency is Critical to Credibility

Without a consistent application of your brand message across multiple communication venues, branding itself is a waste of time.

Consider the following **example of inconsistent brand messaging**:

Recently, I was reviewing the resume of a highly accomplished and well-liked manager (let's call him John). In order to explain individual accomplishments, John's resume emphasized words/phrases like:

- designed new processes
- created frameworks
- developed systems

These words are well aligned with someone who is a creator.

However, when I asked John to verbally explain the foundation of his effectiveness, the verbal response highlighted words/phrases like:

- led high performing teams
- coached and mentored high potential employees
- supported training initiatives

It gets worse.

When I asked John to explain his brand, the reply was:

- strategic thinking that gets results
- highly accountable

John's resume showed a process/task approach. His 1st verbal response highlighted people skills. Finally, John's reply to my request for him to explain his brand was just plain uninformative.

No consistency.

While consistency in messaging has always been important, the present employment market demands it across all communication mediums such as: LinkedIn, your elevator/marketing pitch, cover letters, emails, websites, and Twitter. Even, perhaps, as related to what others have to say about you! As an example…

From time to time, one of my career transition clients becomes so good at applying the tenet of consistency to their brand message that they are even able to prevail upon their significant others, colleagues, and friends to deliver a consistent and compelling brand message…

One such client (let's call him Bob) was a Manufacturing Manager with a reputation for leading significant change. The word "change" was all over his resume. Bob's spouse—Mary—became so adept at carrying her husband's message forward that, when recruiters would call the house and Mary would answer the phone, she would refer to her husband as the "change master!" Finally, one particularly arrogant recruiter called her on it, suggesting that Mary must be "exaggerating" and asking if she "had ever been on a factory floor." After a long pause, Mary calmly admitted that she hadn't been inside a plant in the last 6 months—*since her retirement as SVP Operations for a 10,000 employee manufacturing company*. Bob secured the interview!

What's that? Not really concerned about all this consistency stuff? Just going to use the resume to apply for a few jobs directly?

OK.

Then let's just consider an even more common pitfall…tailoring your resume and job application so much that they actually move away from your brand and core strengths, in other words they move away from the authentic you.

It is easy to make the mistake of inadvertently shifting your brand message during the hiring process.

Let's examine an **example of customizing a brand message too much**:

As a hard charging and talented CFO with strong M&A and team building experience, Sandra had only limited knowledge in the area of international tax. She saw a position opening for a CFO/Controller with significant M&A and international tax/transfer pricing requirements posted on an executive job board. As the position was listed with one of her target companies and she already had several contacts there, Sandra called up her contacts and secured an interview. Prior to the interview, she adjusted her resume, elevator pitch, and LinkedIn profile, shifting her brand message to emphasize the very limited international tax knowledge she did have. She also kept M&A as a focus area and all but eliminated her team building expertise.

You can imagine what happened next.

The first two rounds of interviewing went so well that Sandra was told that the job was "hers to lose" and that only a meeting with the President stood in her path. Of course, in a rare twist of fate, the President was a former human resources executive who was known for turning companies around with employee empowerment and team building. Unfortunately, Sandra's brand message on the resume had shifted almost completely away from her strengths in building teams and now focused completely on number crunching skills and international tax knowledge. So, when she tried to play up her softer, team-building skills with the President, Sandra came across like she was pandering to his interests and being inauthentic. Game over.

The lesson? Tailor the resume for each opportunity, but …

> ***Don't abandon your authentic brand differentiators represented by your two to three core strengths.***

OK. Enough about brand. It's time to move on to resume writing!

Part 2: Write

Chapter 4

Resume Rules

"I know that I do not know."
- Socrates

It's time that you knew what you didn't know. Even if you thought you already knew it. So, open up your mind. Get ready to know.

As you consider my resume-writing counsel, always remember: there are many ways to write a resume. I have written or helped write thousands of resumes. I have looked at thousands upon thousands more. I have learned from career experts. My resumes have been effective in helping clients to *get noticed* and preparing them to *close the deal*. However, I have tremendous respect for differing ideas from other accomplished resume writers. If my advice doesn't resonate, I encourage you to find alternative advice. Just make sure it comes from a source with the highest level of expertise.

After all, this is your career that we are about to mess with.

All right. Enough with the disclaimer stuff. Time to dig in.

Here Come the Rules

There is a science and an art to writing a resume. No question about it.

In this chapter, I will do my best to give you a set of rules and guidelines to live by, in order for you to be maximally effective in crafting your document.

I recommend that you refer back to this chapter on a regular basis.

Keep yourself honest and your work effective—think of this chapter as helping you with your in-process quality checks along the way.

This chapter gives you a set of rules – what to do and what not to do.

Although I am not going to explain my rationale behind every piece of advice, you can be sure there is a concrete reason for it, whether anchored in my experience or in some study where the efficacy of the data was beyond reproach. Translation: years ago, some unfortunate folks suffered so that you could now learn a better method!

Before I spring a bunch of lists on you, consider this priority …

Make. Every. Word. Count.

I don't care if your resume uses few words or is jam packed with detailed content, as are many of mine.

You need to make absolutely sure that there is a reason for every word in the document.

No fluff.

No litany of adjectives.

> **Make Every Word Count**
>
> In creating a first draft, you may be using words freely and with wild abandon. In creating a final draft, you must have a reason for every word you choose to include in your document. I'm not suggesting you have to be brief, just don't leave any necessary words out and please don't put any unnecessary words in. First impressions matter.

Top Resume Truths

The following list is comprised of the macro (i.e. overall) truths to keep in mind during the process of crafting your resume.

Don't forget any of these:

Motivation—Find a way to overcome your anxiety and motivate yourself to write, edit, seek advice and opinion, re-write, and polish off a first-rate product. You are accountable to you.

Branding—Identify your personal brand and how it differentiates you from the competition, then make sure it is presented clearly and convincingly. This is big picture, attention grabbing stuff.

Perfection—There must be zero mistakes on your resume. None. Of course, before "perfection" usually comes "crap." So…forgive yourself early in the process and just get something down on paper. Eight revisions later…perfecto!

Story telling—Ask yourself what career story your resume tells. Does a quick scan down the page as well as a comprehensive, detailed read-through tell the story you want? Put yourself in the shoes of a reader who doesn't have any other knowledge about you except for the information contained in the resume. What is your impression?

Accomplishments—The most powerful indicator of future success is past performance. Detail significant accomplishments on the resume. <u>Accomplishments are the #1 strategy for powerful content.</u>

Numbers—Utilizing quantitative as well as qualitative descriptions is an effective way to quickly convey your effectiveness at getting results. It boosts your credibility. Even if your accomplishments are few. <u>Numbers are the #2 strategy for powerful content.</u>

Consistency—You've already heard about this, but it bears repeating: Your resume's message must be consistent with other messaging, whether via LinkedIn, cover letter, email, verbal dialog, and so on…

Team Approach—Recruit your team now. As previously mentioned, at a minimum, you should be engaging others to help with editing and review of drafts. These team members might even help you remember your strengths, accomplishments, and how you are perceived by others before and during the writing process. You may do much of the writing by yourself, but you need a team to ensure the most effective final product. Go solo and go down.

Professional Resume Help—If all of this is too much for you to remember, consider hiring an accomplished, professional resume writer to help with the process. Questions about this are addressed in Chapter 14. Just remember these three rules: 1) Don't wait until the last minute, 2) You get what you pay for, and 3) Don't expect the professional to do all the work.

Big Picture v. Detail—Your resume must be an effective marketing tool both when scanned quickly and read in detail. Consider that with the successful candidate (the one who gets the offer), probably no more than 60% of the words on their resume are ever read. Of course, if an interviewer does read every word, they had better be good!

The "One Resume" — I developed this resume format, explained in detail in a later chapter. Essentially, it recognizes both the importance of what I call "core strengths" as well as the fact that you will be tailoring/targeting your resume for each opportunity. It also suggests that (with very few exceptions) you should not have more than one resume for any single job search/career transition.

The Process has Value — The actual process of creating your resume will pay dividends in other areas as well. The process can boost your confidence, provide insight into your core strengths/brand differentiators, further define and clarify your value proposition, and prepare you for networking and interviewing. It is OK to tackle the resume early in your search process.

What if you need help understanding or executing an item or two in the above list? Then, get help. You would go get help at work if you needed it, wouldn't you? Since the resume is your primary marketing brochure and you are hiring yourself to create it…go get some help!

Top Resume Myths

These buggers really get my goat. Yes, there are different philosophies, styles, and beliefs held by professional resume writers, but there is also a lot of erroneous material out there. So be careful what you believe.

Here are some of the top myths about resumes:

Myth: Resumes get you interviews.

Truth: Come on. This may have been accurate 30+ years ago, but the resume's significance has declined over time. Certainly, the resume remains your foundational job search tool but, with few exceptions, it must be used properly in conjunction with a comprehensive and well executed job search campaign, including a heavy dose of networking.

Myth: A resume must be one page in length.

Truth: Not necessarily. Certainly, a one-page resume might be a necessity for most recent graduates and many folks who have been doing very task-oriented work for 10 – 20+ years, but an accomplished key contributor or mid-level manager with 10+ years of experience needs to show substance – they are hired, in part, based on the depth of their experience.

Getting onto the second page conveys experience (but don't try to add even a smidgeon of "fluff" just to get there – it has to be content rich).

Some of you will naturally fit into the one-page category and others might pare down their resume at the request of certain recruiters or HR professionals. But very few candidates, other than c-suite executives, will ever get onto page three anymore. We will talk about "addendums" to the resume later – they will provide us a venue for showcasing additional information if needed.

Myth: Online submissions only.

Truth: **There is no substitute for getting your resume directly into the hands of the hiring manager.**

I am well aware of many companies which admonish you with "No phone calls, please" at the end of a job advertisement. And, as many of my friends also work in HR, I am keenly aware that candidates need to be respectful and deferential to human resources.

If you don't believe me, take 75 – 100 hours and run a test – that is about how long it will take you to apply for 100 jobs online. Statistics say that you will receive about five responses (i.e. a 3 to 5 minute phone screening interview) for every 100 resumes submitted online. Note: nowhere did I mention getting an *in-person* interview.

I don't care how beautiful your resume looks OR how perfect a fit you are for the job. In our new world of ATS (applicant tracking systems — the software HR uses to screen and sort resumes), you need to get human eyes to view your resume. Period.

Myth: Key words are a must.

Truth: Key words are important, but...key words just dumped into a resume with no tactical targeting are ineffective. If we truly want to get technical, given all the ATS software which electronically reads, sorts, and ranks resumes, the new normal is to use key phrases of 2 to 3 words each — often computer determined from internal company job descriptions and other documents.

Can you read the mind of the latest software program? Or even the HR recruiter who doesn't have time to job shadow out on the floor (and, therefore, doesn't really understand what the hiring manager is looking for)? I can't. Make sure you have current industry and position specific terminology that is easily picked up if someone were to give your resume a quick scan. Then, spend most of your effort getting a human being to actually take a look at your document.

Myth: I need a different resume for every position opening.

Truth: Not quite. What you do need to do is tailor/target your resume for each position. For an easier and more effective way to accomplish this in most cases, see Chapter 6 for the "one resume" approach.

Myth: I can't use a chronological format because I have a big time gap in my work history or am changing professions.

Truth: Only one of about every 100 resumes I help write uses something other than a chronological format. Even my "one resume" format is still essentially a chronological resume. Chronological resumes make up about 85% of all resumes.

Do you really want to raise a yellow or orange flag with a reader by using something other than the mainstream format?

Recruiters and hiring managers will ask themselves what you might be trying to hide. And, while all the detail in the functional sections makes perfect sense to you, what about a first time reader/interviewer who is trying to determine which of your accomplishments/tasks/bullets go with which companies? When the interviewer starts drawing lines and maps on your resume so they can understand it, it's too late.

Myth: I can't go back further than 10 or 12 years.

Truth: Are you worried about age discrimination? Although you might need to be at least 40 years old to bring such a case in Federal court, the market is so competitive that actual age discrimination now probably begins in earnest at about 32—33 years old! Instead, *evaluate the totality of your experience as it relates to your target audience and positions.*

I have written resumes which cut off at 10 years and others which have gone back 25+ years. It all depends. Do you want minimum wage or are you trying to pay the mortgage? For those of you in key contributor or other exempt/salaried positions, detailing your experience is key.

I do concede that technology sometimes makes earlier experience less relevant, but make sure you consider the brand of the companies you have worked for, responsibilities in each position, and—most importantly—what you accomplished back then.

Ask yourself: **Is my value tied only to recent history and up-to-date skills or is it also linked to substantial and substantive experience which may go back a few years?**

Answer that question and you will have your answer on when to cut off in the experience section.

Myth: I must include my complete work history.

Truth: Unless you're writing a professional biography, there's no need to include every detail of your work history. Of course there are exceptions to every rule, like recruiters who will want everything and the kitchen sink. If they ask for it, give it to them. Otherwise, write the book on your non-work time.

No-Nos

Of course there are differences if we are considering foreign countries, the Federal government, and other exceptions. But, unless you want to torpedo your own search, when writing your resume, DO NOT include:

- Your social security number.
- The *day or month* you were hired and/or left a position.
- The reason you left a position.
- More than one email address or telephone number where you can be reached.
- Job Compensations.
- Live Hyperlinks (generally, firewalls don't like).
- Personal pronouns such as "I," "me," and "my."
- Pictures or photographs (not even of yourself).
- Personal interests.
- Community involvement (exceptions discussed later).
- Personal characteristics such as health, height, weight…
- Potentially discriminatory information such as marital status, religion, ethnic origin, sex…
- Your references…not even "references available upon request."
- *Excessive* shading, parenthesis, columns, lines, boxes, bold, capital letters, underlining, or alternative formatting…

Also, <u>do not</u>:

- Staple pages one and two together (either paper clip them together or leave them loose – your name will be on both pages).
- Print with colored ink.
- Use special colored or pre-formatted paper.
- Mail your resume (very few exceptions).
- Use an older email like AOL or even Yahoo (Gmail is still OK and you can keep your other accounts for personal use like I do).
- Print with anything other than a laser or top quality inkjet.
- Name your file "Resume" (must include first and last name such as "JaneDoeResume").
- Put apartment numbers or PO Boxes (because of hiring discrimination, use only the street address on your resume and give your mailing address once they want to mail an offer).
- Spray your resume with perfume (yes, people have done it).
- Use more than two different font sizes.
- Use more than two different fonts (I prefer using only one).
- Have your name stand out: it distracts from the important content. All the reader cares about is your value — they will find your name and contact information if interested.

Formatting and Organizing Minutia

What's that? You've already had enough with the minutia?

Can't help it. You see, we need to use every advantage to make sure that your content will stand out.

For instance, did you know that you can boost your resume's readability by 2–3% with the right font type and size? What if we make 8 to 10+ small adjustments with similar impacts? That could add up to some serious numbers.

Formatting and Organizing Guidelines

Here are some hard and fast guidelines for formatting and organizing your document, preferably in MS Word:

Font: Times New Roman or something similar. Times New Roman is still considered the most readable font for print communications. Your other option is something similar, like Book Antiqua (what this book is mostly written in), Garamond, or Georgia. Stay away from anything else. You may like the looks of Ariel or Helvetica (commonly used for street signs and other objects which are read far-away), but you aren't the one who will be doing the reading, are you?

Font Size: Stay with 12 point font size, decreasing to an absolute minimum of 11 point if you have to include a bit more content. No lower than 11 point, please. Also, I strongly recommend using the same font size throughout the document.

Your Name: It's tempting to but your name in big, bold font across the top of your resume but you need to resist the urge. Why?

The HR administrative assistant – with $150K in student loans and their MBA from an Ivy League school who couldn't get hired for their chosen profession and is temping in this HR role – has a major chip on their shoulder. They may not take kindly to a big, bold name on top and your resume may never get to the hiring manager. I have seen it in living color, folks … top candidates' resumes placed in the circular file simply because of another person's ego problem

Ask yourself: is your name really part of your value proposition?

If you create compelling content and organize it in an easily digestible format, the interested reader will seek out your name and contact information, no matter what the font size.

Length: One to two pages. Touched on earlier under the "Untruths" section, the length of the resume is usually 1 to 2 pages, with a few executive resumes needing a third page. There is never a need to fill an entire page but, if you are writing onto the second page, a good rule of thumb is to make sure you have enough content to go at least 40% down the length of the page. If you don't, try to cut it back to one page. The length is driven by content considerations but here are some typical guidelines:

One-page resume: students, recent graduates, direct labor workers (paid hourly), early career professionals usually with less than 8 – 10 years of experience.

Two-page resume: professionals, key contributors, supervisors, managers, VPs, and some executives.

Three-page resume: c-suite executives and a few scientists and authors who are significantly well published and patented (although they often could have a two-page resume and an "addendum" of additional pages—we'll discuss later).

White Space: Don't worry about it. You are not interested in your resume getting noticed for lack of content. I am not aware of any studies that point to you having a better chance of getting hired with more white space. Your resume needs to be organized and pleasing to look at to be sure, but content is king.

Did you just have a heart attack in reading about the demise of the importance of white space? Well, white space never was that important as it turns out. Do you remember the 90s when it was common for resume paper to be colored and/or have lines and other images pre-printed on it? Guess why it fell in and out of vogue so fast?

It is true that that kind of paper got resumes noticed more often…but the candidates were not hired any more often! Same with white space.

Chronological Format: Nearly all of you need to have a resume with a chronological format, which accounts for over 85% of the resumes on the market. Anything else may raise a warning flag. Remember, functional and other formats are seldom effective, whether they are pleasing to your eye or not. Key in on your experience and list it in reverse chronological order; list the most recent work history first. Your reader will thank you.

Bullets: You should use a bullet for each separate accomplishment or activity in the "Experience" section. Again, whether you like the looks of them or not, bullets are highly effective in drawing the reader's eye to a particular series of words.

Bold, Italics, Underline, Capital Letters: OK, here is the science: A reader is **most drawn to bold**, THEN CAPITAL LETTERS, *then italics*. Just as with parenthesis, I don't recommend the use of underlining much; it can still really foul up the ATS software sorting and is tricky to use properly. Use these highlighting tools sparingly and preferably not to highlight too many key words or phrases throughout your resume. Here are some general guidelines:

> **Bold**: position titles, core strengths/values, brand statement
>
> CAPITAL LETTERS: company names, your name, address
>
> *Italics*: for lessor sub-titles, notations, catch phrases
>
> Underline and (Parenthesis): preferably not at all

Dates of Employment and Education: Dates must be right justified. That does *not* mean hitting the tab space five times; please set a right tab. Dates are not connected to positions, only to companies. Dates should be represented by years only, not months or days. Unless you are currently pursuing a degree with an expected graduation date or you have graduated within the past 18 months, you do not have to include a date or year for any degrees.

Indents: Indenting by one or two spaces from the left margin can help organize content on your resume for easier reading.

Columns and Tables: Be careful here. I do use columns and tables sometimes, but ATS and word processing programs which differ from your own can foul up your information in these formats.

Top Writing Priorities

This is *how* you will write. I have re-introduced a few concepts from previous pages because I want you to be able to find them here and because they are so important:

Accuracy — Be honest in describing your experience and be conservative when citing numbers. Numbers are so crucial to have throughout the resume but I don't blame you for not remembering if the project took five, six, or seven months. Just say "5+ months."

Focus on Recent Experience — Usually, the length of writing about your most recent 2 to 3 positions will equal the length of writing for all other positions combined. There are exceptions to this principle, certainly.

Choppy Style — Eliminate as many "a" and "the" words as possible, but pay attention to phrase structure.

Perfection — Perfection requires significantly more effort than just running spell check. Have others read over for content and also make sure to read backwards, from the last word to the first, to catch anything spell check may have missed.

Eliminate Personal Pronouns — "I" and "my" do not belong. Of course, neither do "he," "she," "we," or any other personal pronouns.

No Discriminatory Information — Leave out any references to age, religion, weight, marital status, disabilities, race, etc.

Current Terminology — Make sure you use current jargon, especially as related to either technical aspects of the position or cultural speak in the industry. With few exceptions, referring to DOS 3.1 could be a killer.

Verb Tense — I recommend always beginning bullets in the past tense, even with a current position, but you could choose present tense for a current position and past tense for past positions. The summary and core competencies sections are usually written in present tense.

Abbreviations — Be careful about using abbreviations, although a reference to TQM on a manufacturing resume will be easily understood as "total quality management." Typically, include the full name following the first use only, such as with "EQ/emotional intelligence." Also, many companies have their own terminology which is not easily understood outside the culture.

Periods — Periods belong at the end of each bullet. Maybe up to 50% of resume writers will disagree with me on this one, but just try to have a two-sentence bullet without using periods…it's not pretty.

Every Word Counts — If a word does not add value, eliminate it. So, don't use "Work Experience." Use "Experience," avoiding redundancy. Every word counts. And "Work" can sound a bit proletariat.

Use Adjectives Sparingly — Eliminate words like "very," "most," "strong," and "excellent." Choose less subjective replacements or eliminate altogether. As an example, instead of writing "excellent communication skills," write "proven communication skills." Instead of writing "very accomplished," write "accomplished."

Software Programs, Templates, and Margins …

While I keep my own personal opinions regarding various software and high tech companies, I don't let them get in the way of my professional work. Neither should you.

A fairly current version of MS Word is your best bet here.

Economically challenged at the moment?

If you are a student, the student version is reasonably priced.

If you are really doubling down on your budget, almost every library has up-to-date versions free on their public computers, where you can either save your resume to a USB/flash drive or email a copy to yourself.

Worst case, consider going to www.sourceforge.net and downloading Apache's Open Office. But, if at all possible, go with MS Word.

MS Word will allow you to save in a number of different formats. And, while I find most companies either prefer or strongly prefer to have an MS Word document, you may also choose to save in alternative formats, such as rtf/rich text or pdf. While pdfs do increase the chance that your formatting will remain intact and allow readers without a copy of MS Word to view your document, you should consider the following:

> **A note about pdfs**: Pdfs, often preferred internationally and growing in popularity in our market during past years, are often chosen by the resume's author so that a reader cannot "foul up" your content or formatting. Here is the modern day dilemma: the hiring committees in many companies really appreciate being able to mark up, highlight, and make notes on a resume electronically, often using track changes or other tools found in MS Word. If you have sent a pdf, this may present them with an additional step or just be plain frustrating. So, if you really feel compelled to save in a pdf, I might suggest sending two copies of your document: one as a pdf and one as a MS Word document. They can have their pick!

About resume templates in Word or other programs: don't use them.

To set margins on your document: make sure your left and right side margins add up to a whole number or .5 or .25 for ease of future use, such as setting up a right justified tab. Margins on my resumes are typically: .8 left, .7 right, .6 top, and .5 bottom, but you can set your own preferences under "Page Layout."

I won't insult your intelligence with a Word tutorial here, but may make a few suggestions as we go along.

You are now armed and dangerous. It's time to put pen to paper …

Chapter 5

Writing by Section

"Do your best and forget the rest."
- Tony Horton

The results of your "best" are going to look very different from one day to the next. Don't worry about it. The final results will be impressive. Just keep doing your best at this writing workout *every day*.

And remember…you are writing primarily for another reader. So your credibility with that reader is a critical factor.

While "liking" your resume is all well and good, you must follow rules for maximizing your resume's impact when it is read by the hiring manager. Sure, form is important, but don't ever dilute content in favor of form. You must present content that interests the reader.

It's about them. Not about you. Even though it is *your* resume!

Therefore, this next tip, although key to resume writing, is also key to the whole job search process. It is even key to the process of managing your career once you have secured new employment.

In fact, it is so BIG and so connected to everything we are doing here, that it deserves to be included as a tip related to all aspects of your job search…

> ### Perception is Reality
>
> <u>Each person's perception IS their reality</u>—whether you agree with it or not; whether you like it or not. When you are writing your resume, reviewing your draft resume, and preparing to network, interview, negotiate, or perform other career transition activities, you must ALWAYS keep this core concept in mind. Seek feedback from those who will give it to you constructively and honestly. Know how your resume and other messaging comes across. Know how you are perceived. And adjust your messaging accordingly…before it is prime time.

Remember, a resume should clearly and convincingly present your brand/value proposition to the hiring authority. And, as stated earlier in the book, it needs to do so in two ways:

1. **It grabs the reader's attention** (their first scan)—in 7 seconds or less—so that they know your core strengths and want more information. *Stand out from the crowd and get noticed.*

2. **It provides detail to back up your value** (the reader's second pass)—in the form of accomplishments, education, training, abilities, and skills—so that, when the reader spends more time with your resume, they are impressed with your potential to be a top candidate. *Boost credibility by presenting your value via substance; encourage the reader to interview you and set up for closing the deal.*

Writing by Section

Complete one section at a time. In order. If at all possible.

A few of the foundational sections of any resume include:

Heading (your contact information)
Profile (summary of your value proposition and core strengths)
Experience (positions held in reverse chronological order)
Education (partial or completed degrees)

Other sections might include:

Training
Certifications
Technical Skills
Military Service
Conferences and Meetings
Associations
Honors and Awards
Internships
Volunteer Service

Are there other sections you might include? Can you customize your resume with your own, unique sections and content? Sure. But make sure to think critically whether or not there is a potential downside.

The employment marketplace has changed such that companies today are interested in resumes with content targeted directly at demonstrating your background meets their top priorities. In most cases, therefore, adding a section on "Community Service" is going to be a distractor at best. If a company wants to discern your character, the digital world is the place they are going to go to start their research.

Writing each section of a resume — as they appear vertically (top to bottom) on the page(s) — allows you to accomplish several important things...

- **Build upon Success**: Completing the Heading and Profile sections at the top of the resume builds confidence before you dive into the more time-consuming bullet writing in the Experience section. Build the big mo.
- **Promote Brand Synchronicity**: If you write about experience first and write about brand and core strengths second, you will probably end up going back and re-writing about your experience to back up your brand/value proposition. Define and state your brand/value proposition clearly and then write about experience. Of course, you need to have a brand and knowledge of your core strengths even before you begin writing, so make sure you have read Chapter 3. Clearly state and then support your value proposition.
- **Write about the Recent Past**: Since resumes are typically in reverse chronological order (your most recent work history/experience comes before your earlier work history), write about what you most easily remember before moving on to previous positions and employers. Don't tax your memory right away.

Of course, if you get stuck in a certain section, feel free to modify your approach. You could fast-forward to a Training or Education section and complete that before returning to the more challenging Experience section.

Adapt. Modify. Make the process work for you.

For our purposes, we will examine the process of writing each section of a resume as it might typically be read, from page top to page bottom. *Just make sure that, together, the sections tell one story...your story.*

Information Bank

In order to write, you need something to write *about*!

Chapter 1 talked about being organized, including gathering all your "raw material" together before you start writing. This is important.

> **Create an Information Bank**
> Have all of your background information together in one place before you begin writing. Collect old resumes, performance reviews, training records, and other information in one electronic or manila folder. This is often called a "master" or "comprehensive" file of application or job search data.

Here are a few items that might be in your Information Bank:

- Performance reviews.
- Letters of recommendation.
- Training records.
- Personality, leadership, or 360 assessment results.
- Transferrable skills list.
- Brand statement, core strengths, and key words (see Chapter 3).
- Awards and recognition and certificates.
- Patents or publications.
- Design drawings or other work samples.
- List of courses taken in college or higher education programs.
- List of professional association memberships.
- Notepad notes (keep a notepad with you and record your resume-related thoughts during the 30 days prior to writing).

All right. Let's proceed to writing the individual sections!

Chapter 6

Writing: Heading

"Hello, My Name Is _____."
- Found on numerous networking name tags. Author unknown.

No one can screw this up. Right?

Wrong.

How about the candidate who liked recreational parachuting on the weekends and had the email: "deathdefyingdiver@qqqmail.com?" Despite the candidate's actual character, do you think his email will exude responsibility or dependability to recruiters?

How about the well-credentialed individual who insisted on a resume heading of "Sally S. Sample, CPA, CMA, MBA, M. Ed., Ed. D.?" A legend in her own mind…

And the NASCAR enthusiast's email: "redhotRod@qqqmail.com?"

Finally, how about a very particular fellow who known by "Ed" but spelled out his name Edward and included both his middle names on his resume: Edward Ebenezer Elias Effingham? What's that message?

Now, I have nothing against someone having two middle names AND a little alliteration mixed in to boot; I even have a son who meets that test! But how about modifying it for resume purposes? Perhaps something like: Edward E. Effingham or Edward Effingham or even Ed Effingham. I'm all for *more* choices. But I am writing these lines so you will make *better* choices. Our son didn't have a choice when we named him…but he will when it comes time to write his resume!

This section is fairly straightforward. Don't over-think it but make sure it doesn't stand out in the wrong way either. After all, you don't want it to compete with your value proposition, experience, or other content.

For discussion purposes, take a look at this heading from Chapter 1's sample resume.

SARA S. SAMPLE, CPA	000.000.0000
23 LARAMORE STREET	SSAMPLE@QQQEMAIL.COM
ANYTOWN, VA 00000	LINKEDIN.COM/IN/SSAMPLE

This heading contains all the basics: Name, street address, telephone number, email, and LinkedIn profile address. In addition, it includes a professional designation "CPA" (certified public accountant) and an optional double line to separate it from the rest of the resume.

Notice that the name does not appear in bold or in a larger font — or otherwise standout. *Why would you want to compete with other resume content — the words that convey your value?* If a reader is impressed with your content, they will search out your name and contact information, no matter how modest it appears.

While you could add your website or a URL to view a portfolio—make sure to include all the basics or risk being perceived as "out of touch."

The heading should be the same font and size as the rest of the resume: 11 or 12 point Times Roman or something similar, such as Garamond, Georgia, or Book Antiqua. The above heading is in Georgia font and uses small capital letters, which I often opt for, just to give it a bit of polish. In MS Word, simply right click or click Ctrl+D to access the "font" options and you can use "small caps" as well (hint: if you have already typed in capital letters, the small caps function will not work).

Phone: There should be only one phone number—a cell phone—in order to: 1) Route all calls directly to the candidate's voice mail and bypass the chance of any other person answering; and 2) Avoid any confusion regarding multiple numbers. Make sure to have a professional voice mail set up with at least your first name used in the message. "Yo, you've reached 000.000.0000; you know the drill…" does not cut it.

Email: In some metropolitan markets and industries, it is starting to become important which email address you use. I know…really crazy! Gmail is currently viewed the most favorably of the major "free" providers, although having an email address at your own domain name makes a positive statement as well.

There are disadvantages to listing an email from your ISP. The inability to separate out job search activity from personal activity and longer term email accuracy. Once in circulation, your resume will be placed into various databases. If a number of months—or even years—pass, and you change to another ISP, then your email will no longer be valid. I have heard recruiters complain of a perfect candidate-position match, only to find out-of-date contact information (pssst…they won't take the time to call you; it's email or bust!).

If you use Gmail, you can forward all other accounts into it and only have one email page to review each day. Your choice.

LinkedIn Address: Although I will touch on LinkedIn in a later chapter, suffice it to say that, in today's market, a LinkedIn address on the resume is the professional standard. It tells the reader: you are connected to modern technology and professional norms, you are transparent/open to being checked out, and there is another place the reader can go to find out information about you (including your smiling picture and who you are connected to).

<u>Keep this address short so that it doesn't make a statement all by itself.</u>

You have two tactics to keep it short.

Since you should remove any hyperlinks from the resume, don't include the entire URL. Also, you can customize your URL in LinkedIn. Since truncating will not impact the chances of you being "found" on LinkedIn, you can go really short. In the above example, Sally chose "ssample" but, if she could have also chosen something like "ss123."

Economy of words: Each word should add value or be examined as a potential distractor. The phone number is not written as "phone: 000.000.0000" nor is the email "email: ssample@qqqemail.com." There is no need for the words "phone" or "email."

Also, as just noted in the LinkedIn section, you should **remove the hyperlink** (right click in MS Word and choose "remove hyperlink") from email, LinkedIn, and other web addresses, as your entire resume document could be flagged as unsafe to open by a corporate firewall.

Street Address: Although there is seldom any written correspondence sent to the home address, it is important to list a street address. However, *do not* include a PO Box, apartment number, or unit number if at all possible. I know of millionaires who wisely prefer to rent, but I also know of many more hiring authorities who may discriminate against a renter on the false assumption they have a less stable living situation. Yes, unfortunately it happens.

So, if you typically put "Apartment #" or "Unit #" so your mail gets to the correct box within an apartment or condo complex, I suggest leaving it off the resume. There is almost no chance you will have mail sent to this address and, when you make it through the interview process, then you can always let your new employer know of this detail.

OK. You're armed and dangerous. So, jot down a self-reminder about what you just learned that will be most important for you to remember when writing your resume's header.

Reminders About My Resume Header

Chapter 7

Writing: Profile

"Be yourself; everyone else is already taken."
- Oscar Wilde

"Hire me, I'm a good worker" is not going to cut it.

This is where your brand can shine through. This is where you might choose to clearly present your 2 to 3 core strengths to the reader. This section, referred to as either "Profile" or "Summary," can include your personality. But it cannot be made up of fluff, such as lots of adjectives.

Your profile is a golden opportunity—in the "sweet spot" of the resume—to interest the reader. This section will set the stage for how the reader views the rest of your candidacy.

It can be as short as 3 to 5 lines. But it needs to pack a punch.

The profile may be the reader's first impression of you. So, don't blow it!

Remember the importance about being BOTH authentic AND credible? Well, it's akin to including both professional and *appropriate* personal information (such as your personality) in the Profile section.

You need to try and get yourself "into the resume," as many career coaches would advise. But—and this is a big "but"—you better not go overboard! Not too many adjectives, no silliness, not any fluff, and definitely not any odd words that the reader won't understand.

If you are struggling with how authentic you should be, *always err on the side of boosting your credibility with hard hitting professional information, such as* **experience or skills**.

How might you prompt yourself to come up with the right language for writing this section? Ask yourself, in a professional context:

- "Who am I?"
- "How do others perceive me?"
- "What are my greatest strengths?"
- "How do I do what I do?"
- "What strengths and skills will resonate with my audience?"

Then, write. Here is the profile section from the Chapter 1 resume:

> Leadership of both finance and accounting functions with background in manufacturing and public accounting. Proven problem solving and analytical abilities. Expertise in Excel, JD Edwards, Hyperion, and other software tools. Team approach prioritizes integration across departments and maximizes impact of cost control. Direct style balanced by compassion, humility, and fairness.

The Profile gives the reader an overview of the candidate's background and the brand they want to portray. It mentions the candidate's functional expertise or the type of work or positions suited for. It references experience in certain industries or markets.

The Profile may also include items such as the candidate's values, personality, leadership style, technical expertise, software proficiencies, core competencies, training, or even a willingness to learn or be trained.

This is your chance, in 3 to 5 lines maximum, to let the reader know who you are as a professional and what value proposition you are offering.

The Profile can be forward positioned (essentially placing an "objective" *within* the "Profile") toward an area, such as with this statement: "Prioritizing opportunities to utilize LBO expertise in creating shareholder value …" or this one: "Recent RN graduate exploring opportunities to make qualitative impact in the lives of Alzheimer's patients."

What it should not be, however, is solely an objective.

Objectives had their time and place but have been rapidly fading during the past 10+ years; objectives are limiting and their use conveys a sense that you are stuck in the past.

Note that **the first 2 to 5 words and first sentence are most important.** A reader who is scanning the resume for the first time will invariably spend less time on this section and instead be drawn to the experience and education sections. The Chapter 1 example profile, "Leadership of both finance and accounting functions…" suggests both a preference for leadership and an openness to either finance or accounting work as well, setting the individual up for either a CFO/VP Finance type of position **OR** perhaps something along the lines of a more hands-on Controller/Accounting Manager type of position.

The profile needs to be able to stand on its own throughout the majority of the career search, but should almost always be tweaked and customized when applying to a specific position.

When customizing, use key words and phrases from the job advertisement. But don't just cut and paste entire sentences.

We are going to explore customization in much more depth in later chapters but, for now, here's a simple, straightforward example of how the profile we have been examining might be customized when applying for the CFO position at a company with only 40 total employees and one other accounting staff member:

Say the job advertisement includes the following wording…

> "must be hands-on and interested in spending significant time with the G/L (general ledger), making entries and reconciling accounts,"
>
> "will provide ownership with strategic recommendations," and
>
> "should be self-starter, able to work with little supervision."

So, our profile will be customized as follows (Note: changes are highlighted in bold for your reading ease but should not necessarily be bold on the finished version)…

Hands-on leadership of finance and accounting functions. **Balances need for direct and detailed involvement with G/L and cash flow with need to provide strategic direction to senior management. Independently motivated,** with proven problem solving and analytical abilities. Highest level of competency with Excel, JD Edwards, Hyperion, and other software tools. **Takes initiative** to maximize impact of financial management and cost control initiatives.

Adding a Title

Remember 7th and 8th grade? I try to forget. Were you one of the lucky ones who was not assigned a title? Or does "nerd," "jock," "brain," "scuz," "geek," or "boocaloo" ring a bell?

My kids tell me they are more creative now.

Do you remember how some of the kids who were given titles were labeled or branded for perhaps the next several years and had to really work to get rid of them? Sometimes those titles almost "defined" them?

"But, a resume title is different," I hear some of you saying.

Really? How so?

It is still labeling you, locking you into one particular brand.

Now, I'm not putting the kibosh on ever creating a resume title.

I'm just saying, be careful of what you wish for.

Let's consider adding a title to the Profile section. It might look like…

SENIOR FINANCE AND ACCOUNTING LEADERSHIP

Leadership of both finance and accounting functions with background in manufacturing and public accounting. Proven problem solving and analytical abilities. Expertise in Excel, JD Edwards, Hyperion, and other software tools. Team approach prioritizes integration across departments and maximizes impact of cost control. Direct style balanced by compassion, humility, and fairness.

The <u>functional</u> title in the above example draws in the reader's initial attention, making it easier for them to clearly understand the type of position(s) the candidate is seeking.

While 90% of the time I do not recommend adding any title to my client's resumes, it can be effective when applying for specific positions.

Potential downsides are that such a title could be interpreted differently than your intentions or limit your suitability for other positions.

In the above example, the candidate wants the reader to understand that they are open to a variety of both finance and accounting types of positions as long as they are at a senior level. This could be helpful in the event that the candidate is networking inside a large corporate headquarters, in which there are numerous potential opportunities in finance and accounting and each thought of as related but somewhat separate.

Additionally, such a functional might be effective when networking or applying for positions with smaller firms that want one leader on the numbers side who has experience in both areas. But, there are dangers lurking as well…

What if the word "senior" is interpreted incorrectly?

Perhaps one larger company's "Finance and Accounting Team Leader" position may actually have more responsibility and better pay than another smaller company's "Chief Financial Officer" or "CFO" position? Could the word "senior" in this title begin to *exclude* the candidate instead of including them? Absolutely.

And yet, this particular candidate may not even want to bother with anything other than senior level positions.

I can respect that.

I just want this candidate to have the choice to decide whether a position is suitable or not—instead of a reader deciding for them.

As a general rule of thumb, <u>try to stay away from using titles at the top of the resume</u>.

However, if you must force the reader to pay attention or you are applying for a specific position, use a <u>functional</u> title as in the previous example. Do *not, never, don't-you-dare use a specific position title*, such as "CFO," "Controller," and "Accounting Manager." Please note…

A "functional" title gives you some wiggle room, while a "position" title can be severely constraining.

There is one instance when using a functional title becomes almost a necessity, however. This occurs when the candidate's *relevant* experience for a particular opening is many years ago and is preceded by more recent, but less relevant, experience.

Let me give you an example.

One of my clients spent the first 12 years of her career in accounting positions, reaching the level of Controller for a small manufacturing firm. Then, for the last 10 years, she focused more on IT and systems positions, reaching the level of Systems Manager.

Her present career search focus was to get back to work in accounting again, perhaps for a smaller firm wanting a part-time Controller or Accounting Manager. The client had held onto her CMA (Certified Management Accountant) designation and had updated her skills via several recent seminars.

However, if my client had not chosen to use the title of "Accounting Management" on the first page of her resume, the reader would have spent most of their attention on the client's recent and impressive systems background.

The reader may never have made it to page two and, therefore, probably never would have considered my client as a serious candidate for an accounting manager position.

The client's *accounting* message would never have been considered.

Incorporate Your Professional Brand

Remember all that work you did in the Self-Assessment and Branding Chapters? Well, it's time to put it to use!

The Profile section, placed in the most viewed "sweet spot" of the resume, is prime real estate when it comes to advertising your professional brand.

This is your chance to let the reader know your value proposition or what you can offer a potential employer.

It's time to take a first stab at writing your resume Profile in the space on the next page.

Or, type it right into your Word resume document, as it might be easier to refer back to the key words and language you developed in Chapter 2 and Chapter 3.

Hint: you might want to keep in mind the questions posed a couple pages ago: "Who am I?" "How do others perceive me?" "What are my greatest strengths?" "How do I do what I do?" and "What strengths and skills will resonate with my audience?"

Take a deep breath, do your best, and commit to numerous revisions before the final version.

First Draft of Resume Profile

Chapter 8

Writing: Technical Skills

"I fear not the man who has practiced 10,000 kicks once, but I fear the man who has practiced one kick 10,000 times."

- Bruce Lee

We have come a long way from nearly a century ago when Frank Parsons observed that we defined professional value and career development almost solely in terms of skills.

Today, companies are much more focused on the *results* you have achieved and, therefore, your potential for achieving future results.

So, for 90% of you, a "skills" section that appears near the top of many resumes only serves to add clutter, not value. Skills are usually discussed within the Profile and Experience sections.

Don't worry if you're part of that 10% who needs a "skills" section; just keep reading because help is on the way!

The focus on past results aligns with the rise of behavioral interviewing during past several decades: <u>companies examine your past behavior to predict future performance</u>. Therefore, specific skills are often tied to *how* you achieved certain results or *how* you performed a function.

Sometimes they are even mentioned in the Profile section as in the Chapter 1 resume, which notes: "Highest level of competency with Excel, JD Edwards, Hyperion, and other software tools."

Including a Technical Skills Section

So, when should you include a separate section for technical skills? The following are just a few examples that cry out for highlighting technical skills on the resume and, perhaps, in a separate section…

- **Recent Graduate**—especially if just coming out of a technical program, may very well wish to highlight relevant skills in a separate section.
- **Engineer**—whether on the process or design side, may need to show a high level of competency with certain concepts and tools.
- **Software Engineer**—may choose to showcase technical expertise in several separate sub-sections, such as "hardware," "software," "systems," and the like.
- **Health Care Technician**—needs to demonstrate proficiency on a number of instruments required in their daily routine.

So, what should you title a skills section? Well, here are a few thoughts:

Technical Skills
Core Competencies
Technical Competencies
Areas of Technical Expertise
Software
Design Instrumentation
Laboratory Techniques and Protocols
Technical Abilities

Stay away from titles or descriptions that will date you, such as using the word "Computer" in the title or "DOS 3.0" in a list of skills.

And, while we are on the subject, every Tom, Dick, and Hortense who is over the age of 40 (and that includes me!) should NOT include a "software skills" section to show that they can use MS Word and Internet Explorer. It's sort of assumed at this point, with rare exception. Including such a section would only suggest you were out-of-touch.

How should you make your list? Completely up to you. You could use strings of words separated by commas. You could use the column/bullet approach. Here I am less concerned about the reader remembering a manageable number of skills (as opposed to wanting them to remember you're your 2-3 core strengths).

That having been said, I strongly recommend you force rank your list to highlight your top 2 or 3 technical skills.

If your list includes more than 4 to 6 skills, I would highly recommend organizing them into 2-3 titled sub-lists, allowing the reader to quickly digest your areas of skill proficiency without having to be assaulted, on a first scan of the resume, by 15+ different items.

Finally, when making any kind of list, remember that readers will be reading/scanning "top to bottom" even a tad before "left to right."

In this example, the words "Oracle," "Hyperion," and Advanced Excel" appear in the three most readable positions.

	TECHNICAL COMPETENCIES	
• Oracle	• Advanced Excel	• Legends V
• Hyperion	• Cash King 3.0	• YGT Database

In the next example below, the words "Machining," "Engineering," and "Design" head the sub-lists and allow the reader to overview the section quickly.

TECHNICAL COMPETENCIES

MACHINING	ENGINEERING	DESIGN
• CNC Programming	• Statistical Process Control	• SolidWorks
• ANSI 15.4 Certified	• Engineering Change Orders	• CADD Max 3.3
• Machine Operation	• Finite Element Analysis	• Axel Blueprinting
• Tolerances to .0001	• Mechanical Vibrations	• V-Prototyping

---

NOTE: The above example also shows the need to **spell out acronyms**, at least the first time they are used in a resume, for improved understanding by HR and other non-technical persons. "Statistical Process Control" = "SPC" while "Engineering Change Orders" = "ECOs" and "Finite Element Analysis" = "FEA." The acronyms would be easily understood by an engineer or technical staff person, but those people aren't the only ones involved in the hiring process!

Where should you put a "Technical Competencies" section? It should be right after your "Profile/Summary" section if critical to your value proposition—as in the case of a software engineer or a new graduate of a CMA/Certified Medical Assistant program, for example. It also often follows the "Education" section, especially if less critical to your candidacy.

If you aren't sure about where to put it, just cut and paste it into a couple different places; try it out in several locations. Chances are a solution will become visible.

Of course, you will also want to field test your resume with trusted advisors, some of whom may work in a related field and be able to guide you with such decisions.

OK, so whether it is fixing broken machinery, creating Excel macros, operating a forklift, or designing websites in WordPress, it is time for you to list any of your technical skills which may appear on the resume, whether they comprise a separate section or not...

My List of Technical Skills

Additional ideas about incorporating technical skills in the resume can be found in Chapter 15, as it pertains to my "one resume" concept.

Chapter 9

Writing: Experience

"There is no substitute for hard work."
　　　　　　　　　　- Thomas Edison

Experience is THE MOST critical component of your resume.

I don't care if it is a volunteer internship for four hours a week…If your experience relates directly to the position requirements of a job opening … Ding! Ding! Ding! … you become a potential candidate.

Companies have a HUGE talent pool from which to draw for the "good jobs" so it is highly unlikely you will be considered for an interview without demonstrating what you can do. It's about creating trust.

Let's begin by examining an important and oft asked question…

How Far Back Should You Go?

I briefly covered this common question in Chapter 4 but, as it is one of the most often asked questions, we'll revisit it here with more context.

As a rule of thumb, very few of my mid to senior level resume clients will list any experience further than 15 or 20 years back. After all, it usually just isn't that relevant.

And my more technically inclined clients—whose employment prospects depend much more heavily on remaining current with the latest software tools in their respective professions—often decide not to mention any experience beyond the last 10 years. It just all depends.

Take Charlie, for example. He was one of the few clients I ever helped construct two separate resumes. One of the resumes went back 10 years. The other went back 40 years. This doesn't make sense to you? Well, let's take a quick look at Charlie's case …

Charlie, a very youthful-looking 75-year-old, was the past president of four different companies. He was financially secure and had two distinct career directions he was pursuing, both within the PC board industry: assembly line quality inspector and management consultant.

For the past 10 years, Charlie had held three different quality control positions. Therefore, we only included this experience on the one-page resume targeted at individual contributor quality control gigs.

However, in 1965, Charlie was one of the first scientific minds to settle down in a quaint little locale now known as Silicon Valley. He was a successful entrepreneur in the wafer and PCB industries and so, 40 years later, he still had much sage advice to offer to potential client companies. When someone in Silicon Valley heard Charlie's name, they would customarily make a little bow of respect to the "wafer king."

Therefore, we included nearly all 45 years of Charlie's work experience on the three-page resume and accompanying addendums, which listed patents and board positions at other companies. We adjusted Charlie's value proposition to the particular market he was targeting. By the way, he received offers to work in both venues—he was that good.

So, how long is the experience section? As you can see, it all depends…

Company Title

The company or organization title is typically left justified and leads off each sub-section of experience. USE CAPITAL LETTERS (BUT NOT BOLD) FOR YOUR COMPANY TITLE. This allows it to stand out without overshadowing the position title, which is usually in bold.

As every word on the resume counts and we are aiming for a high degree of understanding with both readers who are quickly scanning as well as taking a more thorough look, I recommend shortening the title as appropriate, without losing the identification power of the words. Therefore, if a candidate worked at "L.L. Bean, Inc.," list the title as "LL BEAN." Likewise, if a candidate worked at "Wang Laboratories, Inc.," truncate the title to "WANG" or "WANG LABORATORIES." However, if the same geographical area boasted several companies by a very similar name, as in the case of multiple family businesses located in one area, then the "Inc." might be kept to distinguish between them.

What about in the case where a company name has changed due to merger or acquisition? While there are exceptions to every rule, place the prior company name in lower case italics following the current company name. For example, if you were hired by Magellan Industries eight years ago, and three years ago Magellan was bought out by Rocky Mountain Enterprises, then it is preferred you would list your company as: "ROCKY MOUNTAIN ENTERPRISES *formerly Magellan Industries*," with no comma in between. This promotes improved readability and clarity.

Further, if you have worked for the same company for 30 years and the company name has changed four times, it can be tempting to list four separate companies on your resume.

How this may be perceived, however, is anyone's guess.

At best, a reader might be mildly confused when it came time for the interview. At worst, a reader might misinterpret your clarification efforts as an effort to twist the truth into something more favorable to your candidacy. Be safe and opt for listing the most current company name, with perhaps the most prominent former name listed in italics. If it is truly, truly important that the reader is aware of all the M&A and name changing activity surrounding your employer, then find a way to work it into the text in the lines following the company name.

The location of the company and dates of employment follow on the same line as the company name, with the name of a city/town appearing in lower case, such as:

HRD INDUSTRIES, Anytown, CA	2005 - 2012

Dates are always right justified and not just moved over using multiple strikes of the indent or tab key. In the latest version of MS Word, access the "Tabs" section either by right clicking or via the "Paragraph" function above the top ruler.

Position or Job Title

The position title (also known as "job title") is important—it is of high interest to most readers.

Use bold (but not capital letters) for your position title.

In combination with using capital letters (but not bold) for your company title, this will allow the reader to easily delineate between the two, while prioritizing the position title.

Try to keep the position title short and highly readable.

If you have a longer title, consider truncating or clarifying with non-bolded italics following the title.

For example, if your formal position title is "Senior Manufacturing Engineer for Production of Switch Mode Power Supplies," first determine how important it is to highlight the product line (you will no doubt be mentioning it in your bullets, but the question is how much you need it to stand out) and then choose between these two options:

Senior Manufacturing Engineer

or

Senior Manufacturing Engineer — *Switch Mode Power Supplies*

<u>Always be honest regarding your title, but don't feel the need to use the exact wording of your formal position title.</u>

Otherwise the readability of your resume and power of your brand may suffer.

This can be especially true if your job duties have shifted over the years. By some estimations, nearly 25% of all Fortune 500 company workers have their roles/duties shifted an average of 30% or more each year…while their titles and job descriptions remain static!

So, it could actually be inaccurate and misleading to use your formal position title.

Take, for example, the person who started in the warehouse as a Picker/Packer (an actual title) four years ago. They may have moved into a logistics analyst role two years ago and yet still have the formal title of Foundry Warehouse Associate III.

In this case, I would suggest using one of three options on the resume:

Logistics Analyst — *Foundry Warehouse*

or

Logistics Analyst / Warehouse Associate III

or

Logistics Analyst
Warehouse Associate III

If the first option is used, then you could always list the former Warehouse Associate position later, with each having several descriptive bullets.

The second option is typically used when someone is working two different functions simultaneously (perhaps the individual still helps out as a Picker/Packer during periods of peak volume).

The third option allows ease of readability and offers the idea that the candidate was promoted from the bottom position to the top one. In this case, list descriptive bullets for both positions together following the titles.

Additionally, if you have had multiple positions at one company, it is your choice whether to list all the positions on your resume or simply the last/most current one(s). I write resumes both ways, depending on the candidate and what they have for a brand.

Certainly, when filling out an application for employment or answering detailed questions about work history, a candidate should always consider listing every position. However, remember that a resume is a marketing piece—a "professional brochure" if you will—and, as such, needs to be honest but also promote a clear, succinct, and understandable message.

Company or Position Descriptions

While not mandatory, sometimes it adds value to give an overview description of either the company, the position, or both. Readers often find this useful in getting a sense of the size of company, the type of product, or your overall role. Just make sure you don't insert a description as simply a space filler. And, if you use a description for one company or position, you need to do the same for each one on the resume, maintaining parallel form.

Let's consider the following example:

> **Controller / Accounting Manager**
> *Managed finances for 3 divisions totaling $21M in revenue. Responsible for operating plans, annual forecasts, reporting functions, financial statements, and daily flash reporting.*

First to note in the above example is the candidate's position title. Their formal position title was simply "Controller" but, because the Accounting Manager's position was eliminated due to budget constraints, the candidate ended up doing the Accounting Manager's duties as well.

So this extended position title is actually more accurate and informative than simply that of "Controller."

The description is actually a merger of company and position descriptions. And the description doesn't even really get into details about the company's product or market...because the only areas of relevance for a Controller type of position would be the number of divisions and total revenue (financial information), giving a reader a quick, yet informative view into the breadth of responsibilities of this particular candidate.

The description goes onto the third line, which may be a bit lengthy; it really depends on what the candidate is trying to accomplish.

The italics allows the description to stand out but not take away from the bullets (the main event) or overshadow the bolded position title and capitalized company title.

Such a position or company description can serve other purposes, as well.

For instance, while it is not advisable to put certain information on a resume such as salary or why a candidate left a position, if there was a compelling reason to describe a unique situation, it could be accomplished here.

Perhaps the company, once employing 900 workers, sold off divisions and downsized to a skeleton crew of 30 for last six months before closing.

If you were one of the 30 workers selected to stay with the company to the end, you could describe this as: *"...following downsizing of 900 positions, selected to serve as one of last 30 employees to close down business operations..."*

Just make sure the description is making a positive, key point.

Remember: Every word counts.

OK, you knew it was coming. It's time to jot down a complete list of all the companies and all the positions you have ever held. Only then you will be able to determine which ones have value and need to be included in the resume.

Then, once you have your final list, give some thought to whether a reader would find value in a brief, italicized description of the company or position or both.

My List of Companies Worked At and Positions Held

Your writing ability is all "warmed up" now. So let's move on to creating the content of the Experience section in the form of bullets…

Chapter 10

Writing: Bullets

> *"I've missed more than 9,000 shots in my career. I've lost almost 300 games. 26 times, I've been trusted to take the game winning shot and missed. I've failed over and over and over again in my life. And that is why I succeed."*
>
> - Michael Jordan

As with Michael Jordan, most of us can connect our failures to our successes. This inspirational quote calls on every one of us to be resilient, to learn, and to persevere following failure. The key is trying to do your best every day. The key is taking action. Consistently.

Keep this quote in mind as you write the bullets that make up the heart of your resume. *Don't judge yourself; that is the hiring manager's job.*

Instead, commit to detailing your accomplishments. But also remember that your actions need detailing, too. Companies hire people who get results. Companies also hire people who take action.

Bullets Promote Content

Bullets follow the position title(s) and provide accomplishment and task details to back up your brand's value proposition.

"But I like the look of a paragraph-style description better," you protest.

Well, so do I. But it's not about what we subjectively "like." It's about what is going to get results. And **bullets are proven to draw in the reader's eye to the content**—which is king. Therefore, bullets are the preferred choice for almost all resumes.

A few parameters for using bullets...

- Start each with a past tense action verb.
- Have no more than 4 to 6 bullets in any series (after a position).
- End each with a period.
- **<u>Describe specific and measurable accomplishments/results.</u>**
- Place the two most important bullets at the top of a list.
- Include an action component as well, giving detail to how you realized the accomplishment.
- Use numbers/numerical values (no matter how big or small) in the bullet to describe your actions and/or accomplishments
- Place the most important words (sometimes the accomplishment and sometimes the action) at the very beginning of the bullet.
- Use a choppy style, eliminating words like "a" and "the" if possible.
- Worry less about length; more about content. One line bullets are OK *as long as the words convey value*. Remember, resumes must both: grab the reader's interest on a quick scan and present compelling and detailed content upon further reading.

Review of Sample Bullets

Let's take a moment to look at a few bullets from the "after" resume sample in Chapter 1…

Sample Bullet #1

> - Renegotiated 3 primary vendor relationships, without sacrificing "loyalty factor," to effect average of 5% or $215K annual savings.

This bullet is strong and succinct. It begins with an action verb, describes the candidate's actions or tasks, shows a tangible result, and utilizes numbers. Should the candidate expand the detail about how they "renegotiated?" Perhaps if it was a complex negotiation or they were known for a unique negotiating style or they were in a different role (such as that of a "Buyer"), but this CFO/Controller candidate captures exactly what they need to in this case.

Sample Bullet #2

> - Organized all financial systems for Mexican subsidiary, completing all related tax returns for first year and incorporating transfer pricing model.

This action/task-oriented bullet is well written. While it doesn't refer to a specific accomplishment, it begins with a strong overview of the action and follows with more detail about the specific tasks involved. The choice of the lead word "organized" resonates with the reader because a finance/accounting professional must thrive in a highly ordered and organized world all day. Could the bullet have included numbers? Sure, but there are plenty of other bullets in this resume with numbers. Could the bullet be made more succinct, leaving out the detail following? Perhaps. But not all accounting and finance folks are involved with transfer pricing. The detail adds value here.

Accomplishments are most compelling, but can be hard to determine for most individual contributor jobs, which are often more action or task oriented.

Are you nodding your head right now? That's perfectly fine.

Some of you will be hard pressed to come up with specific accomplishments which relate to your actions. Just do your best.

Remember, even action/task-oriented positions relate to the bottom line—whether through individual or team efforts. Note: a bullet can start with: "Teamed with 3 co-workers to …" (Note: remember to use numbers whenever possible and *always use their numerical form*)

Consider the areas of accomplishment for the task-oriented positions below and ask yourself, "What are my areas of accomplishment?"

- **Bank Teller**: accuracy, cross selling, customer satisfaction
- **Assembler**: quality, productivity
- **Machine Maintenance Tech**: machine up-time, response time
- **Retail Clerk**: accuracy, efficiency
- **Customer Service Desk**: calming upset customers, solving problems

You may have to dig deep to come up with specific and measurable accomplishments to put in your resume and use in your interview. But the dividends will be huge.

Just remember to develop your own resume content.

Resist the urge to just "copy and paste" the contents of your job description onto your resume. Reviewing job description wording can be useful but you will need to further develop your bullets to make them compelling. Let's examine another bullet from the sample resume in Chapter 1.

Sample Bullet #3

> - Reduced scrap by 86%, utilizing lean concepts, for average $28K+ in annual savings. Initiated idea of "efficiency committees" for each department, which eventually led to consolidation of lines and outsourcing of non-essential functions, resulting in additional savings.

This bullet is also well-developed.

It begins with the accomplishment and then expands into additional detail in the second sentence. Numbers are involved up front, although the person may not have had a figure available to describe the "additional savings." Note: If you have a general idea of a number but don't remember it exactly, use a conservative approximation, as this candidate did with "$28K+."

This bullet, as with most other accomplishment bullets, is versatile; it could present either the action or the accomplishment first, depending upon which is most impactful. For example, it could be modified to:

> - Initiated idea of "efficiency committees" for each department, which eventually led to consolidation of lines and outsourcing of non-essential functions. Additional lean efforts led to 86% reduction in scrap or average $28K+ in annual savings.

"Action" AND "Result" in each Bullet

Think of each bullet, optimally, as having an "action" and a "result." Try your best to include both in each bullet. Once your have written your bullets, review each to determine whether the action or the result should be stated first.

While it is usually evident whether action or result/accomplishment is more powerful for each bullet, remember that you could switch their order if it would be more compelling when applying for a particular position.

Overwhelmed? It can feel that way. But you owe it to yourself to present the best possible first impression when entering the employment marketplace. After all…

There is no job offer for the runner-up.

Uncovering Accomplishments

It can be challenging to uncover your accomplishments, let alone to promote yourself by writing about them!

Here are a few strategies when trying to identify accomplishments:

- Look at past performance reviews.
- Ask your co-workers or former supervisors whom you trust.
- Think about the teams you have served on, your roles on the teams, and what the team accomplished.
- Remember professionally difficult or challenging moments.
- Remember moments when you were praised.
- Keep a pad of paper and pen with you (or nearby) so it is always easy to jot down ideas when they pop into your head.
- Make a list of your strengths and then how you have used each.
- Ask yourself specific questions (consider the questions in the next list) or have a trusted friend ask you specific questions and then write down or record your answers.
- Design your own strategy or system to help you remember your accomplishments.

You might consider asking yourself the following questions to prompt a recall of your accomplishments:

- Did you recommend, design, or implement a new method, system, process, form, or procedure? By what means did you do so and what happened as a result?

- Have you identified problems? Did you suggest or implement solutions? If so, what was the result?

- Was your work in a fairly common position, but perhaps you did your job differently in some way? If so, what was the result?

- What impact did you make in terms of time, money, morale, safety, or accountability? What was the specific result?

- Did you solve internal or external customer problems? Did your contribution engender a "smoother running" operation?

- Have you promoted, cross-marketed, or sold? If so, what were the metrics you were held to and how did you perform? Was it a difficult market? Did you face "jungle" conditions?

- Still having a tough time? Ask yourself: what am I most proud of and what did people compliment me on?

Now that you have remembered some accomplishments, it's time to write about them!

Am I hearing some of you protest? OK, you always have the choice of calling one of us resume writers to help you out. The problem with that? Most higher-quality resume writers will still require you to either write about your experience or speak to us about it or both!

Certainly, when I have engaged with someone to work on their resume, I plan on spending at least a couple hours total on the phone with that client, in addition to having them write about their experience and/or having them provide me with old resumes.

Also, I require each of my clients to fill out a 12+ page form right up front…and those questions aren't about their experience!

So, even if you choose to engage a professional resume writer to help you out, be ready to provide them with some well thought out content.

The quality of your resume is related to the quality of your effort, one way or the other!

Natural vs. Structured Writing Approaches

Simply put, there is no right or wrong way to develop your bullets.

Rather, there are two approaches: "natural" and "structured."

I have used both approaches successfully.

It is really a personal preference of which will work best for you.

A *natural approach* means that you just start writing. When writing, you might find that you think of other ideas for bullets or your bullet might start expanding such that it transforms into two or three bullets. This is a less structured type of approach.

It can, however, lead to important missed details unless the writer reviews the bullets several times.

A *structured approach* means that you utilize a more methodical system for developing bullets, typically creating the various parts of a single bullet in linear fashion. You might use a system such as PAR (see below) to help you develop the various parts of a bullet.

The potential downside here is that it lacks efficiency and, in being so detailed and compartmentalized, you could miss the bigger picture.

PAR

A common *structured* approach to bullet development that has been used for years by major outplacement and career consulting firms is the PAR, or Problem-Action-Result, approach.

Here is a sample of what a PAR might look like and the corresponding bullet:

Problem: Addition of "boom and bust" semi-conductor business grew overall revenue rapidly, but margins suffered as a result of losing track of actual production costs as related to output.

Action: Senior management met and decided to task Cost Accounting position with identifying costs and suggesting appropriate ways to save without impacting output or quality. Cost Accounting position researched and identified costs on both material and labor sides, as well as considering monthly output targets. Developed recommendations and reported back to senior team.

Result: Recommendations implemented by line managers with savings ranging between $5K and $8K each month during a sustained period.

From the above PAR, the candidate developed the following bullet:

> - Identified actual production costs for both material and labor, correlating recommendations for savings with monthly output targets. Implemented recommendations saved between $5K and $8K per month over 3-year period.

Whatever approach to bullet-writing you choose—including those of your own creation—the best results come from being deliberate and consistent in your process.

Action Verbs

I'm not going to waste space here by providing you with a list of action verbs. You'll get better results with more variety by simply Googling "action verbs" or some other derivation. Everyone and their brother has come up with a list.

Besides, there is something much more important than coming up with an exhaustive action-verb list: **choosing the *right* action verbs to begin your bullets**.

The sample resume in Chapter 1 uses: led, directed, determined, spearheaded, organized, improved, enhanced, identified, reduced, and researched. Essentially, as each bullet was written, an appropriate action verb was chosen, keeping in mind both the bullet and the bigger picture of what was wished to be conveyed as the actual brand message. Each action verb in this sample is different. But it doesn't have to be…

Redundancy in the defense of a resume's brand message is no vice!

A strategy of utilizing a few of the same action verbs to begin multiple bullets reinforces a message to the reader that those actions are among your strengths.

Similarly, related words can really drive home a point. And these are easy to find: simply right click with your cursor on a word and choose "Synonyms" or, like I still do sometimes, dust off the old thesaurus!

To illustrate the potential power of using redundancy and related words in tandem, let's look at an example. Say a design-engineering candidate really wants to emphasize their ability to create new products and processes. The action verbs on their resume might be biased in favor of "create, design, and develop."

The bullets on their resume might start with:

COMPANY 1
  Position 1
- Created...
- Designed...
- Instituted...
- Created...
- Re-designed...

  Position 2
- Designed...
- Researched...
- Utilized...
- Developed...

COMPANY 2
  Position 1
- Developed...
- Created...
- Organized...
- Created...
- Designed...
- Implemented...

This example is heavy on a message that this candidate's strengths lie on the creative/design side. The words used to begin their bullets would help them to *get noticed*.

But, if this candidate chose to apply for other types of positions such as those that were more focused on supervising and managing teams, these words would not resonate and there would be no interview.

Choose your action verbs wisely.

So, what action verbs are you going to use?

Guerilla Tactics for Writing Bullets

Still stuck?

Here are a few more bullet-writing tactics for getting you started and keeping you on track:

- To get ideas, go online and look at sample resumes, LinkedIn profiles, job descriptions, and position announcements that relate to your own professional experience.

- Talk with a friend and have them ask you interview-style questions about your work. Record, either in audio or in print, your responses (you could even use a Skype-like program and save it for future review!).

- Choose five action verbs most relevant to each position and then fill-in-the-blank after each verb.

- Write down a few words to describe the heart of each bullet. Worry about the details of numbers, action verbs, and the like at a later time.

- Take a break and begin again when your mind is less cluttered.

- Purchase a sample resume book to generate ideas (some libraries carry these in the reference section).

- Budget a 1 to 2 hour block to visit your local library and enjoy some dedicated quiet time to focus on your task.

- Bring a pad of paper or recording device with you during your daily travels or workout routine to record random ideas—just be safe and don't use while you are driving or doing another dangerous activity.

- Don't worry so much about the fancy words—resumes are more effective in your own words anyway.

Now it's time to try a bit of writing. Review the most important aspects of your last job and identify actions and results, whether working alone or in a team. Then, briefly jot down observations (form your "bullets" later). <u>After</u> you have done some writing, then add in some numbers!

Information for Creating My Bullet #1

Action	Result

Information for Creating My Bullet #2

Action	Result

Information for Creating My Bullet #3

Action	Result

Chapter 11

Writing: Education

"There is no elevator to success. You have to take the stairs."
   - Zig Ziglar

A college degree has become a requirement of most good paying jobs.

I don't like it, but it's a fact. Before we get into writing the Education section, you need a bit of background to make good career choices going forward.

In 1982, 1.5 million Americans earned a bachelor's degree or above. In 2013, 2.7 million Americans earned a bachelor's degree or above. A reasonable increase of degrees over a 31 year period. But a closer examination of the numbers reveals an alarming trend.

In 1982, 12% of these degrees were master's level or higher. In 2013, about 30% of these degrees were master's level or higher.

The master's degree is quickly taking over…at a time when higher education costs have skyrocketed and employers are picking up less of the tab.

The responsibility is all yours.

While I am a huge proponent of higher education in general and technical training/community college education specifically, such trends make me sick to my stomach.

Whether you can remember it or not, there was a time, not so very long ago, when hard work, ingenuity, and good decisions were all you needed to become successful.

My two grandfathers could attest to that. But things are different now.

If you already have a degree, now is the time to apply the manifesto of hard work, ingenuity, and good decisions.

*If you do not have a degree, now is the time to seriously consider completing a <u>**marketable**</u> degree or technical certificate.*

And, if you do go back to school, <u>do your research</u>.

Don't think that just because you are choosing a bachelor's in business over sociology or an MBA over an MEd that you will be marketable.

That was 15 years ago and this is now.

So, what are your options?

<u>Take advantage of quality programs at community colleges and public universities to keep costs down.</u> And, even if you already have a degree, make sure it is still relevant. If not, explore the potential of earning certifications or perhaps a two year technical degree.

Don't just look at the internet to identify those professions with increasing demand. Because, even if demand is increasing by 15%, some schools are looking to cash in and may be boosting supply by 30%! (*Example: Last year, in my home state of Maine, there was a healthy increase in demand for medical assistants, with 70+ openings. But private and public schools graduated 470+ individuals with medical assistant degrees!*)

So, again, do your research. Make an intelligent decision.

Of course, a degree by itself will not guarantee you employment or upward career mobility. But one thing is for certain: a lack of education will dramatically decrease your chances of landing a decent job and will probably cost you hundreds of thousands of dollars in lost wages over your lifetime.

Sorry for admonishing some of you. But it is *that* important. So consider your fastest, most inexpensive way to the right degree that can boost your job search chances. And take action. Now.

OK. Let's give you some guidelines for writing the "Education" section.

An Important Section

Such a small section. Such a big impact.

The "Education" section is the second most viewed part of a resume, after the "Experience" section.

It must be easily readable, presenting your degree(s) succinctly and, typically, in reverse chronological order with your most advanced degree placed at the top of the list.

I prefer to have the entire contents of this section centered but formatting is up to you.

Usually, **the name of the degree will be in bold** and listed first on a line, followed by the name of the college or university, and followed by the city and state in which the campus is located. There should be at least a half space between each degree listed.

By the way, while we are speaking about the "Education" section... although there are exceptions, training and non-credit courses do not typically belong here. We will discuss this in a bit.

Now let's examine some specifics...

Abbreviating the Type of Degree

In most cases, abbreviating your degree (such as: BS, AS, MBA, or PhD) actually allows for greater readability by hiring managers and ease of being found by recruiters scouring the web. Especially if you bold the degree name, as I previously suggested.

If you like, you may choose to use periods in your abbreviation. I usually do not use periods in an abbreviation only because some search and sorting programs have historically found candidates quicker if they are left out. The choice is yours.

Similarly, while other resume writers have certain rules, I don't have much preference as to separating your degree type from the major.

I have used commas, hyphens, empty space, and "in"...

> **BS, Accounting**
> **BS – Accounting**
> **BS Accounting**
> **BS in Accounting**

Of course, sometimes it is commonly recognized to abbreviate the entire degree, such as with: MBA.

Following are a few more examples of an abbreviated degree:

AS, Accounting
AAS – Engineering Technology
BA in Physics
BA, Sociology
BS Chemistry
BS – Business
BSME
BSMET
BSEE
BSN
MS Management
MA, History
MS – Finance
MBA
MPA
PhD in Organizational Leadership
EdD, Counselor Education

Are there as exceptions to the abbreviation rule? Of course.

If potential readers of your resume are unfamiliar with an abbreviation, spell out the type of degree in full.

For example, an MPA is fairly widely known as a Master of Public Administration, while an MPPM is a lesser-known abbreviation for a Master of Public Policy and Management. I routinely use the MPA abbreviation but will use the full spelling of the MPPM degree on a resume.

Another exception would be receiving a Certificate in a field of study. It is advisable to spell out the word "Certificate" instead of trying to abbreviate.

Minors, Concentrations, and Courses

Most of the time, I don't recommend having minors or other core concentrations compete with the degree major, even if the major does not relate directly to your targeted profession.

Hence, the type of degree and major field of study should appear in bold, with all other references to coursework appearing in plain text.

Are there exceptions?

Of course.

What about the anthropology major who's minor in accounting becomes the ticket to open the door to be interviewed for business-related positions?

That candidate may or may not present their major in bold, but they will certainly want to draw the reader's eye to their minor as well. In their case, the minor is almost more important than the major!

Two of the most effective ways to help a minor, concentration, or group of courses standout are to italicize and/or position the relevant words on the line underneath the major.

Consider these four examples:

BS History with *Minor in Accounting*, HGD College, Denver, CO

BS in History. *Minor in Accounting*. HDG College, Denver, CO

BS—History, HDG College, Denver, CO
Minor in Accounting

BS, History with Minor in Accounting, HDG College, Denver, CO
Select Courses: International Tax, Transfer Pricing, Audit I & II

Partially Completed Degrees

Partially completed degrees need to be listed on the resume, no matter how much time has passed. With rare exception, they will only add to your perceived value as a candidate. Whether you completed four courses or 40 credits toward your degree, it demonstrates to the reader that you value higher education, are interested in professional development, and have the ability to learn in a formal, classroom setting. It may just be the deciding factor in whether you are offered an interview.

You may either use the number of courses completed or the number of credits completed to describe your progress toward a degree. Note that I typically advise against placing the degree in bold in these instances.

Often, my clients' resumes will indicate the number of credits they have completed. So, if an individual has completed 10 courses worth three credits each, then the words "completed 30 credits" would appear on the resume.

For those individuals who are concerned about the fact that they have completed only two or three total courses, there is the option of simply stating "coursework" instead of accounting for the number of courses or credits earned.

Irrespective of the descriptor you choose, you should state the name of the degree or major for which you were/are studying. If you have not yet declared a major, new may alternatively write "general studies."

Unlike my preference for showing degrees in bold, I typically do not use bold in the case of partial degrees...unless a degree is to be conferred in the next semester or two, as with the last of the four examples here:

> *42 of 48 credits completed towards AS Business*, SWR College, Gary, IN
>
> Coursework in Business, SWR College, Gary, IN
>
> 13 courses completed, SWR College, Gary, IN
>
> **AS Business** — expected graduation May, 2015, SWR College, Gary, IN

High School Diploma or GED

The resume writing world is somewhat divided over whether or not to include a high school diploma or GED if that is your only degree.

Today, with such a high percentage of individuals completing their high school degree, there is less and less of an argument for including it on the resume. However, an alternative point emanates from my experience helping outplacement clients who lived in rural America and worked hard in lower skill occupations.

Frequently, the employers in those communities had numerous applicants who had not completed high school. Therefore, it was useful to include such a degree on the resume for their local job search.

Finally, just to be clear, even if you have completed a few college courses, you should not include your high school degree or GED but, instead, list those college courses. This is due to the fact that, excepting today's "dual enrollment" high school honors students who sometimes take college courses in high school, it is generally assumed that you have completed high school in order to enroll in college.

Placement of the Education Section

If you have completed a degree within the past 18 months and it is relevant to your job search, the Education section should follow the Profile section. Otherwise, it belongs immediately following the Experience section.

GPA

In this era of grade inflation, everyone earns a "B."

A "B" is now considered average. Show up for each class, turn in mediocre work on time, and fudge the essay questions on the exam. It often translates into a "B." Of course, some colleges offer more rigorous programs than others. Some courses are more rigorous than others.

Now, I don't mean to put anyone down if they have pursued higher education and/or have earned their degree—no matter what the school or program of study.

On the contrary, I have great respect for the students of today who face substantially increased life pressures and are working their way through any sort of higher education or training beyond high school, irrespective of their program or grades.

But, <u>*completing*</u> the degree or certificate program is what really matters. Not the GPA. Employers know that and are unimpressed by a "B" or even a "B+" with a few exceptions. So, most of the time…

I advise not including GPA on your resume.

The exceptions? If you graduated from a heavy-duty program (notice I said "program" and not "college") such as engineering, chemistry, or physics, you could consider including a GPA as low as 3.3 or 3.4. Otherwise, resist the temptation to put down anything less than a 3.85.

Also, if you have graduated with your bachelor's and master's degrees, certainly you would either choose to include *both GPAs or neither*.

Disagree with my advice? I can respect that.

Just remember, once your resume hits the streets you cannot take it back. Also, *remember that the resume is not for your consumption.* So, be proud of your 3.5 GPA, have a certified copy of your transcript ready in case employers ask for it, and omit your GPA from the resume. For the most part, you should follow that same logic with any honors received.

College Honors and Awards

Similar to GPA, unless you were inducted into Phi Beta Kappa (not a different honor society), made magna or summa cum laude, or earned the equivalent of a Rhodes or Fulbright…be proud of your honors and awards, but please leave them off the resume. Otherwise, you risk coming across as arrogant and sophomoric.

Also, if more than 8-10 years have passed since you earned your degree, you would probably be well advised to remove the "3.9 GPA" and "summa cum laude" from the resume. At that point, your accomplishments and experience should be speaking for you.

Academic Projects

Consider including one or two academic projects if they have value to your candidacy.

Examples might include: a Capstone Paper, original research, an engineering design and/or build, a practicum, an internship (unless included in the Experience section), or a team project.

If you do choose to list an academic project, consider including a brief, one or two line description so that it is easy for the reader to understand the work you were engaged in and, if appropriate, the process you followed. You might also make mention if it was a team project.

And, if the project related to an area of interest for the potential employer, you might want to have a copy of the final paper ready as a supplement to your resume.

Please note that companies are particularly interested in individuals who are able to achieve results while maintaining smooth and productive team relationships, so group or team papers and projects will often resonate with perspective employers.

Date of Graduation

I usually leave off graduation date on resumes. It's less about trying to hide age and more about including only essential information.

Remember, the resume is akin to a marketing brochure and, as such, does not purport to provide 100% of your professional or educational history. That's what applications for employment are for.

Of course, there are exceptions.

Consider including a date if you are a:

- Current student with an expected graduation date.
- Recent graduate (within the last 18 months) who chooses to place your education section before the experience section on the resume.
- Technically-oriented candidate for whom a degree in the last several years will show proficiency in the latest concepts, technologies, methods, and/or tools.
- Candidate who left work for a few years to earn your degree.

Your Studies Away

Employers typically only care about where you earned your degree. However, if your semester or year abroad was in the Galapagos Islands conducting research on Chelonia agassizii and you're applying to work at the International Sea Turtle Research Association, you should include that information on the resume.

Or, perhaps you previously attended an Ivy League school for a couple years but then had to transfer to an in-state university due to financial realities. You could make mention of this fact in the education section.

The bottom line? Put yourself in the shoes of a discerning recruiter or hiring manager and ask yourself whether or not listing your semester abroad or studies at another college come across as pretentious or valuable. I bet you're smart enough to make the right choice.

Omitting a Degree

I do not believe in "dumbing down" a resume by omitting an aspect of your education. There have only been two or three exceptions out of the thousands of resumes I have worked on or reviewed professionally.

The one that comes to mind belonged to a senior manager/scientist with two PhDs and four master's degrees. He was, as I recall, in the process of going for a fifth master's!

I didn't want that individual candidate to be perceived by hiring managers as someone who is constantly distracted by pursuing additional education. In addition, several of the individual's degrees did not relate to the field they were pursuing. We settled on including one PhD and two master's degrees.

As the advice contained in this chapter is now fresh in your mind, please take the next few minutes to jot down some ideas or even a draft of how your education might be presented on your resume.

Ideas for Content and Format of My Education Section

Chapter 12

Writing: Extra Sections

"With great power comes great responsibility."
- Voltaire

You have the power to add any sort of section to the resume of which you can conceive. Just remember Voltaire's words.

When pondering the addition of a section to your resume, presumably after the "Education" section, ask yourself questions like these:

- Does it support my professional brand?
- How will it impact the reader?
- Is it essential (or pretty darn close) to getting me hired?

If you have a positive answer to such questions, you have the green light to add it to your resume.

Let's explore what "other sections" you might consider including …

Training

This is the most common additional section to the resume and is often utilized to either supplement or offset the "Education" section.

Of course, you won't want to simply state the obvious (if you are a truck driver, for instance, you don't have to list defensive driving training—it is assumed you have it). Instead, make sure such a section would enhance your value as a candidate (perhaps you have taken advanced defensive driving for FEMA level IV emergencies). A "Training" section must add real value to your candidacy. You can provide detail and dates for your training or you can simply list subject content.

Example of a Training section that follows and supplements Education:

EDUCATION
AS, Engineering and Avionics Technology, UBV Community College, Anytown, TX

TECHNICAL TRAINING

Flight Controls and Recorder	GPS and Compass	Turbine Overhaul
Electronics Troubleshooting	Control Calibration	JIT Inventory KL System
LN-9 Inertial Navigation	Digital Autopilot	Prevention of Collisions

---

Example of a Training section for a production candidate who never completed high school. Items are bulleted to engage the reader:

TRAINING

- Lean Manufacturing
- Kwick Kaizen 1-2-3
- 9 Step Team Process
- EMT
- HAZMAT
- ChemClean
- JHG Machine PMs
- JIT StockMover II and III
- Logistics Traffic Mod I

Example of Training section for a seasoned IT manager/director, with broad technical knowledge and management expertise:

RELEVANT TRAINING

NTL Human Interaction Laboratory III	Situational Leadership II
ITSM Foundations	Tivoli Identity Manager V2.1.1
Silicon Advanced System Administration	1561 Designing Directory Infrastructure
HACMP/6000 Operating System Principles	HGF Storage Data Implementation

---

Ask yourself:

What training have I completed that could add value to my resume?

Associations

You might include a section for either the professional or the industry groups to which you belong, or both.

Perhaps you have even held leadership or committee positions within these organizations. Maybe you worked on a few projects or you helped organize a training.

The key, again, is to make sure it *adds value to your candidacy* and doesn't suggest that you might be distracted at work.

A "Professional Associations" or "Industry Associations" section might also include regional meetings or conferences attended, although you could instead choose to create an additional "Conferences" section if you had enough compelling material.

Certifications

Listing "MSCE" ("Microsoft Certified Engineer") might just get you interviewed…or even hired!

Here is an example of a rather Spartan certification section. Yet each of the certifications, by itself, is significant! Someone with these credentials is going to *get noticed…*

CERTIFICATIONS
CompTIA Security+
MS Systems Engineer
Information Technology Architect Certification

I have witnessed candidates who prominently displayed PMP, CPA, and Six Sigma Black Belt (or another certification) secure interviews and get job offers much quicker than candidates who didn't have those certifications or didn't make them easily visible on the resume.

And, I have witnessed the opposite, as well.

Ask yourself:

Does the hiring manager require a particular certification?

Although it's rare, certifications can occasionally work against you.

After all, you certainly don't want to be perceived as just being adept at amassing a bunch of certifications to the detriment of actually accomplishing anything!

Know the market and what it wants.

Then you will know if including such a section is even in your best interest at all.

Additionally, you need to consider the placement of such sections on the resume. Typically, these extra sections are placed either after the "Education" section or before the "Experience" section.

And, please, do not list any expired, dated, or basic-level certifications that even your pet cockatoo might list on its resume.

Finally, please understand that the significance of certain certifications is sometimes linked with the organization that endorsed an individual's qualifications. In these cases, you will want to mention the organization's name and any other relevant information.

For example, CPAs and lawyers are typically licensed in a particular state. In these cases, the organization's name and state should be listed and, in the case of a CPA, their license number should also be evident.

If you do choose to include a Certifications section, make sure it draws the reader's attention to something of significance.

Hiring managers are savvy enough to know when someone may be trying to pad their resume and this doesn't reflect well on a candidate's character.

Company Honors or Awards

The big challenge with including an "Honors" or "Awards" type of section is that a candidate may be perceived as more focused on their ego/winning recognition than on an employer's priorities or on achieving results.

Of course, many honors and awards are conferred exactly because an individual has achieved results above and beyond an employer's performance expectations.

If you choose to include an honors and awards section, I would strongly recommend a brief, one or two line explanation of the accomplishment that led to the recognition.

And, certainly, you'll want to make sure that you only include honors and awards that are significant. How do you know if they are significant or not? Ask your colleagues and other trusted advisors who will be reviewing your resume.

All that being said, **honors or awards, if mentioned at all, are usually best *written into accomplishment bullets*** in the "Experience" section.

By including them in the "Experience" section, they can be included in the resume, are placed in the context of job performance, and don't draw attention away from your experience.

A bullet referring to an honor or award would usually begin with a description of the actions and results that led to receiving the honor and *then* mention the actual recognition near the end of the bullet.

You might even find that, once you have written such a bullet, there is really no need to make mention of the honor or award in a separate section after all.

Military Service

If you are just leaving military service—whether after 20 years or four years—and you're seeking employment in the private sector, your military service should probably be described under the experience section itself.

Alternatively, if you served your country in the armed forces for a period of four to eight years and that service ended 15 or 20 years ago, you could account for it under a separate "Military Service" section.

Should you choose to have a separate "Military Service" section, it might be placed directly after the "Experience" section or even after the "Education" section.

A "Military Service" section does not have to be formatted similar to the "Experience" section. Especially if your military service does not relate closely to your job search objective, you might think about keeping this section rather short, with either a couple one-line listings of functional position titles or perhaps a very short paragraph describing your service.

While including a "Military Service" section on the resume has been back in vogue now for many years, there was a time when it was often omitted. Don't try to hide your service but, if you are applying to be a field representative with an organization named "Citizens for Unilateral Disbanding of the Armed Forces," you might want to leave it off the resume. Of course, you might also be wasting your time applying for a position with that organization!

Certainly, even if you leave your past military service off the resume, you could always mention it in the interview if you sense it would give you a tactical advantage. Who knows…relating to the unlikely example in the above paragraph, perhaps you find out during the interview that the organization actually has a veteran hiring preference just because those who served best understand the horrors of conflict.

While it is natural to be proud of serving your country, it is critical that you remove your ego from the resume and focus instead on the resume's impact with the hiring manager. If including a brief military service section on the resume will be an advantage in helping you to stand out then, by all means, make sure you create one.

Community or Volunteer Activities

Most of you would be treading on thin ice to include this section.

So be very careful here.

Over 25 years ago, including such a section could have bolstered the perception of your character and leadership. Not anymore.

Most companies *expect* you to have unimpeachable character.

As for your outside-of-work activities and interests? They just plain don't care.

In fact, today's employers want you focused on completing their tasks as efficiently as possible and are often concerned that too many outside interests or part-time/moonlighting jobs could lead to work place distractions.

Even if an employer touts "community service" as part of its cultural values statement, I typically do not recommend you include such a section on the resume anymore. In most cases, there is just too much risk.

However, if the position requires community involvement as part of the actual job itself, you will want to include such a section. Banking branch manager, non-profit executive, fund raising/development officer, commercial lending officer, real estate agent, insurance agent, office supply vendor, and small business development/sales specialist are just a few of the positions that cry out for you to include a "Community Involvement" section.

As with other resume sections discussed in this chapter, the choice is less about your ego and more about the hiring manager's requirements.

Ask yourself:

Am I seeking a <u>position</u> for which community or volunteer activities are clearly required or very closely related?

If your answer is "yes," then add this section to your resume.

Athletic Involvement

Ah, to be young!

If you are an athlete currently attending a high school or college and are seeking an internship or if you are a very recent high school or college graduate and are seeking fulltime employment, you might consider including a short "Athletic Involvement" section.

Of course, you could also list your involvement and/or other school activities immediately following your degree in the "Education" section instead.

It is really a matter of personal preference.

There is no doubt that playing a varsity sport could be perceived as a boost to your candidacy—both in terms of leadership potential and health/fitness.

Certainly, if you achieved significant athletic honors, noting that on the resume could have a high impact.

Just be mighty careful here.

Listing your involvement in sports could also be perceived as unsophisticated. Especially if it relates to your JV or intramural involvement.

After all, your experience and educational qualifications are the main event.

So, if you find yourself with limited resume space and a choice of whether to include your two years on the varsity croquet team or an additional engineering team project, your decision should be a no-brainer…<u>choose the project</u>.

Also, if you have completed ironman distance races…congratulations. Just leave them off your resume. I did.

Combining Sections

Should you ever combine two or three sections into one?

Professional resume writers respectfully disagree on if this is a good idea.

While I typically don't recommend it, I believe it depends on the individual and their particular situation.

There are two compelling arguments *against* combining sections:

> *1) Section searching and sorting:* Recruiters or other individuals may search for you by section heading keywords or sort your resume in an electronic database by the same criteria (following this school of thought, *you might also want to keep your section headings to one or two words maximum*). I am typically less concerned with this argument, however, because of my belief that you need to get the resume in front of the hiring manager in order to get noticed.

> *2) Readability*: Having separate sections for "Education" and "Training" could add clarity and be more easily digested by the reader than a combined section of "Education and Training."

My own exceptions to this rule typically revolve around either space limitations or offsetting a weak, but required, section. The latter of these exceptions is perhaps the most compelling.

One example might be the individual who just misses the educational requirements for a particular position but has significant training—well beyond that of most candidates. I might then propose an "Education and Training" section on their resume.

Perhaps the job advertisements are specifying an Associate's degree and you only completed three semesters but also have a certificate and other company-sponsored training in the latest technical tools. If you can get your resume directly in front of the hiring manager, they might be convinced to interview you if they read:

EDUCATION AND TRAINING

Certificate in ProEngineer Wildfire 5—JKK Community College
15 credits in Mechanical Design—GHC University
Solidworks 3D Aero-Space Design—Boeing
AutoCAD LT 2015 Pre-Release Test and Training—AutoDesk

Another example of such an exception would be an accomplished process engineer with significant training and expertise in six sigma and lean manufacturing but without a college degree.

In this case I would give consideration to combining the education and training sections in order to offset the lack of degree as well as to show the individual's openness to future learning in a formal/classroom setting.

Such a section might look something like:

SELECT CERTIFICATIONS AND TRAINING

PMP Certificate
Six Sigma Black Belt
Motorola Invitational Process Improvement Series
GE Advanced Lean Manufacturing Concepts I and II

In the above example, the first two lines denote certifications and the last two show training.

In addition, I have employed the use of the word "Select" in the title to guide the reader into perceiving that this candidate has more to share but doesn't want to clutter up the resume.

Indeed, the four items listed are significant and would have a positive impact with the reader…as individual items and collectively.

Note: Be aware, however, that the above section title is getting a bit lengthy…remember my advice about keeping it to one or two words maximum if at all possible. As you can see, sometimes there are a couple competing guidelines to follow.

I will leave it up to your best judgment whether you need to make an exception and combine two or more sections together.

You just might want to test your ideas with a few trusted advisors…before the market either validates or rejects your decision.

Before you can make any decisions about adding additional sections to your resume, you will need to take a close look at all the items that might populate a section or, in the alternative, at least be mentioned within some other section on your resume.

What else about the "professional you" might a reader want to know?

Since you have been learning about the relevance of adding additional sections to the resume in this chapter, its time you jot down a few notes to yourself about what potential sections or pieces of additional information might be valuable to the reader.

My Training, Associations, Certifications, or Other Information

Chapter 13

Gaps in Employment

*"Oh I'm lookin' for my missin' piece
I'm lookin' for my missin' piece
Hi-dee-ho, here I go,
Lookin' for my missin' piece."*

Shel Silverstein

Many of us experience some sort of gap in our work history.

The reasons can vary: reduction in force/getting laid off, pursuing a higher education degree, temporary illness or injury, starting a family…

Unfortunately, there is a perception by employers that a gap in employment makes a candidate much less desirable. So, such a gap must be dealt with on the resume.

While we aren't going to get into a full blown discussion of job search marketing strategy in a book dedicated to resumes, here are my thoughts…

Paramount here is resisting the temptation to run wild into the pucker brush of alternative resume styles, including a functional resume style.

Chronological formats comprise over 85% of all resumes and are much easier for the reader to interpret. Any other format risks raising at least a yellow or orange flag with the reader. In my own resume-writing practice, no more than one or two of the 100 or so resumes I work on each year is formatted in an alternative style. If you do choose to use an alternative style, please consider calling upon the services of a qualified resume writer.

OK, so now let's take a look at how to deal with a gap in employment on a more traditional, chronological format.

Years Matter, Months Don't

Resume writing evolved many moons ago such that, for some time now only *years*—and not months—are associated with a candidate's experience at each company.

While you should be completely forthright if asked about *months* details in either an interview or on a job application, months should be left off of resumes; they only serve as a distraction to the main focus—your suitability for the position opening.

This tactic alone typically solves a number of employment gap problems on the resume.

Let's take a look at an example that involves a one and a half year gap in work history…

Let's say a candidate worked at Company JHG from 2004 until being laid off in a RIF (reduction-in-force) during March of 2009. The candidate had a challenging job search, lasting 18 months, which finally ended when Company VBN hired them in September of 2010. The candidate's resume would therefore look something like this:

COMPANY VBN, Anytown, CO **Position** • Bullet 1 • Bullet 2 • Bullet 3	2010 - 2012
COMPANY JHG, Anytown, WY **Position** • Bullet 1 • Bullet 2 • Bullet 3	2004 - 2009

A reader might assume that the individual ended one job at the end of 2009 and started another, after the holidays, in 2010!

And, once given the chance to actually speak with a human being in the form of an interview, the candidate could choose to explain the gap in employment if asked. Most of us can relate to someone who had a difficult job search experience during the economic tailspin of 2009 – 2010 and, probably, so can the interviewer.

But you don't even get a chance to tell your story if there is no interview!

You see, an emerging hiring trend after the Great Recession has been the comeback of long-dormant discrimination against candidates who have a significant gap in employment—let's say longer than six months. In other words, extended time off can translate to even more time off! A completely unfair, but real, Catch-22.

While many of us Boomers and Gen-Xers grew up with the false idea that any lengthy gap in employment meant that someone might not have had a strong work ethic, the LBO- and M&A- led corporate downsizings of the mid 1980s through the early 1990s dispelled this notion for a generation to come.

Hiring authorities began to understand that boardroom shenanigans often had no real link to the value workers were providing to an employer.

And the subsequent increase in the off-shoring of jobs only served to cement this point.

For 20+ years, it was accepted that the ranks of the unemployed included top talent.

Not anymore.

Unfortunately, **the market for "good jobs" has become so insanely competitive that many employers are using additional criteria to weed out even qualified candidates** — they are turning back the clock and discriminating against folks who have been unemployed for six months or longer.

Your resume typically won't even get past the first seven-second scan with a gap in employment. The solutions?

>1) **Leaving out months on the resume** as described above (which has been the norm with most resume formats for 10+ years anyway).
>
>2) **Speaking with a real person at your target company** — preferably someone with hiring authority (this is usually accomplished via networking).

Obviously, even if you implement solution #1, you're still going to need to implement solution #2; you will need to network in order to have someone actually *read* your resume.

Whether you like it or not…

Networking needs to comprise at least 75% of a full-time job seeker's daily activity.

This is critical.

Of course, you also need a first class resume to begin networking. So, here's another strategy you should consider, as well…

Gap Fillers

If you are presently experiencing an employment gap and it is expected to exist for longer than 4 to 6 months, I recommend you seek out some professionally-related part-time or volunteer work, as well as other training or professional development activities to supplement your longer term job search efforts.

Depending upon the quality of such activities, you may very well want to list these on the resume—either in the "Experience" or another section.

At a minimum, when asked a related interview question about what you accomplished during your gap in employment, you will then have something to point towards.

Following is a list of some activities that, in addition to your own job search, you might consider doing during an extended time off from work (and which a hiring authority might view favorably).

Potential "gap fillers" include:

- Part-time or temporary work.
- Consulting—paid or voluntary.
- Volunteer work—related or unrelated to your profession.
- Involvement in a professional or industry organization.
- Blogging—via LinkedIn-related or other established sites.
- Starting your own blog and/or website to offer your professional perspective and free advice.
- Writing some short two- to three-page white papers to attach to your LinkedIn profile or website.
- Taking or teaching a university course.
- Taking or teaching a continuing education course (CEU credit oriented).
- Taking or teaching a course offered by a professional association.
- Securing a certification via either coursework or testing, such as PMP or MSCE.

There are many other activities that will help you to feel good about yourself and help you maintain balance during the stressful time off.

The above list is just a sample of activities that may have the added benefit of going on your resume, or at least helping your candidacy in the eyes of hiring authorities. Can you think of other "gap fillers?"

Longer Gaps

If the gap is even longer (let's say 2 to 3 years), and relates strictly to personal reasons (perhaps end-of-life care for an elderly parent), then it will be evident on the resume. As a matter of course, the explanation for such a gap is usually not found on the resume.

Exceptions?

Sure.

You could include an explanation in the italicized position description that alludes to the previous gap, such as with *"Hired into customer service position following planned time off to care for elderly family members."*

You could also refer to/explain a lengthy gap in either a cover letter or accompanying email.

Again, however, the importance of securing a conversation first—via networking—cannot be overstated here.

Don't be screened out of the interview process.

Find a way to speak directly with the hiring manager to explain your value and your return to the work force.

Chapter 14

Other Considerations

"The road to hell is paved with works-in-progress."
- Philip Roth

You have to start writing your resume.

And you have to finish, too.

That's why I've put together this chapter to help you tie up any loose ends. So you can get started on actually using your resume!

Topics we'll touch on include: how to list staffing agency employment on the resume, the importance of showing "hard skills" on the resume, the "video resume," getting unstuck, and hiring a resume writer.

Employment Agencies

"Temping" or temporary assignments should be included on a resume. Any part- or full-time employment through a staffing firm or employment agency allows you flexibility with how to present the work on a resume. As long as you disclose the type of employment, there are a couple ways you might account for this experience (and there's no reason you should be ashamed—temporary staffing firms even exist that specialize in placing c-suite level executives). Here are two ways a candidate, who worked in two different assignments through the same staffing agency during a three-month period, might present their experience…

KLL STAFFING AGENCY, Anytown, AR 2010
  Position – *at ARG Company*
  - Bullet 1
  - Bullet 2
  Position – *at VCW Company*
  - Bullet 1
  - Bullet 2

Or…

ARG COMPANY, Anytown, AR 2010
  Position – *through KLL Staffing Agency*
  - Bullet 1
  - Bullet 2

VCW COMPANY, Anytown, AR 2010
  Position – *through KLL Staffing Agency*
  - Bullet 1
  - Bullet 2

Hard Skills

Up-to-date hard skills have made a comeback. They will get you hired.

You have to show them on your resume.

While soft skills are still important, hard skills will be critical to your perceived value. They should be included on the resume, either within the "Experience" section bullets or in a separate section.

Hard skills have made such a comeback that even Sociology and Anthropology majors have a shot at not having to work six part-time retail jobs if they have *advanced* hard skills in a couple of programs such as: Excel, SPSS, Access, or QuickBooks. Imagine a Geology major earning $50K+ per year right out of college doing underwriting or some other analysis. Imagine that.

I know, I know. College admissions said that Geology majors had a 90% placement rate at the time you took out $150K in loans. They just didn't say in which field you would be working or if the position would pay more than $11.50/hour or if you would even be using your degree…

So, what are you waiting for? Your local adult education program has Advanced Excel taught by expert instructors for $75 to $125 per session.

Of course, hard skills can be related to a specific field, such as the latest 3-D or solid modeling software as related to a design engineer's position or…the latest version of JD Edwards or Hyperion as related to a CFO's position or…HVAC technical repair skills and tools as related to an HVAC technician's position or…You get the picture.

Now, go make sure you have the hard skills that will set you apart in the market, the hard skills that will help get you noticed. And make sure they figure prominently or, at least, are visible on the resume.

The Video Resume?

No.

I keep getting questions about video resumes several times a year so I mention the genre here to educate you now. Before long term damage is done to your reputation. Let me be perfectly clear: **do not do it.**

There is an exception to every rule…except this one.

A few of my clients have learned this lesson the hard way. Please note that a couple of them even hired out professional videographers and career coaches to ensure a high quality, finished product. It never worked the way it was intended. Because it is an "intent versus impact" problem-in-the-making. It relates back to our old friend *perception is reality* with a vengeance. Even if the finished product is extremely well done and is favorably received by five of the six members of a hiring committee, if it has a negative impact on the remaining individual, they will make it their mission to torpedo your candidacy.

Finally, even if used in conjunction with your written resume, the video resume does not allow for an easy scan by the viewer. The reader will not be in control of "how" and "when" they digest the material.

Even though our mission is to influence the hiring manager, a cardinal rule is to have the interviewer believe they are in control of the process.

Although video resumes have evolved considerably since the torched potential career of one individual who shall remain anonymous out of respect (I refuse to use his web-based and much-viewed video resume as an example anymore), there is simply too much at stake, in terms of your reputation, to risk moving forward with such a project.

Just don't do it.

If You Are Really Stuck

Maybe this book is more than you bargained for.

Or you're simply stuck in terms of coming up with basic content for your resume. Whatever the case, the following are a few ideas that might help you out of a writing jam and kick start your effort:

*O*Net* (www.onetonline.org): This powerful government website allows you to access tens of thousands of detailed position descriptions. Simply type in your past or present positions into the "occupation quick search" box at the top right corner of the page and you'll generate a list of similar occupations. Clicking on one will bring up a summary report that offers you a wealth of phrases and words to describe the very knowledge, skills, and abilities that you already have!

Many of my clients also utilize this site in their career exploration phase, researching position particulars, including how much each job typically pays and whether or not it is expected to enjoy the strong growth over the next 10 years. Note: at the bottom of each position-description page you'll find links to other, similar positions and to the appropriate www.bls.gov page for your state's salary data.

<u>This website will also provide you with more information than you ever wanted to know *about the jobs you have already held*</u>. A simple cut and paste of key job details and phrases into your own resume will provide you with a base of content for your resume. Easy as pie.

Warning: As with other options involving cutting and pasting content onto your resume, I would highly recommend that you customize the O*NET language.

A resume needs to be authentically "you" to work effectively on your behalf.

Job advertisements: Why not hop on over to a meta-search engine like www.indeed.com or www.simplyhired.com, type in your former position titles, and read the job ads for current openings? I'm betting that the language they use is fairly representative of the tasks and duties you performed in those positions.

Again, cut and paste, but be sure to customize. You're off to the races.

Sample resumes: There exist entire books with nothing but sample resumes in them. Often, these books will specialize in presenting samples from certain professions or industries.

Special Note: Always, always, always be respectful of both an individual's and resume writer's intellectual property. Even if you intend to customize, never lift material directly from a sample resume.

Why not make a small investment and buy one of these books to give you ideas about alternative resume formats, as well as wording? Just make sure that you don't take wording directly from the samples (did I say that already?). Instead, use the samples' wording as a guide to help you develop your own.

Colleagues: Contact your professional colleagues who have held positions similar to yours in the past. Be forthright, honest, and open with them about your need for resume writing help and your interest in reviewing their resume for ideas pertaining to wording. As with reviewing sample resumes, you should strictly respect the intellectual property of these colleagues and not copy verbatim from their resumes.

I think you'll find that a number of your colleagues will be quite amenable to letting you view their resumes.

Some may even give you permission to utilize wording from their resume and/or offer to help you with ideas for your own resume.

Hiring a Resume Writer

Full disclosure: I am a resume writer for hire.

I suppose I didn't need that disclaimer. After all, I did write this book and I am unapologetic about sharing my views to benefit your job search. But I just couldn't resist!

While I only take on a limited number of clients at any given time and have frequently turned down business because my services and/or personality were not a good fit with a perspective client, the views expressed here are my own. If you *do* choose to seek out the assistance of a resume writer, I hope that my words here might provide some guidance but, please, do your research and speak with a number of prospective writers. OK, now for my thoughts…

You get what you pay for.

Most of the time, this old adage rings true.

$150 may be a lot of money to you. Often times, however, that'll only get you a snazzy new format, a rearranging of your own words, and a few fancy new phrases that you might have to look up in order to understand. It may look great to you…and be no more effective than what you had before!

Depending upon your particular geographic market, your job search situation, and your professional level, you could easily expect to pay a minimum of $250-$350 per page for a quality job. Senior managers and executives might expect a starting range of 50—100% more than that.

Sticker shock?

Again, **you get what you pay for.**

And ... you will still have work to do!

Even at those rates, you will still have to work at producing content, even if it's via conversations with the resume writer. What?!

That's right. Many top-of-the-line resume writers will give you homework. I do. Expect to have one or two conversations with the writer, in addition to providing the written content that they request. Otherwise the resume will not be authentic.

You must be in the resume.

As an example, each of my clients initially fills out a twelve-page questionnaire detailing their personality preferences, values, objectives, and character traits. The form does not ask any information about the particular positions they've held. I give clients additional homework following our first conversation.

<u>If a resume writer does not require you to do homework and/or be engaged in the process, you should question how experienced they are and/or how customized the resume they create for you will be.</u>

There are no discounts for existing resumes.

There are typically no discounts if you already have a resume.

And, probably 95% of my clients already have a resume. 95%.

In addition, I would estimate, in any given year, 25−40% of them have already paid another resume writer! Usually, they chalk up that experience to learning a valuable lesson: you get what you pay for.

Your previous efforts at resume writing and decisions to pay for poor quality work do not necessarily make a high caliber resume writer's job any easier.

Pay for a resume, not a cover letter.

I have no problem with a resume writer charging you for writing a customized cover letter or even including it as part of their service.

But, as each cover letter (not letter of introduction) is unique to each position application, providing you with one cover letter is necessarily providing you with a great deal of value in your search.

Base your decision to hire the resume writer on what they can help you create in terms of a professional and effective resume.

Certifications and association memberships can be a plus.

Then again, just as with any other profession, someone can take a course, go through training, or be certified…and yet still not be able to provide a high level of quality.

And someone else with no certifications but a boat load of experience could provide a superior service.

That having been said, certifications are one good starting point in your search. A few resume writing certifications you might be aware of include: CPRW, ACRW, and MRW.

A couple of associations that I think highly of and which include much of the nation's resume writing talent within their membership ranks include PARW and NRWA.

It isn't a bad strategy to contact a professional association of resume writers.

Association websites will even typically list members by specialty or geographical area. Again, this is just a starting point. But it can be a good one.

Make sure you "fit" with the resume writer.

Do not expect the resume writer to become your best friend, your career coach (unless you're paying them for that service as well), or your personal counselor. They are providing a professional service and you are the client. To that end and, although you are the client who will be paying for a service, please realize that the resume writer will be the one in charge of your relationship.

On the other hand, I highly recommend that you have an initial sense of fit with the particular resume writer, as your experience will be greatly enhanced. This is personal work you will be embarking on. If you are not comfortable with the resume writer—their personality and/or their process—it may be a long road ahead for both of you.

Payment up front.

Many experienced resume writers require full payment up front.

I know I do.

And while I have a satisfaction guarantee and am open to re-doing work, I don't do financial refunds. Have I ever had a dissatisfied client? Not that I'm aware of. And I plan on keeping it that way!

Expect a professional product and experience.

If my previous lines seem slanted in favor of professional resume writers, please accept my sincere apology. For while resume writers are earning a living, *most of us are engaged in this work to make a difference in your lives*. You are the client. And, as the client, you should expect and receive a professional product and treatment for your investment.

The client is not always right but the client always comes first. As it should always be.

Best wishes on your search.

I hope this helps. *I have the utmost respect for other career coaches and resume writers.* We may have healthy and professional disagreements about the most effective way to write a resume or help you get hired, but this is the norm within any profession.

Whomever you may choose to work with, I am hopeful that you will come away from the experience with as much respect and appreciation as I have for my fellow colleagues.

Chapter 15

The "One Resume"

"20 percent of focused effort results in 80 percent out come of results!"
- Vilfredo Pareto

Why not use Pareto's Rule to your advantage?

Over 95% of my clients do. They have one foundational resume for their career search. They perform simple customization as required.

They use the "one resume" concept that I created based, in part, on Pareto's Rule; the rule that has led to decades of success in sales and fundraising. I will explain the rule in more detail in just a couple pages but for now, let's consider the "one resume" difference.

If crafted correctly, this "one resume" can maximize the effectiveness of your written brand message as well as simplify your life when it comes to customizing your resume for each position opening. It helps give hiring managers what they want. Do you like *easy* AND *effective*? I do.

While networking and applying for positions, this one, versatile resume can be utilized *without making changes* perhaps up to 75% of the time. When a more targeted message is required, it can easily be customized.

Gone are the days of a candidate needing two or three entirely different resumes or having to use a "functional" or other alternative style-resume, which may be less effective with hiring managers. This resume style *forces* the reading of the candidate's top 2 to 3 *core strengths*.

Core Strengths = Brand Differentiators

That's right. Your top 2 to 3 core strengths differentiate your brand. Therefore, they also present your value proposition.

<u>You need to identify a maximum of 2 to 3 core strengths.</u>

Each should be clearly understood simply by its name.

Let's compare the top "Profile" sections of the "Before" and "After" resumes in Chapter 1 this book, as the latter is an example of the "one resume" concept.

Not only is the "Before" version poorly constructed, but the brand message is not clear and there are no fewer than *16 different bullets* that highlight the candidate's strengths. *Sixteen!* Can the average reader even remember 8 or 10 different items in a list, let alone 16? I think not. Even if a reader could connect with all 16, would they paint a coherent picture of the candidate's value proposition and brand? No way.

The "After" version of the Chapter 1 resume highlights three core strengths: *Budgeting/Forecasting, Cost Accounting,* and *Cash Management.*

The reader is much more likely to remember three strengths instead of sixteen.

Notice that most of the words comprising the 16 bullets in the "Before" resume are still included in the "After" version. But now, they clutter less and inform more. The "After" resume allows the candidate to go for positions like Controller, Accounting Manager, or even Consultant; the candidate is not "locked in" to CFO positions only. Of course, the resume could be customized for CFO or VP Finance positions, as well.

"Before"

Chief Financial Officer

Objective
Senior CFO seeking top accounting management position or lead accountant for smaller, growing firm. Experienced in cost accounting and computer systems, with record of improving efficiencies and bottom line profitability, as well as cash flow. Responsible for risk management initiatives. Strengths:

Budgeting/Forecasting	Hyperion	Vendor Mgmt.	Conversions
G/L and Reconciliation	Team Leadership	Monthly Reports	Research
Cash Management	Cost Accounting	JD Edwards	Audits
IPO Experience	Contracts	International Tax	Bank Relationships

"After"

Leadership of both finance and accounting functions with background in manufacturing and public accounting. Proven problem solving and analytical abilities. Expertise in Excel, JD Edwards, Hyperion, and other software tools. Team approach prioritizes integration across departments and maximizes impact of cost control. Direct style balanced by compassion, humility, and fairness. Core strengths:

BUDGETING/FORECASTING

Delivers accurate forecasts and budgets based on customized systems that analyze organization-wide data and align with market events. Financial statement preparation and reporting integrated with up-to-date forecasting to allow for monthly review by senior management and stakeholders.

COST ACCOUNTING

Develops close working relationships at all levels to leverage expertise in cost control and reporting. Automates systems and analyzes data to realize savings and improve accountability.

CASH MANAGEMENT

Leads creation of detailed, automatic revenue and expense tracking systems as foundation to effective cash management, even in difficult situations. Maintains credit and vendor relationships during tight cash flow situations while incorporating "no risk" cost reduction strategies.

You may not care for the "paragraph" about each strength. You may be partial to bullet lists of your technical skills. Don't worry. We'll address your concerns. First, though, let's take a deeper look at Pareto's Rule and why it is so powerful when applied at the top of the resume…

Pareto's Rule

Pareto's Rule is often called the 80/20 Rule or even the 90/10 Rule.

> ### The Power of Pareto's Rule
> Choose to apply Pareto's rule of efficiency to every aspect of your career transition. Identify the 20% of your networking contacts in which to invest 80% of your time. Identify the 20% of your example stories for the interview that connect with 80% of the hiring manager's priorities. You get the picture. Deliberately apply an 80/20 (or 90/10) rule for maximum efficiency and results.

The "one resume" style may be somewhat familiar to you already. The look has evolved from the old "executive resume" style from the 80s. Whether you are an executive or not, you might recall perusing sample resumes that look somewhat similar. Some of my colleagues refer to these similar versions as "hybrids" or a combination of "chronological" and "functional" resume styles. A key difference between my "one resume" and these or other resume styles is the development of the 2 to 3 "core strengths" to differentiate your brand.

Of course, each of us has many strengths. But only 2 or 3 strengths are linked to most of the results we produce at work. To sum up:

80% of your professional value or impact come from just 20% of your total strengths.

Core strengths are part of your authentic, professional fabric. They are a golden opportunity for you. They will define your own unique career brand, so be careful when identifying them. Lest you turn a golden opportunity into fool's gold.

2 to 3 Core Strengths vs. 15+ Total Strengths

Why should you not list all your strengths?

Because memory and focus are limited.

Ever notice that telephone numbers are seven digits long instead of eight? Ever notice that roadside billboards and internet advertisements stay on point with one or two messages instead of many? Ever notice that, when you pick up a content-rich brochure that dives into detail, it is formatted to force your focus back to only 2 to 3 key points? And these examples just relate to the *printed* word.

What about a person's ability to remember more than 2 to 3 takeaways from a conversation? Think about a person whom you recently met for the first time: can you remember more than one, two, or three different things about them or about the conversation? It's just not possible.

Of course, each person has many professional strengths. They come from our character, personality traits, technical expertise, experience, and other factors. Most of us have well over 15 professional strengths that we can offer to a prospective employer. But if you list *all* of your strengths in a table near the top of your resume, the reader may be impressed at first…and then will be unable to recall what differentiates you from the rest of the applicants. Because it is just too much.

NOTE: If you need to provide detail, notice how a short paragraph following each core strength will allow the reader to take a deeper dive the next time they pick up your resume.

Every successful product or service brand is anchored by up to 2 or 3 differentiators offering specific value for the consumer.

You need to do the same thing with your resume. That's why, years ago, I developed the concept of the "one resume" — to help differentiate and clearly present each of my client's 2 to 3 core strengths to prospective employers.

The concept has helped clients *get noticed* and *close the deal*.

The Resume's "Sweet Spot"

Fact: The top third of the resume's first page gets the most attention.

Some resume writers refer to this area as the "sweet spot."

That's why the old "Objective" section used to be placed in that area. That's why your "Profile" (akin to "Summary") section is placed in that area now. That's why a recent college graduate moves their "Education" section up to immediately follow "Profile." Therefore, you must make sure that your 2 to 3 core strengths are placed in that area.

NOTE: *You get to choose how your 2 to 3 core strengths are presented.*

There is no right or wrong way. Approaches utilized by my clients have included: bullets, quotes from references, paragraphs, and list headers, to name a few. In just a little bit, we'll explore what a couple of these might look like.

While the sample resumes in this book largely reflect a paragraph approach, do not feel constrained by that bias.

Present your 2 to 3 core strengths in the format that will be most helpful to your candidacy.

Keeping You Honest

That's right. The "one resume" keeps <u>you</u> honest. How so?

Well, it can be sooooo tempting to apply for positions that are really just outside of your wheelhouse. The further you are from your core strengths, the less likely you will be to even get a sniff of interest from a prospective employer. And, imagine if you are actually hired for such a position—one that doesn't align with your core strengths. What will your longevity be at that company? What will your sense of success or fulfillment be during the short time you are employed there? Focusing on 2 to 3 core strengths will improve your process qualitatively.

Priority: Technical Skills

We've discussed technical skills (which are often "hard" skills) previously, but what about as they relate to the "one resume" concept? What if the market <u>demands</u> you list your 15+ technical skills in the resume's sweet spot? No worries. Here are three options within my "one resume" format…

Option 1: Create headers for areas of core technical strength.

<u>Use this option when the market could care less about your soft skills and solely determines your value by technical strengths</u>. Arrange your technical skills under 2 to 3 headers representing areas of core strength. These 2 to 3 headers represent your "core strengths" as defined by applying Pareto's Rule.

This method, previously discussed, lists all of your technical skills, and leverages the Profile to provide additional context. If the reader wants to capture a quick snapshot of your technical strengths during the few seconds they might spend on a scan of page one, this option's three-header approach shown on the next page should fit the bill.

OPTION 1 EXAMPLE
(Including Profile statement):

Quality focused CNC programmer and machinist with versatile training, including milling machines, lathes, jigs and fixtures, tool room, and engineering design. Completes tasks on time and to tight tolerances. Keeps work area organized, clean, and setup for next shift. Highly motivated to learn new machining and manufacturing techniques. Collaborates and communicates easily with all personality types. Training and knowledge includes:

MACHINING	ENGINEERING	DESIGN
• CNC Programming	• Statistical Process Control	• SolidWorks
• ANSI Y 15.4 Certified	• ECOs and Documentation	• CADD Max 3.3
• Machine Operation	• Finite Element Analysis	• Axel Blueprinting
• Tolerances to .0001	• Mechanical Vibrations	• V-Prototyping

---

Option 2: List technical skills as one of your 2 to 3 core strengths.

<u>When it's important to list both technical and non-technical core strengths and you have limited space</u> (such as with a one-page resume), this hybrid option might do the trick. Note that "Software" represents the area of technical strength in the following example.

OPTION 2 EXAMPLE
(Including Profile statement):

Motivated BSME graduate with proven work ethic and ability to solve complex technical problems. Background includes software support, training, and design. Effective in team, individual-contributor, and lead roles. Appreciates need for cross-functional cooperation. Focused on exceeding expectations of internal customers. Skilled at quantitative analysis. Core competencies include:

PROJECT ENGINEERING / PROTOTYPING

Training in development of new product features, prototyping, solid modeling/3-D and 2-D CAD, managing RFP writing and vendor selection, collaborating with consultants, and writing reports.

SOFTWARE

Excel Macros, Pro Engineer Wildfire 4.0, SolidWorks, Dassault Compiler ADV, MatLab, MS Project and Access Math CAD, HTML, Visual Basic 2013, SafetyLink, C++ Vector, and ViscosityPlus 2.0.

Option 3: Allow for two separate sections in the sweet spot.

<u>Perhaps you want to showcase both your technical and non-technical skills equally</u>. While you can always customize your resume later for specific positions, this strategy can be especially helpful on a foundational resume utilized primarily for networking. In addition, some of my clients who have been open to a range of positions: "individual technical contributor," "supervisor," or "manager." This option will do the trick...*if you are not hired for one type of position, you may be hired for the other*!

OPTION 3 EXAMPLE
(Including Profile statement and Functional Title):

IT Security and Systems Architecture

Achieves optimum levels of IT security, consults and builds system architecture to best practice standards, and develops technical proficiency in high potential team members. Seeks to partner with other highly accountable and motivated technology professionals in an environment that promotes continual learning and growth. Energized by solving complex problems to the root and implementing systems to identify and mitigate future challenges. Strengths include:

IT SECURITY MANAGEMENT

Drives improvements in safety of information and integrity of systems to provide uninterrupted usability, even during catastrophic events. Prioritizes achieving triple-redundant backups via simple, easy-to-configure processes. Utilizes Six Sigma philosophy to promote continuous accountability and process improvements.

SYSTEMS PLANNING

Focused on strategic systems planning anchored by proven expertise in platform architecture, with competencies in: identity administration, IT security, Active Directory, Level 3A firewalls, databases, and data centers. Leverages network of colleagues & vendors to identify best practices. Leads analyses, customizes solutions, and executes changes.

TECHNICAL COMPETENCIES

SECURITY DESIGN	SYSTEMS ARCHITECTURE	NETWORK ENGINEERING
• Selected Access	• Catastrophic Planning	• CISCO Wireless
• Ti67 Restrictions	• Disaster Recovery	• Remote Access
• PCI and HiPPA	• Active Directory	• WAN Accelerators
• Power Systems	• Mainframe and UNIX	• VLAN Layout
• VBR Firewalls	• Vendor Management	• Topology Discovery

> ### *Core Strengths are Authentic*
>
> Your core strengths must be authentic. They must be you. Certainly, you will be customizing them for each position opening, thus enhancing their credibility with the reader. Right now, though, focus on making sure they are simply "core" to the value you offer. They must be part of the authentic you.

Formatting Considerations

There are many ways you might "dress up" your core strengths. Be creative...in the *right* ways. Examine the following example's formatting and then, on the next page, I'll point out a couple concepts I applied.

EXAMPLE
(Without Profile/Summary included):

ARCHITECT OF EMERGENCY PREPAREDNESS STRATEGY

Creates detailed and user-friendly action plans integrated with larger strategies to realize highest levels of readiness for small to catastrophic events. Researches and applies best practices. Involves other departments and organizations in planning and drills. Proven ability to "see" and analyze potential threats. Aligns planning with resource allocation. *Factors in total landscape of variables when designing strategies.*

CHAMPION OF CONTINUOUS IMPROVEMENT INITIATIVES

Increases efficiencies and promotes smooth-running operations via critical review and enhancement of existing systems and processes. Bridges gap between expected and actual results by creating simple solutions to complex problems and by developing tools to measure effectiveness. Incorporates lean and Six Sigma methodologies right down to the work group levels. *Realizes new efficiencies via system improvements.*

DIRECTOR OF SEARCH AND RESCUE TEAMS

Leads emergency-related operations requiring full engagement across departments by zeroing in on core challenges and bottom-line objectives. Always remains open to suggestions for shifting tactics in the moment and encourages cooperation at the highest levels. Resolves conflict swiftly and keeps others' professional dignity intact, while finding a productive way forward. *Builds teamwork through open dialog and action.*

So, two formatting concepts in the example on the previous page are: title expansion and mini-tagline. A description of each…

Title Expansion: Usually, less is more. So, I would typically use "Emergency Preparedness" only. But the word "strategy" relates to working with the big picture. And "architect" defines a role.

Mini-Tagline: This comes at the end of the core strength description. In the example, "*Factors in total landscape of variables when designing strategies*" affords the reader a quick, punchy, alternative explanation of this core strength if they don't wish to read the entire paragraph.

What are YOUR Core Strengths?

You're probably wondering how to determine your core strengths. Well, there is no one right way or infallible process. But, wait! ***If you completed the exercises in the early chapters, then you can go back and review your answers to find clues about your core strengths.*** *(Your 2-3 core strengths may even be plainly evident!)* Alternatively, you could keep a few of these guidelines in mind during your explorations:

- Core strengths may or may not shift every few years, depending upon your acquisition of new skills. This is especially true for individuals with specific technical expertise.
- Core strengths represent skills and abilities you have in the present moment, not those you expect to have in the future.
- Core strengths are an authentic part of you. If they relate to your character or personality, their development may have even started when you were growing up.
- Core strengths must have specific work examples to back them up. Additionally, it can be useful if your reputation among peers and supervisors connects to one or more core strengths.
- Core strengths are described in your own words. Don't worry about trying to conjure up some fancy words because they won't be representative of the real you!

Trouble Cutting Down to Three

So, what if you believe you have four, five, or more core strengths and just can't find a way to cut down to two or three? These questions may be helpful to ask yourself before making a final decision:

- Do two of these strengths naturally fit together or at least closely relate to each other? If so, what word or words would you use to *describe the combination of strengths*?

- Does the market of potential employers care about each of the four strengths equally? If not, which are the two or three *most important strengths from the perspective of potential hiring managers*?

- Would past or present coworkers rate each of these strengths equally? If not, *how would your peers and supervisors rank your top four strengths*?

If you answered the above questions and still believe you have four distinct core strengths, here are options to include them on the resume:

- Choose to showcase two or three of the strengths but write the remaining one or two strengths into the Profile paragraph and into some of the key bullets in the "Experience" section.

- If you can't combine two of the strengths into one but those two strengths are related to each another, create a single category name and list each strength as a subset of that category.

- List two or three of the four strengths on the resume, keeping the fourth one in reserve. When applying for particular positions which are aligned more with the fourth strength, replace one of the three core strengths already presented with the fourth strength which you were holding in reserve.

- List all four core strengths on your resume! The world is not going to come to an end. (Just don't tell me about it.)

Now it's time to describe each of the core strengths you have identified. The descriptions are for use on your resume, while networking, and during the interview. Keep them brief and clear.

My Core Strength #1 and Brief Description

My Core Strength #2 and Brief Description

My Core Strength #3 and Brief Description

Chapter 16

Resume Supplements

"Would you like fries with that?"
- McDonalds

These six words make up perhaps the single most effective question in marketing history. They influence the customer to buy more.

And that's exactly what you are trying to do with the hiring manager.

I hope the McDonalds employee who came up with that supplement to their standard order-taking script was richly rewarded. Because the company certainly has been. Marketing genius.

You want to serve up a resume that will make the hiring manager hungry for more. Why not give them a side order that will satisfy, cementing their decision to call you in for an interview?

Side orders are, essentially, **"addendums" to your resume**. And they can take the form of <u>anything from a list of people who are your references, to a physical work sample, to a portfolio of your work</u>.

Please note, however, that any supplement to the main course of the resume better *not distract*. It must instead complement.

Also, the timing of presenting your supplemental material is important. Sometimes, it should be delivered right up front with the resume. This is especially important when you might be perceived as a weaker candidate who would not otherwise be interviewed. At other times, it is more tactical to hold back and present your material during the interview itself or even after the fact. More on that later.

Because supplements can be incredibly powerful and utilized in a variety of ways, I'm going to provide you with several cases "from the files" to get you thinking about how you can find a way to use them to your advantage. Consider these cases:

High Tech

In the early 2000s, I served in the lead outplacement role for dozens of layoffs in the connector and PC board manufacturing industries. Hundreds of assembly workers would be laid off at one time as their jobs went overseas. When the numbers of displaced workers climbed into the thousands in a compact geographical area, it was only the most skilled who were hired at the last few remaining competitor companies.

Although my team and I created top notch resumes and provided detailed interviewing guidance for these candidates, the most successful candidates were those that brought a **physical work sample** in with them to the interview. After all, it is easy to claim on a resume that you are one of the best solders around, but a physical sample proves it. The candidates who brought work samples with them to their interviews often started work on the next shift.

Highly Skilled Tradespeople

One of the companies I helped close down a few years ago boasted some of the most skilled welders I have ever come across. Their expertise was in high-purity stainless welding—they helped build large vessels and systems for both the bio-pharma and brewing industries. In fact, their welds were so good that, for the most part, you could not even tell where the seams were! Seriously. That's why these welders could often earned well in excess of $100K per year, including overtime.

A few of the up-and-comers who weren't as well-known took pictures of their work and emailed them to potential employers or provided **links to webpages that showed pictures of their exquisite work**. The result? Several companies found it hard to believe that the photos weren't doctored up! Once they conducted reference checks, however, they quickly opened up their checkbooks

Traditional Manufacturing

Fairly recently, I was hired to provide career transition support for 200+ employees who worked for a market-leading, custom stationery and wedding invitations manufacturer that had been bought out and was being closed. When most people hear the words "stationery" or "paper," they relate it (often incorrectly) with lower skilled workers and ancient equipment. And it's true that many of the numerous Heidelbergs at this plant were over 50 years old.

But, as I said, this company was market leading because of their quality, custom work. When an A-list actor was about to receive an Academy Award…when a member of a royal family was planning their wedding…when a major political or business figure was planning an event…they all called this company. When these humble machine operators brought **discarded work samples** to their interviews, potential employers were impressed.

Interviewers shifted their stereotypical views of workers in the paper and card industries and instead saw these candidates as workers committed to the highest levels of quality and teamwork. The physical work samples served as effective supplements to the candidates' resumes when it came to them getting noticed in the right ways.

Long Term Care CNAs

CNAs can have some of the most physically demanding jobs out there…for little pay and less recognition. Often times, they are wrongly typecast as individuals who don't have the expertise that is often ascribed to RNs and others with more credentialing. And, what about their profession's reputation for relating to the customer? Well, they often carry the additional stress of being wrongly accused of thievery by the same elderly patients and families they are serving! So, it is really impressive when a CNA presents hard evidence of their high-quality, customer satisfaction-focused work.

Years ago, I gave career advice to a number of newly minted CNAs and suggested they keep any thank you note they were given. Several of those CNAs did just that. So, when their facility closed, each CNA had a pile of these notes. Then, each CNA arranged the papers into a **"portfolio scrapbook" of thank you notes** and brought it along on interviews! They impressed the heck out of the hiring managers!

Look, your well-written resume is going to give you an edge. But why not open up a bigger lead on your competition?

> *I challenge you to get creative in coming up with some effective supplements of your own.*

Let's examine six types of resume supplements that could give you an edge. They include: portfolio, physical work samples, web-based work samples, letters of reference, reference list, and addendums.

Portfolio

Portfolios are not just for artists.

They can be an effective tool for just about anyone who has a group of work samples to put together.

For instance, design engineers, tradespeople, and recent college graduates are several groups that are often significantly advantaged by the use of portfolios. Sometimes, the portfolios of these groups are even more important than their resume! Consider...

- Design engineer clients of mine have often selected 6 to 12 drawings to include in their portfolio and have sometimes included a link to an online version to show solid modeling/3-D designs.

- Woodworkers, boat builders, and machinists I have worked with will sometimes chose to take pictures of their work and have those pictures available in either a physical or online portfolio.

- Recent college graduates who I have advised will often put together a portfolio that includes major papers and project reports, especially if the content of those reports is of interest to a hiring company or the documents demonstrate advanced formatting and writing skills.

As long as it is created thoughtfully and appears professional, a portfolio is always useful to your candidacy.

Note: In days of old, portfolios used to be bound with impressive-looking covers that cost an arm and a leg. Certainly you will want to have your work samples professionally presented. But for around $20 you can find something at your local office supply store that will look just fine.

Physical Work Samples

You may not have enough high-quality work samples to include in a portfolio.

But that shouldn't hold you back from sharing those couple samples that you do have available.

As long as they are impressive, work samples can make the difference between getting the interview and getting a rejection letter. They can make the difference in nailing the interview or going home empty handed.

It's your choice.

A physical work sample could be an object, a picture of an object, or a document that you designed, prototyped, or modified.

Examples…

- A machinist could bring one or two finished metal pieces to an interview or they could bring pictures of their work.

- A mechanic who overhauls motors for a living might not be able to bring in an entire motor, but they could bring in "before" and "after" pictures.

- Even those individuals who are only responsible for a portion of the work on an object can benefit, as presenting such an object can prompt a discussion about the candidate's role in its development or manufacture.

Physical work samples can actually make you feel more comfortable in the interview itself because they are familiar to you, they allow you to feel more confident in describing your work.

Web-based Work Samples

Web-based work samples can be some of the most impactful and versatile of all. If they are visual and involve color or pictures, the quality is often superior to that of the printed page. Digital images of web pages or electronic copy can be conveyed via e-mail, CD, or links. Blog entries and the like are a two-for-one special: they show subject matter knowledge or expertise and demonstrate communication skills. Also, such samples show your comfort with using current technology — a must in almost any job search today. I could go on about advantages but should mention the potential disadvantages too. The disadvantages are market related: the pace at which information is processed and the increasingly strict cyber security considerations. For instance:

Convenience: Even though it just involves a few clicks to see a web-based work sample, some interviewers would actually prefer to have physical, printed work samples instead of links because they can quickly glance at material you hand them in the interview instead of having to sign on and spend extra time getting to a web page.

Accessibility: As is the case with the Federal government and a number of other larger employers, the PCs and terminals that hiring managers have on their desks have built in security constraints that prevent users from accessing all but the most secure of sites.

Firewalls: Firewalls can also pose a problem, so I typically don't recommend including live hyperlinks in the resume or application materials. If your e-mail attachment contains hyperlinks, there is a good possibility that those attachments may be stripped from the email by the corporate firewall and never even reach the hiring manager's desk.

Keeping disadvantages like these in mind, it is still important to consider the web as a vehicle for sharing supplemental materials and showcasing your strengths.

Letters of Reference

As with cover letters, if you are targeting potential employers that have more formality to their application processes (such as the government or education employers), then you should ask for and collect at least four letters of reference from former supervisors, peers, and others with whom you worked.

Other considerations prompting you to ask others to write testimonials on your behalf could include:

- Your company is closing the doors for good and you expect to lose track of many of your references.

- Your references are retiring and not prone to giving out personal contact information or staying in touch.

- You have a conviction or other very big negative to address.

- Your references are VIPs who do not typically take phone calls.

- Your references are overseas in another time zone.

Other than the above reasons, I generally don't recommend that my clients ask for letters of reference anymore.

Why not?

Let me count the ways …
- A reference can be initially flattered and pleased to write you a letter but, if prone to procrastination or faced with circumstances that require putting the writing off until the future, their positive feelings can turn negative in a hurry. Guilt, frustration, and anxiety can enter your relationship with that person.

- A reference may be well spoken but not well written. What if the letter a reference writes for you is just plain embarrassing? This has happened to numerous clients of mine.

  Unfortunately, you will often be forced to use that letter because the hiring company almost always still wants to talk with the individual reference, irrespective of whether there is a letter. And, if the reference finds out that you didn't forward their letter to the company, the relationship you have with that reference may be damaged beyond repair.

- Perhaps your reference writes an absolutely glowing letter…with several minor spelling errors. Even if you choose to gently point these out to them, chances are probably 50/50 that their re-written letter will also contain a mistake. Egad.

- Since hiring companies almost always want to speak on the phone with your reference in order to answer specific questions, your reference can feel like they're being abused. After all, they just slaved away at writing you an awesome letter!

  Even though they know it's not your fault, you become guilty-by-association.

- What if your reference writes a great letter but happens to frame one of your authentic strengths in an embarrassing light. Several clients of mine have had this happen.

  An example? One reference wrote in their letter that "Gary has had the most significant impact on collaboration and morale of anyone I've ever managed in my career. His team commitment is so strong that, when we go off site for our biweekly group sessions at the pub, we often have to have someone drive him home." I know. Hard to believe. Yet, unfortunately, this could happen to you, as well.

Here are some guidelines you might consider if you need to ask others to provide you with reference letters:

- Make your request well in advance of your job search.

- Provide your reference with a copy of your resume.

- Don't be surprised if your reference asks you to write your own letter—for them to sign. This is often the case with supervisors who are just not that well-written; they want to give you a strong letter of reference but are fearful their poor communication skills will reflect poorly on you and them. By the way, it is perfectly OK for you to write a letter under these circumstances and can even work in your favor as you get to choose the words!

- Ask for an electronic copy. If provided with a printed copy of the letter, scan and/or take a picture with your smart phone so that it is available to send electronically.

- If you are impressed with the letter, consider asking the reference to cut and paste part or all of it into a LinkedIn recommendation that will show on your profile.

- Just in case the information is omitted from the letter, ask your reference for their phone number and e-mail. Also ask for permission to share the phone number with potential employers who might want to have a phone dialog.

- Let your reference know that, given the nature of today's job search, they may also be called by the hiring company. Of course, you might also mention that you'll do your best to give them a heads up before this happens.

- Get down on your knees and thank the reference for agreeing to write a letter. It is a really big deal!

Reference List

A list of references is a necessary supplement to any resume. Once you are a finalist for a job, the company will want to talk to your references. So take the same care here that you have in preparing your resume. Here are some considerations for developing your reference list:

- It is preferable and most respectful to call or have an in-person conversation when you are asking someone to be a reference for you. Always follow up with a note of appreciation.

- You might be faced with the prospect of needing a certain person to be a reference, even though they are not your biggest supporter. In that case, practice the art of graciousness. Deftly inquire if the potential reference would feel comfortable with speaking to just a couple of your strengths on which you both agree. You might also delicately-but-directly ask if they would be able to provide you with a "positive reference." FYI, it is nearly impossible to recover from somebody giving you a less-than-positive recommendation.

  Finally, to limit the risk of the person being completely uncomfortable with being put on the spot and/or having to turn you down, you might break a communication rule and, instead, email them with your request. Write something like: "I would really appreciate you serving as one of my references — who might be contacted by a potential hiring company. If you feel comfortable providing a positive testimonial on my behalf, please just let me know and I'll add your name to my list of references. I appreciate your consideration and respect your decision."

- Keep your references in-the-know about your job search progress. They are among your biggest cheerleaders. Your references will become vested in your success and feel appreciated if you acknowledge their importance in your process by asking for advice and networking contacts from time to time.

- It is preferable to have 8 to 15 total references, even though you would typically only share about 4 to 6 of these on any given reference list you provide to a target company. Why? Think about it. If you only provide three names to the hiring company, there is a possibility they won't be able to reach one of the references.

    More importantly, you want to <u>create a targeted list of references for each open position.</u> Having multiple names to choose from allows you flexibility to customize each list. Remember that "perception is reality" concept? It permeates all things.

- Prioritize having a minimum of three references who have supervised or managed you. Other possible references include: peers/coworkers, subordinates, internal customers, team members, professors and trainers, vendors, customers, and any others who have firsthand knowledge of your professional skills and abilities.

- Don't include personal references on your list. There are career coaches who do suggest having personal or character references, but I am not one of them. Of course, there are exceptions…

    One of my former clients had completed years of volunteer mission work in Guatemala. After a full career in the corporate world, she wished to secure a position doing international mission work. So, her minister and other volunteers who had accompanied her on mission trips went to the top of her reference list.

- While you should ask your references for both phone and e-mail contact info, <u>only provide a phone number on your reference list for each person</u>.

    If you provide an e-mail you run the risk of requiring a lot more work from your references. How? Instead of calling references, recruiters will try to make their own lives easier by emailing a lengthy list of questions and expecting written responses.

It is more efficient for your references and better for you to have them engaged in a 10- to 15-minute phone call with the recruiter.

An exception to this rule, of course, is if your references are located in a distant time zone. In those cases, you should make a note to that effect by their name(s) on your reference list and provide an appropriate email address.

- Do not include the address of any individual reference. This is way old school. The days of a company mailing any forms to your references have long since gone. To provide addresses would only be dating yourself and distracting the reader.

- Order the references on your targeted list for maximum impact. If you don't really want the company to contact your last boss but feel you have to have their name on the list…place their name in the fifth position from the top. Maybe you have a networking contact who is already employed by the company to which you are applying? Place their name in at the top of the list.

This is the information you should provide for each person on your reference list: *name, current title, current employer, and phone number.*

Concerned that your reference doesn't appear to have any connection to you because of time passing since you worked with them? Even if you aren't concerned, I recommend including a very brief sentence that would describe your relationship with the reference. For instance, you might note that the reference was your direct supervisor, that you worked with them on an intensive six-month project, or that they were customer of yours at a former employer. Context helps the reader.

No other information is necessary unless, of course, you choose to use my "targeted reference list" format…

"Targeted Reference List" Format

More than 10 years ago, I developed a reference list format to boost a candidate's perceived value and allow flexibility in how and when it might be used. It is simple, straightforward, and will turbo-charge your reference list.

So, why not try bulking up your candidacy with this supplement?

Simply put, you will just add one short sentence after each of the references on your list. That sentence will identify a maximum of one or two strengths you possess—*as viewed from the perspective of your reference*. This last part is critical because, as you well know by now, each person's perception is their reality. You need to ask yourself (or your reference) what each of your references would identify as your one or two top strengths.

These strengths could be hard or soft skills, they could be representative of your accomplishments, they could connect to your character, or they could showcase your potential. <u>As long as they are from your references' perspectives</u>.

Here's what happens when you use my "targeted reference list" format:

1. An ordinary list of names now becomes a true addendum to the resume. Even before anyone calls a single one of your references, they are reminded of your strengths. These strengths may also be found on the resume or they may not be.

   For instance, one of your references may believe you to be "one of the easiest persons to work with" among everyone they have ever known. This is a powerful testimonial. It relates directly to "fitting" with a company culture and getting along with others—both critical to today's hiring managers. Yet, if you said that about yourself in your resume, you risk coming across as arrogant.

2. Even if no one ever calls a single reference on your list, they can have a quick read about what your references would say. It's almost like you have provided an additional page to the resume. It is valuable information that doesn't have to clutter up the main course.

3. In the event that one of your references is called, they will be asked the same list of 15 to 20+ questions that every other reference will be asked. No doubt about it. And, no doubt your reference will sing your praises when giving their answers.

    But each of us is a creature with a unique sense of priorities and vantage points. It is possible—in fact probable—that the hiring company will <u>not</u> include on their list of standard questions a query that asks about your most important strengths *from that reference's personal perspective.*

    With my format, however, the company representative/recruiter who is calling your references is almost compelled to ask about the one or two strengths that are noted by each reference's name.

    And, when your reference responds to the question, their voice tone will change and there will be passion and force behind their answer, *because the subject matter is important to them.*

    It's like their testimonial on your behalf goes from being black and white to color. Or going from 2-D to 3-D. It's almost as if they will be reaching through the phone with an exclamation point!

    You will have their absolute strongest endorsement...*because it comes from their perspective.*

    Their perception is their reality.

On the following page, I have included an example of my "targeted reference list" format.

sample "Targeted Reference List"

SALLY S. SAMPLE
13 WRENS WAY, MOUNTAINHIGH, CO 00000
SSample554@gmail.com | 000.000.0000 | linkedin.com/in/sss554

REFERENCES

Ed Example, Logistics Director—The Americas
XYZ Company
000.000.0000
Ed led our logistics group for 4 years at XYZ Company and was my direct manager. He can speak to my resourcefulness and that I fit easily with all personality types.

Theresa Test, Director of Order Fulfillment
XYZ Company
000.000.0000
Theresa manages order fulfillment at XYZ and was my internal customer for 3 years. She knows my record of on-time delivery and cross-functional collaboration.

Ida Illustration, International Account Manager
ABC Company
000.000.0000
Ida was a senior manager at ABC. We teamed up on a global distribution project during which Ida witnessed my conflict management and de-escalation skills.

Mike Model, Warehouse Supervisor
ABC Company
000.000.0000
Reporting to me for 6 years, Mike is knowledgeable concerning my work ethic and participatory management style.

Tina Trial, Customer Relations Manager
VRN Company
000.000.0000
Tina was a vendor I teamed with to reduce transportation costs at VRN. She has witnessed my ability to conduct win-win negotiations.

Charles Case, Senior Materials Specialist
FDS Company
000.000.0000
As the decision maker at a major customer of XYZ, Charlie and I teamed up to forecast demand, eliminate bottlenecks. He can speak to how I handle pressure.

Addendums

During the last 10 years, there has been a rise in the use of addendums to the resume. They can really set you apart. And, addendums are standing the test of time because they add value without adding pages to the actual resume.

I suppose, in some ways, one could view each of the aforementioned resume supplements as an addendum. In fact, I routinely refer to my targeted reference list format as an "addendum" to the resume. But the word "addendum" typically refers to one or more pages of content that supplement the resume by diving deeper into a particular area or providing additional context of something that is mentioned briefly on the resume.

Examples of addendums would include:

- An expanded list of patents, designs, and or inventions.
- An expanded list of publications or writings.
- A list of volunteer or community service activities. As you have read earlier, these activities are now routinely left off of a resume except when such involvement is a direct requirement of the job… such as with these representative positions: bank branch manager, salesperson, small business manager, and nonprofit manager or fundraiser.
- Creative designs, drawings, or artistic renderings.
- An expanded list of professional development and trainings attended or facilitated, including workshops, seminars, and courses.

So you see, the term "addendum" does represent a broad license to create additional marketing materials and/or list additional relevant information to support your candidacy.

If you are contemplating a major career change or shift into a new area where your expertise or experience is almost exclusively by way of volunteer or personal experience, an addendum almost becomes critical to your marketing efforts.

Because you'll need to "show" your proficiency in the new area.

And, by creating an addendum—which is <u>not</u> an actual page of the resume—you are afforded the flexibility to use the document tactically and according to the timing of your choice.

Timing is Everything

You should consider the timing of using your supplements.

For maximum effect.

Of course, and as stated earlier, if you're struggling just to get an interview for a particular position, you may not want to hold anything back. In that case, it might be wise to send in all your material in the very beginning. Even if the hiring company is only asking for your resume. Because, when your prospects at securing an interview are dim, you really have nothing to lose.

For the most part, however, you should be extremely tactical about the timing of using a resume-supplement during the hiring process.

The right timing can make a world of difference. Consider this case…

Becky had done her homework. She knew that the hiring process included two interviews. She knew she was a fairly strong candidate for the position but also that she had some stiff competition. In the job advertisement, the hiring company had asked for a cover letter and resume so that's exactly what Becky sent in. No more and no less.

Becky had networked with several people at the company to ensure her resume was viewed by the hiring manager and so, after submitting the cover letter and resume, she was called in for a first round interview.

She thought she did well in the first interview and was told that she would be contacted next Tuesday about whether she would be coming back for a second interview. Becky sent thank you notes out to each of the people she interviewed with and waited patiently.

Getting Anxious
Next Tuesday came and went without a word. On Thursday, Becky called and left a polite voice mail for the hiring manager. She simply said that the first interview had "peaked her interest" and something to the effect that she was "looking forward to hearing from you when it is time for the next step in the process." The next weekend came and went without a word from the company.

During the middle of the next week, which was two weeks after her first interview and a full week after the day the company told Becky they would get back to her, she started to get a bit anxious. But Becky was smart enough to know not to transfer her anxiety over to the hiring manager. She was aware that, during the last 5 to 10 years, most companies' hiring processes have become notoriously unpredictable and often quite drawn out.

Becky allowed herself a few more days of waiting and then she sent an e-mail.

The Addendum Difference – Round I
The follow up e-mail Becky sent was just two or three sentences long. In it Becky reiterated her high level of interest in the position and her feeling that her skills and background were an excellent fit with their requirements.

She also included a list of names in my "targeted reference list" format.

The next day, the hiring manager called and apologized for the delay.

He noted how appreciative he was that Becky had sent along the list. Reading about just a couple of her key strengths from the reference list had reminded hiring manager about their interview and why he was interested in Becky in the first place.

Her candidacy was back on track and, during the following week, Becky interviewed a second time with the company.

The Addendum Difference – Round II
To this second interview, Becky brought along another one page addendum. This one was about two-thirds of a page in length, with content not found on her one-page resume, and coalescing around "skill training" that Becky had received over the years. It even noted the Excel and Access courses she was currently taking through the local adult ed. program. Much of the interview's discussion focused around Becky's training and how important the ability to continually learn was to success of the position for which the company was hiring.

Becky was able to close the deal during the second interview when the company made her an offer on the spot!

The two takeaways from this story?

1. Create a targeted reference list and other potential supplements <u>now</u>.

2. Use the supplements tactically, when the time is right.

While the concept of a "targeted reference list" is fresh in your mind, jot down the names of four professionals (current or former bosses, peers, subordinates, customers…) who you might ask to be on your list. Then, think about how each of those persons perceives you and try to predict *what each of them would identify as your top two strengths*. Remember, you are considering what you think *they* would say, not what *you* would want them to say.

Name of Reference #1 and *their* Perception of your Top 2 Strengths

Name of Reference #2 and *their* Perception of your Top 2 Strengths

Name of Reference #3 and *their* Perception of your Top 2 Strengths

Name of Reference #4 and *their* Perception of your Top 2 Strengths

Part 3: Customize

Chapter 17

Customizing

"Give the people what they want..."
 - The Kinks

We only hear and see what we want to hear and see.

To *get noticed*, your resume must use words that speak the hiring manager's language. It must:

- Be customized/tailored for each job to which you are applying.

- Contain the key words and phrases from the job advertisement.

- Be in alignment with the position's hiring criteria.

The hiring manager's perception is the hiring manager's reality.

Feeling a bit "put off" because you already have what they want and don't feel you should have to make an extra effort to spoon feed the recruiters and hiring managers? OK.

But if you don't customize your resume, then it will be "filed" along with 100+ others which also did not stand out. In the circular file.

Because the hiring manager does not have time to read every resume for every position. They will decide your resume's fate during a quick "scan" ... of 7 seconds or less. So make it easy for them.

Include the words and phrases they are looking for.

> ### *Know How You Are Perceived*
> Choose to assess how you are and will be perceived—as a candidate for a particular position or even as an employee. You can take self-assessment tests. You can ask colleagues for honest feedback. While you should still remain authentic and true to yourself, you need to factor in how others will perceive you (on paper and in person) in order to customize your resume, speak their language, and make it easier for them to hear your message and open a dialog. *Perception is reality.*

This is not about being fake.

It is about understanding others' realities. It is about being smart enough to find a way to *get noticed* and build a foundation for effective communication. You might say it is really just about being courteous.

You see, each person simply has a different lens through which they translate what they read or experience. So, each person's perception is different. And, each person's perception becomes their reality.

You may perceive that your resume doesn't need customization to be noticed.

That is your reality.

But your reality is not nearly as important as the hiring manager's.

And the hiring manager has identified certain criteria essential to performing the tasks and meeting the objectives of the open position.

They know what they want.

So, give it to them!

You have already invested considerable time and energy in creating a powerful marketing tool. But, with all due respect, you did not write your resume for your own consumption. You wrote it to get noticed by others at your target companies. Therefore, for each position you go for, the resume must have key words and phrases related to what that particular company wants. In addition, some key words and phrases are more important than others. Some even might be grouped together to form common themes or relate to common areas.

As you analyze the job advertisement and conduct additional research about the company, position, and potential co-workers, keep in mind that these key words and phrases will usually relate to 1 of 3 different areas:

- *Results* that they are expecting the new hire to achieve.
- *Skills* that are necessary to perform the position's tasks.
- *Fit* with the culture.

Let's examine the importance of each area.

Results

You already get this, but let me state the obvious...because you really, really need to get this: *Companies hire people to solve their problems or prevent new ones from happening.* Don't ever lose sight of that fact.

They <u>won't hire you</u> just because you need a job and are a great person. They <u>will hire you</u> if they believe you can impact their bottom line.

You have to convince them that you will get results.

And one of the best predictors to determine whether you will deliver the goods in the future is to examine your track record in the past. *Emphasize your accomplishments that relate to their present needs.*

Whether the results they are looking for are related to...being 100% accurate in keeping financial records, satisfying the needs of each retail customer who enters a store, developing new product designs and prototypes, or improving the profitability of an entire division...your resume needs to show that you have achieved similar results in the past or at least that you have the skills to do so in the future.

> ### Take Away Their Pain
> Choose to customize your brand or marketing message to show you can eliminate or prevent problems specific to an industry or hiring company. Candidates who can identify a company's pain points—and then promote themselves as a solution—increase their chances exponentially.

Struggling with this concept as related to *your* position? Consider this example: Not sure how a sales person takes away or prevents pain? By making enough profitable sales so that the company won't go belly up!

Skills

It is your responsibility to acquire and keep current with the skills necessary to get the job done correctly. That's right. It's <u>your</u> responsibility.

I know it's not fair. I know that companies used to pay for your training, education, and re-training. But, with few exceptions, these are different days. *You need to come fully assembled and with batteries included.*

You need to list the skills they want in plain sight within your resume. And, please pay particular attention to the "hard skills," which are typically technical, often in groups, and have made a roaring comeback lately.

Examples of hard skill groups:

- Excel, QuickBooks, TaxPro 4.0,…
- Commercial Driver's License, HAZMAT,…
- JD Edwards, Hyperion, SPSS, Excel macros,…
- MIG, TIG, and Fluxcore; metal fab; mechanized welding,…
- HVAC, electrical test, ladder logic,…
- International tax, transfer pricing, Corptax TPA,…

And, hard skills are often connected to certain training or certification requirements, which usually have accompanying acronyms:

- PMP = Project Management Professional
- CMA = Certified Medical Assistant
- SPHR = Senior Professional Human Resources
- CPA = Certified Public Accountant
- MSCE = Microsoft Certified Engineer
- CDL = Commercial Driver's License

Of course, you should be careful about using acronyms on a resume. If you do choose to use them, please spell out the name in its entirety the first time it appears in print. Don't make it difficult for the reader.

Special note for new college graduates and others with possibly limited experience and accomplishments that relate to the hiring company's needs: **You won't get hired unless you have the hard skills a company wants.** Don't complain. Sign up for that adult ed. course. And get hired!

Fit

Every year, in national surveys, hiring managers rank "fit" as a very important criteria for deciding to hire candidates.

And, it just makes sense. Consider just 2 reasons …

- Retention of talent continues to be a significant problem, especially among workers early in their career. Companies invest in getting a new hire up to speed in the first few months but when workers don't feel a "fit," they may jump ship…
- Managers are commonly overloaded, leaving limited time for dealing with cultural or "people" issues. People who "fit in" are prized as "easy keepers" and contribute to positive morale.

Here are a few sample key words and phrases to include on your resume that might relate to fitting in with a company and its culture:

- Takes initiative
- Task-orientation
- Calm under pressure
- On-time delivery
- Learns easily and quickly
- Mission or values driven
- Fast paced environment
- Succeeding as a Team
- Entrepreneurial
- Continuous improvement
- Customer satisfaction focus
- Works with little supervision
- Resourceful and dependable
- Solves conflicts independently

> **Fit with an Organization's "Personality"**
>
> You have a unique personality. So does each organization and/or department; it is called their "culture." The words you use to describe your personality should be similar to the words that describe your target organization's culture or you shouldn't waste your time applying. But, if there *is* similarity, be sure to include those words on your resume to broadcast your potential "fit."

Research, Research, Research

You cannot over-research a particular company or position.

You can make the mistake of under-researching, however.

You need to bring the same commitment of detail and organization to your research that you have previously brought to your resume development. Otherwise, your research will be a waste of time and your resume will not be customized with the words to get you noticed.

Watch out for these common research traps:

- Researching the position but not the company.
- Relying solely on internet-based research.
- Believing everything you read—especially on a company's site.
- Assuming that the job ad and/or job description is up-to-date.
- Assuming that a company's culture permeates the entire organization equally and that no sub-cultures exist.
- Ignoring important research criteria such as: pay, morale, pace of the work, personality of the manager, and work hours.

- Not speaking with current or past staff, vendors, or customers.
- Assuming you know what you don't know.
- Not speaking to the competition or not networking with people in similar positions at different companies.
- Identifying so many key words and phrases that you lose sight of the most important ones to highlight on your resume.

Be smart. Spend more time on researching and applying for a few jobs which seem to really synch with your background and that you have a shot at. Yours should be a qualitative approach.

Don't know where to begin in terms of web-based research?

The Riley Guide site has been around since 1994 and contains a wealth of job search information, much of it written by career coaches themselves. At www.rileyguide.com/jsresearch.html, you will find help whether you are researching a particular industry, trying to come up with a list of target companies, or actually researching companies as you customize your resume to apply for positions at each one.

Visit the Library's Reference Section

This is a must for any job search and it can be absolutely critical when conducting research to customize your resume and target your approach for each particular position.

The reference section of your local or regional library can be the key to meeting all your research needs.

You can use any public library's resources just by walking in and, if you have a library card, the databases and other web-based tools may also be made available for use on your home computer. Instead of paying to access some of the best online databases, go to the library!

In addition to the online databases, the reference section of the library is also a repository for valuable printed material.

Some of the more useful bound resources still funded in larger libraries include: manufacturers' directories for each state, regional business magazines with articles on specific companies, top 100 best places to work periodicals, and directories of professional and industry related organizations.

Tip: For faster, friendlier service, show your appreciation to the reference librarian with a personal note or batch of gluten-free cookies!

Here are just a few of the better databases, which are commonly found in the reference section at your local library:

EBSCO Host: An index of magazine, biz journal, & newspaper articles.

InfoUSA or *ReferenceUSA*: A detailed business database of 100 million small to large sized employers.

A to Z Databases: A database of 30 million companies.

Thomas Register: A database of manufacturing companies and products.

Hoovers: A database used by many salespeople that includes information on over 75 million companies.

CorporateInformation.com: A database of financial information on 39,000+ public companies worldwide.

Not sure what information to seek out either when conducting online research or through discussions with networking contacts?

Following is a sampling of areas of research you might prioritize to help you customize your resume as well as develop your interview strategy.

Company Research:

- Recent events — newsworthy or otherwise.
- Mission and vision.
- Values and culture, including continuous improvement initiatives.
- New products or services.
- Customers, vendors, and competitors.
- Common software or systems used across the company.
- Performance management system and philosophy.
- Names of current or past employees to network with.
- History and stability of the company, including market position.
- Morale and employment reputation.
- SWOT analysis.

Position Research:

- Top 2 – 3 objectives to accomplish in 3 – 6 – 12 months.
- Most important skills — hard and soft.
- Biggest challenges and barriers to success.
- Reporting and key working relationships.
- Compensation structure.
- Software or other technical competencies needed.
- Sub-culture and/or management philosophy of the department.
- Professional behavior and attire norms.
- Ongoing projects and initiatives.
- When — in the business cycle — the position will be filled.
- Manager's personality and style — normally and under stress.
- What the company is looking for — specifically.
- Who is involved in the hiring process.
- Terminology that is often used and that which is not.

Visiting the library may pay other dividends for you as well. Some possible advantages to you include:

- Free internet and free or low cost printing and photocopying.
- Personal computers so you can work on your resume. Hint: You may want to email it to yourself so that you always have access and don't need to use a CD or USB drive.
- Limited distractions and chance to *force* yourself to work on your resume or do a "quiet" job search while there.
- An alternative to staying cooped up in the house.
- A chance to dress presentably and work in a "professional" space.
- The occasional free workshop on aspects of job searching.

So, what are you waiting for?

ATS/Applicant Tracking System

You heard it here first, folks…

There is no way to beat today's ATS.

Period.

For those of you not familiar with the term, an ATS is a system, either software or web-based, that the vast majority of companies use to attract, accept, sort, screen, and manage the multitude of resumes they receive for each position opening. One way or another, over 95% of all resumes submitted online travel through some sort of ATS—most of which are largely designed to *screen you out*.

If you rely solely on the online application process—even if you customize your resume with key words and phrases—you have less than a 5% chance of getting noticed. In other words, for every 100 online applications you submit, you would garner 5 positive responses.

I'll save you the gory details of my extensive sleuthing except for this: algorithm changes in 4 of the big 5 applicant tracking systems over the past 20 months—combined with new features that often leave selection of resumes to the systems themselves—mean you cannot win this fight.

Hey, just because you are responding to an online ad for a store clerk position as Susie's Local Hardware Store, don't think you are exempt. After all, the online job board that listed the position ad is anchored by ATS software. That's right. There's no escape.

Many of my colleagues who are senior managers in human resources will not admit it publically, but privately they acknowledge this fact: <u>you must get your resume directly to the hiring manager to get noticed</u>. It is not that HR isn't doing their job. They are working overtime! But with HR staff cuts every year and tons of qualified applicants, HR is in an untenable position and forced to rely on ATS. By the way, guess what HR professionals do when they are looking for a job? They network and try to get their resume to the hiring manager!

So, let's be clear. You are not customizing your resume to try to beat an ATS. You are customizing your resume so that when you get a copy to the hiring manager, they will want to interview you.

Networking has no substitute.

Analyzing Job Advertisements

You must analyze the job ad for key words and phrases to put in your resume. This will help you to *get noticed* and secure an interview. Further, it will set you up to discuss how you can impact their bottom line, thus improving your chances to *close the deal* and secure a job offer.

Today,<u> most successful candidates for professional positions customize their resumes</u>. You need to do this.

Here is a customizable, step-by-step system for analyzing job ads:

1. Print the job ad and read it thoroughly.

2. Highlight words and phrases that appear multiple times throughout the job ad, especially if they are found in several sections.

3. Underline the highlighted words and phrases which appear near the beginning of a section or a series or a list; these are the most important of all.

4. Note any common themes, groupings, or linkages between the highlighted words.

5. Use a free word cloud creator such as www.wordle.net to double check your work. Just cut and paste the entire job ad into the program. The words that appear most often in the ad will be emphasized in the resulting visual image; the larger the size of a word, the more frequently it appears. While the frequency with which a word appears in a job advertisement does not guarantee it is a key word, it does suggest closer examination.

6. Begin resume customization, inserting key words and phrases, but be careful not to come across like you are pandering.

One strategy is to combine the key words and phrases with those you already have in your resume.

7. Review your resume to make sure it still honestly and accurately represents you.

REMEMBER: Don't lose authenticity when boosting credibility!

OK, now let's look at a sample job ad in which the key words and phrases have already been put in bold by a job seeker…

Job Ad with Key Words and Phrases in Bold

Executive Director of WXQ Nonprofit

Overview
The Executive Director (ED) of WXQ Nonprofit will focus externally on **fundraising** and **community building**. The ED will also focus on creating a culture of **continuous improvement**—achieving **performance** targets for the organization, including **service delivery**, **fundraising**/revenue and expense targets. The ED manages and teams with Operations, Public Support, HR, Finance, and Service Delivery department managers. The ED acts as the WXQ's **principal fundraiser**. Over 60% of the ED's time is spent in **community relationship building**, **fundraising**, and overall **visibility**.

Duties and Responsibilities
- **Achieves fundraising goals** for **annual campaign** and **capital projects**. Teams with community leadership to grow adequate and diversified financial resources.
- **Builds strong external relationships** with key organizations and community leaders to increase organization's visibility and financial support. **Cultivates relationships** with **external constituents**, including donors, governments, corporate partners, and civic organizations.
- Leads operational enhancements, with emphasis on creating and sustaining culture of **continuous improvement**. Builds high performing teams to boost morale, focus limited resources and efforts, increase efficiencies, and maintain high level of accountability.
- Ensures strong **visibility** for the WXQ in the service area. Increases **community awareness**, participation and commitment to WXQ by being an **active community participant** and ensuring regular local media communications.
- Meets all assigned targets and goals, including cost containment, revenue generation, and operations to deliver highest quality **service delivery**.
- Partners with related nonprofits and other organizations to ensure coordinated outreach, **service delivery** and **visibility** within the community.
- **Grows capacity** for **service delivery**, recruiting 150+ new volunteers.

Experience Requirements
Minimum 5 years related experience in the non-profit sector, business, or sales.
Proven track record in **raising significant financial resources**.
Development of teams, consensus, and **continuous improvement** initiatives.
Demonstrated ability to exercise good and timely judgments in complex situations.
Strong skills in communication and influencing, along with public speaking and writing.

Experience Preferred
Experience **raising major gifts of $10,000+**.
Experience **establishing a planned giving program**.

Education Requirements
4 year college degree. Master's degree preferred.

Choosing Key Words and Phrases

As the above example illustrates, many job ads can be problematic. With so many content-rich words, which ones should you choose?

You must create and use your own methodology or system, such as the one suggested on the page before the job ad.

Even then, it can be challenging. And, with other *hidden* key words and phrases not in the job ad, it becomes essential to network with others.

> ***Network to Uncover "Hidden" Key Words and Context***
>
> Do not expect all key words to be included in the job ad. Discover "hidden" key words and context by networking with current or past employees, vendors, customers, and contractors. Analysis of the job ad alone won't cut it.

Important Themes within this Job Ad

After both analyzing the job ad and networking with others familiar with the position, the following themes emerged:

Fundraising: revenue generation is a clear priority for the ED.

Leadership: "management" is implied but "leadership" is required.

Relationship Building: partnerships are key to organizational success.

Community: this is a visible, high profile community position.

Continuous Improvement: this position will lead such a cultural shift.

Service Delivery: this terminology represents the service to customers.

The next two pages show how a resume might be customized with the key words. See if you can tell the difference in the "before" and "after" versions...

Resume Before Customizing with Key Words

DISTEN DAVIES
22 FIELD DRIVE, ANYTOWN, CT 00000
distendavies@gmail.com | 978.238.9923 | linkedin.com/in/davies5

Results focused with non-profit management and fundraising background. Develops effective relationships at all levels of an organization, with community partners, and donors. Hands-on leadership, project, and financial management experience in challenging environments marked by significant change.

EXPERIENCE

ON YOUR WAY UP, Anytown, NY   2006-2013

Executive Director
Engaged to restructure staffing, operations, and balance sheet for non-profit with 5,300 individual and 64 corporate customers, 54 staff, and $625K annual budget.

- Led comprehensive reorganization driven by clear performance and behavioral metrics. Turned over 48 out of 54 staff in 4 months to support new direction.
- Managed challenging finances to positive cash flow for the 3rd time in 17 years, increasing earned & total revenue, cutting costs and repositioning organization.
- Negotiated with mortgage holder and developed business plan to cure default with 3 year win-win workout plan. Liquidated non-performing assets for $290K pay down of debt.
- Teamed with consultant and volunteers on $424K capital campaign.

SYCAMORE DISASTER RELIEF, Anytown, CT   1999-2006

Executive Director
Development Director
Responsible for operations, human resources, and finances of two newly merged business units, serving 6,300 customers. Led development of county-wide identity.

- Instructed 40+ workshops and courses throughout NY and southern New England. Trainings included: Major Gift Solicitation, Board Development, Planned Giving, and Disaster Fund Raising.
- Pioneered concept of Industrial Support Committee, involving area CEOs.
- Served as 1 of 8 national disaster fundraisers on projects such as Hurricane Andrew and the Mid-West Floods. Led initial phase of $80M campaign.
- Increased revenues by 105% in 2 years and lessened dependence on one source from 75% to 32%, while increasing revenue from source. Established major gifts and endowment programs. Increased volunteer staff from 180 to 335.

EDUCATION AND TRAINING

BS in Organizational Leadership, MNV College of Management, Brooklyn, NY

Certified Fund Development Executive, National Board of FDEs, Arlington, VA

Resume After Customizing with Key Words

DISTEN DAVIES
22 FIELD DRIVE, BURLINGTON, MA 00000
distendavies@gmail.com | 978.238.9923 | linkedin.com/in/davies5

Achieves fundraising goals and leads continuous improvements.

Delivers sustainable growth, anchored by individual gifts of $10K+, planned giving programs, and operational leadership. Develops effective community relationships and partnerships, increasing the organization's public visibility and service delivery effectiveness. Hand-on style and commitment to team building.

EXPERIENCE

ON YOUR WAY UP, Anytown, NY   2006-2013
  Executive Director
  Led fundraising increases—in annual appeal, major gifts, and planned giving—and co-developed capital campaign. Created culture of continuous improvement.

- Increased annual giving by 112% or $67K through major gifts strategy and raising community profile. Efforts at growing service delivery capacity and controlling costs resulted in positive cash flow for only the 3rd time in 17 years.
- Teamed with consultant and volunteers on $424K capital campaign.
- Restructured staffing, operations, and balance sheet for non-profit with 5,300 individual and 64 corporate customers, 54 staff, and $625K budget. Raised community visibility and established numerous partnerships. Developed new business plan and spun off non-performing assets for $290K debt reduction.

SYCAMORE DISASTER RELIEF, Anytown, CT   1999-2006
  Executive Director
  Fundraising Director – *Major Gifts and Special Campaigns*
  Increased earned, and donation revenue, leading 2 newly merged businesses with 6,300 customers. Raised organization's visibility across all county communities.

- Served as 1 of 8 national disaster fundraisers focusing on securing major gifts of $10K to $100K+. Led initial phase of $80M campaign.
- Increased revenues by 105% in 2 years and lessened dependence on one source from 75% to 32%, while increasing revenue from source. Established major gifts and endowment programs. Increased volunteer staff from 180 to 335.
- Pioneered concept of Industrial Support Committee, building relationships with area CEOs and soliciting advice for continuous improvement initiatives.
- Taught major gifts, planned giving and other workshops to 40+ audiences.

EDUCATION AND TRAINING

BS in Organizational Leadership, MNV College of Management, Anytown, NY
Certified Fund Development Executive, National Board of FDEs, Anytown, VA

So, concerning the two resumes you just perused:

- Did you notice the key words and key phrases that were inserted into the revised resume?

- How about the tagline at the top of the resume?

- Did the reordering of some bullets stand out?

- Did you pay attention to the title change in the second organization/company?

Remember that the resume's purpose is to get you noticed, to grab a reader's attention long enough that they are interested in knowing more—whether that involves re-reading it more carefully, checking out the candidate's LinkedIn profile, scheduling a five minute phone screen, or inviting them in for an interview.

To be certain, the above candidate has a much improved chance of getting their resume noticed after customization...*as long as they get it into the hands of the hiring manager.*

A Word of Customizing Caution

There is an exception to every rule.

While I would still highly recommend you err on the side of significant customization to target your resume for each open position, you may want to keep one thought in mind...

If you are unable to secure either an interview or an offer and want to be considered for other positions within the company, *there is always the potential that your resume might be tailored so much to one position that you would not be considered for another.*

Now, many larger organizations expect resume customization for each position and even allow replacement of an uploaded resume on their ATS. But take more care with smaller companies, where everyone knows everyone else. And, be especially mindful if you are less focused on one position and are marketing yourself to the company as a whole.

There is nothing wrong with a job search strategy of trying to get hired by one of several target companies, irrespective of the job. But customizing your resume could actually backfire in this particular case.

Use your best judgment on a case-by-case basis when customizing.

Chapter 18

"Core Hiring Motives"

"The first step in exceeding your customer's expectations is to know those expectations."
- Roy H. Williams

Time to customize the "one resume" with "core hiring motives."

Because, even if they are hiring for the same job, multiple hiring managers will each want something slightly different. So, you are going to give each one exactly what they want. You want to make it easy for each different hiring manager to see you as a top candidate.

And call you for an interview.

I developed the simple concept of "core hiring motives" many moons ago as a complement to the "one resume" and "story telling interview" concepts. **This concept helps provide a bridge between** *getting noticed* **and** *closing the deal.*

Both the "one resume" and "core hiring motives" concepts are anchored in Pareto's Rule, sometimes known as the 80/20 rule.

But, while my "one resume" concept presents your 2 to 3 *authentic* core strengths, the addition of my "core hiring motives" concept makes you more *credible* by customizing your core strengths to fit the top priorities of the potential employer. They work so well together...**1+1=5**!

Remember, **you must be both credible AND authentic** in your resume and in all aspects of your career transition.

Ease of Customizing

The "one resume" format makes it easy to customize your resume for each job opening. Why? Because…

Each candidate has 2 to 3 core strengths.

and

Each hiring manager has 2 to 3 core hiring motives.

Show the prospective employer that your core strengths align with their core hiring motives and you will likely end up with an interview.

The "one resume" format has 2 to 3 core strengths clearly visible in the "sweet spot" of the resume so <u>just modify those core strengths to reflect the company's 2 to 3 core hiring motives</u>.

Identifying Core Hiring Motives

As you probably have 15+ total strengths to offer a perspective employer, the hiring manager and company often has 15+ total requirements and qualifications for each position.

Of course, almost no candidate will have 100% of what the prospective employer wants.

So the most important analysis is determining which 2 to 3 of the 15+ total requirements and qualifications are most important to them. You need to use your critical thinking skills here.

Essentially, I'm asking you to revisit Pareto's 80-20 Rule.

Each hiring manager will use their own, unique process and criteria to define their top 2 to 3 hiring motives for a position. Just like you did when you developed your 2 to 3 core strengths using your own, unique process and criteria. In other words, just as you identified your own unique brand, each hiring manager develops their own unique hiring criteria! <u>Match your brand to their hiring criteria and...you *get noticed*</u>!

Of course, the hiring manager may not even be conscious that they are narrowing down their 15+ total requirements, but they always do it. They have their top priorities for the job and those top priorities become their core hiring motives; those top priorities are what they will base their hiring decisions on.

Now, instead of getting all worked up about identifying the complexities of a hiring manager's process and how their mind works, allow yourself to open your own mind, ask the right questions of yourself and others, and just *observe*.

Identifying the core hiring motives for a position opening may take some intention and time, but it will be easier than you think if you can keep an *open mind*.

As you are reviewing the job advertisement (and other key documents), researching on the web, and — most importantly — networking with individuals who have knowledge of the position and company, you will need to ask yourself and others the right questions.

These 6 groups of questions will help you ID their core hiring motives:

1. HISTORY: *What were the keys to achieving good performance for the last successful person in the position? How are your strengths different then that individual's? Has anything shifted with that position, the company, and the business objectives since another individual formerly held the position?*

2. GOALS: *What will the one or two most important measures of success be for the position during the first three months on the job? During the first six months? During the first 12 months?*

3. CULTURE: *Does there exist a significant cultural or communication/ process requirement that every company employee must prioritize? If such a requirement exists, how does it compare in importance to the top measures of success for the position?*

4. SKILLS: *Are there two or three technical skills or abilities that are absolutely mandatory? If such a technical requirement exists, what is the level of proficiency expected or required? Are there corresponding certifications or training that are a must?*

5. SOURCES: *Are there differences or discrepancies in criteria as indicated by different sources — the hiring manager, networking contacts, the job advertisement, the job description, web research, networking contacts, and individuals who previously held the position? Are these differences material in nature? Which sources are most credible?*

6. **PAIN:** *What pain does the hiring manager feel or want to avoid? What is their major discomfort that you can help alleviate? Or, if all is going smoothly for them at the moment, what potential discomfort can you help them avoid? Finally, how might such pain be measured?*

<u>This last group of questions, focused on the hiring manager's existing or potential "pain," may be the most important of all. Answer those questions and you will be close to identifying their core hiring motives.</u>

Customizing Your "Core Strengths"

This is relatively simple in most cases, as you may be applying for position openings which align well with your strengths. However, often the open position will be somewhat different than jobs you have held in the past. To help you understand how you might customize your core strengths during such a transition, consider these examples…

Example 1: *Senior Manager: VP Operations transition to General Manager*

Our first example involves a VP of Manufacturing Operations with an engineering background, track record of improving both quality and efficiencies, and advanced people management skills. Let's say she is applying for a plant manager position that is tasked with both making improvements to the bottom line and also developing the organization's most promising talent. She has identified three core hiring motives: "realizing continuous improvements," "developing top talent," and "liquidating non-performing products."

Examining the "Before" example below, we can see that the first and third core strengths align pretty well with the first and second core hiring motives, respectively. But the core hiring motive known as "liquidating non-performing assets" does not have a correlating core strength. One needs to be created almost from scratch so it can take the place of the current strength: "leads new product development." Other slight wording changes position the candidate as more of a general manager/leader than a senior manager/engineer. If is the candidate determines that one of the core hiring motives is more important than the others, then the motives may be re-ordered accordingly.

On the next page, examine the "before" and "after" example. Notice how the candidate simply weaves the core hiring motives in with her existing wording, <u>boosting her credibility and also remaining highly authentic.</u> Lesson: *Don't feel the need to use <u>exact</u> wording from the job ad.*

Example 1: "Before" Core Strengths (without "Profile" paragraph)

INNOVATES PROCESS IMPROVEMENTS
Engages entire workforce to achieve reduced inventory and lead times, improved quality, and lower costs. Integrates value stream mapping, Kaizen, waste elimination, and other lean tools. Analyzes and simplifies complex systems, develops KPIs, and drives innovative solutions.

LEADS NEW PRODUCT DEVELOPMENT
Introduces profitable new products on time and within budget. Guides 'concept to launch' process, including product selection and revenue projections. Delivers new product on time through constant communication, milestone tracking, and potential problem analysis.

ENGINEERS HUMAN RELATIONSHIPS AND SYSTEMS
Solves problems and creates new synergies through employee engagement. Relates to others in their own preferred style when possible. Develops motivation and reward initiatives.

Example 1: "After" Core Strengths (without "Profile" paragraph)

LEADS CONTINUOUS IMPROVEMENTS
Initiates and leads sustainable improvements by engaging entire workforce to achieve reduced inventory and lead times, improved quality, and lower costs. Ensures senior managers integrate value stream mapping, Kaizen, waste elimination, and other lean tools. Simplifies complex systems, develops KPIs, and drives innovation.

INVESTS IN PROFITABLE PRODUCTS
Eliminates non-performing products through careful analysis of ROI, market potential, integration with brand, and customer loyalty. Invests savings to increase margins on already profitable lines and introduce profitable new products on time and within budget. Willing to make unpopular decisions to sustain long-term profitability and build brand. Re-organizes and re-allocates workforce, machinery, and capital, facilitating a smooth change process.

DEVELOPS EMPLOYEE TALENT
Leads talent development by identifying and investing in high potentials. Believes in relating to others in their own preferred style. Develops motivation and reward initiatives. Prioritizes systematic mentoring of high potentials by current leadership and subject matter experts.

Example 2: *College Grad: Anthropology transition to Underwriting*

This example involves a recent college graduate with a liberal arts degree and mostly retail work experience who is trying to make the transition to business. She is applying for a position as an underwriter trainee with a large insurance company because she was unable to secure a position within the field of Anthropology. After reviewing the job description, searching blogs, and speaking with other recent graduates who are working in similar positions, the candidate has identified three core hiring motives for the position: "intermediate Excel," "excellent project management skills," and "attention to detail." In addition, the candidate understands that all hires will be going through a 13-week training program.

Examining the "Before" example on the next page, which shows a brief "Profile" paragraph, we can see that the second and third core strengths align pretty well with the second and third core hiring motives, respectively. But the core hiring motive known as "intermediate Excel" lacks a corresponding core strength. This needs to be created almost from scratch so it can take the place of "customer focus." Other changes in the wording of the "Profile" paragraph position the candidate as trainable and already possessing some skills that competing business majors do not.

This candidate chose to take two adult education classes to learn Excel at an advanced level and also volunteered to do some basic statistical work for her professors during her last semester, when it was apparent she would not be hired in her field of study. Smart moves. This candidate will most likely be on the short list for a call from a corporate recruiter, even though her major is not in business or accounting.

On the next page, notice how, on her space-limited resume, the candidate has listed core strengths without definitions. It wouldn't add much value to a candidate with little experience. The reader is still "forced" to notice that this candidate has what they want. Game on.

Example 2: "Before" Profile and Core Strengths

> Conscientious and reliable in completing tasks and projects on time. Helpful attitude contributes to team problem solving. Database experience. Takes responsibility for own learning and achieving quality outcomes. Develops ideas with big picture in mind. Adapts to other cultures. Intermediate Spanish. Core strengths include:
>
> - Customer Focus
> - Detail Orientation
> - Team Projects

Example 2: "After" Profile and Core Strengths

> Focused on accuracy and detail with ability to quickly learn new skills and processes. Recent training in advanced Excel, including pivot tables and macros. Conscientious and reliable in completing tasks and projects on time. Helpful attitude contributes to team problem solving. Database and statistical modeling work for two professors. Core strengths include:
>
> - Advanced Excel
> - Project Management
> - Detail Orientation

Example 3: *IT Lead: Network Administration transition to Helpdesk*

This example involves an IT lead who has recently been involved in network administration but who is shifting over to work in a helpdesk capacity. *Please keep in mind that, often, in technical fields, core hiring motives are related to "areas" of technical competency in which various skills are represented.* After reviewing the job description and speaking with several peers who made a similar transition, the candidate has identified two core hiring motive areas for the position: "hardware and software" and "systems and certifications." In addition, the candidate has a good grasp on the priorities of various technical skills represented by those areas.

Examining the "Before" example on the next page, it is evident that the candidate shows some of the individual technical skills found in the two core hiring motive areas, but that he will require re-positioning under different technical area titles. In addition, the individual needs to name more skills for the "hardware and software" core hiring motive area. Since IT or other technical professionals often have a wheelhouse that is much larger than that represented on any given resume, this should not be a problem. And, if there is a technical skill this candidate is lacking for such a move into a related but different profession, he can always seek out the appropriate training or certification courses.

The "After" example on the next page shows the two areas representing the two core hiring motives and also offers several other insights. This candidate wisely chose to keep one other column visible, as his network administration skills might be useful at a small- to mid-sized firm that prizes versatility. In addition, notice the title change to this section now incorporates the word "Helpdesk." (Please note that the formatting of the technical skills typically calls for the capitalization the first letter of each word—this is not standard formatting for other resumes.)

ADDITIONAL INSIGHT: In addition, the candidate also adds the words "Expertise," "Proficiency," and "Knowledge" to three software programs in the first column (assumed to be found on the job advertisement as utilized by the hiring company) to indicate his level of mastery with each. "Expertise" suggests the highest level of mastery, "Proficiency" suggests a working comfort with, and "Knowledge" suggests the candidate has been trained (formally or informally) in the software but has not used it much or at all. Such distinctions are typically appreciated by readers who often times tire of reading technical resumes in which candidates try to inflate their skill mastery.

Finally, this candidate has wisely chosen to include a note in bolded italics just following the columns. Often, network administrators would have less experience working directly with non-technical employees who rely on support from the helpdesk. But not this candidate.

Even though communication and people skills were interestingly absent from the job advertisement (which can be common with hiring technical professionals—technical skills are often very heavily weighted to the exclusion of "soft skills"), this candidate is savvy enough to insert it into the resume nevertheless. While he will probably be a weaker candidate on paper than others who have been working directly in a helpdesk capacity during recent years, if this candidate can get his customized resume in front of the hiring manager he has a real chance of beginning a conversation.

Example 3: "Before" Core Strengths (without "Profile" paragraph)

TECHNICAL COMPETENCIES

Network Administration
- 175 Workstations and 25 Servers
- Enterprise Anti-Virus Server
- Firewall-Switch Design
- Wireless Networks
- Disaster Recovery

Systems Engineering
- Windows and NT Servers
- Active Directory
- VMWare/VLANS
- DNS and DHCP Servers
- Comptia A+ and MSCE

Example 3: "After" Core Strengths (without "Profile" paragraph)

HELPDESK AND TECHNICAL COMPETENCIES

Hardware and Software
- Mobile: Android and iOS
- Remote Access and Cloud
- Laptops: PC and Mac
- MS Office Suite Expertise
- JD Edwards Proficiency
- Salesforce Knowledge

Systems and Certifications
- Comptia A+ and MSCE
- Windows and NT Servers
- DNS and DHCP Servers
- Active Directory and LDAP
- MS Exchange
- Mac OS Levels I and II

Network Administration
- Disaster Recovery
- Firewalls-Switch Design
- WAN Accelerators
- Enterprise Anti-Virus
- Topology Discovery
- Wireless Networks

Experience with hardware and software configuration, installs, training, and troubleshooting. Proven listening, de-escalation, and coaching with non-technical internal customers.

Adding Core Hiring Motives from Scratch

What if you aren't starting with the "one resume" format? But you still want to use the power of the "core hiring motives" concept? No worries. You'll just have to insert language that speaks directly to the hiring manager's 2 to 3 core hiring motives. Your format will still end up looking like the "one resume" but you just won't be customizing your "core strengths," since you have not defined them yet.

In the previous chapter, you learned how to customize a resume with key words and phrases taken from the job ad and other research. We even identified six of the most common themes to include in the resume: Fundraising, Leadership, Relationship Building, Community, Continuous Improvement, and Service Delivery. Well, you will still want to customize your resume according to the strategies presented in Chapter 17. However, you will now need to take it one step further. You need to identify the top 2 to 3 "core hiring motives" and then...*you need to use the "one resume" format to show you are the candidate most aligned with those "core hiring motives."*

So, review the common themes and read the job advertisement in Chapter 17 once again. I think you might now identify that the two areas of "**leadership**" and "**fundraising**" clearly stand out. Now, you would not be wrong to simply use those two words.

But two sub-themes seem to offer important context in this example. Leadership seems to be linked with change, specifically the kind that builds a culture of "continuous improvement." And fundraising seems to be focused specifically on bigger gifts, which are realized by cultivating "major donors." Adding in these two sub-themes to offers a *stronger connection* with the top priorities for this position opening.

On the next two pages, look at the resume we customized in Chapter 17 and how it has been modified to include the two "core hiring motives."

Reprint of Chapter 17 Keyword-Customized Resume

DISTEN DAVIES
22 FIELD DRIVE, BURLINGTON, MA 00000
distendavies@gmail.com | 978.238.9923 | linkedin.com/in/davies5

Achieves fundraising goals and leads continuous improvements.

Delivers sustainable growth, anchored by individual gifts of $10K+, planned giving programs, and operational leadership. Develops effective community relationships and partnerships, increasing the organization's public visibility and service delivery effectiveness. Hand-on style and commitment to team building.

EXPERIENCE

ON YOUR WAY UP, Anytown, NY   2006-2013
Executive Director
Led fundraising increases—in annual appeal, major gifts, planned giving—and co-developed capital campaign. Created culture of continuous improvement.

- Increased annual giving by 112% or $67K through major gifts strategy and raising community profile. Efforts at growing service delivery capacity and controlling costs resulted in positive cash flow for only the 3rd time in 17 years.
- Teamed with consultant and volunteers on $424K capital campaign.
- Restructured staffing, operations, and balance sheet for non-profit with 5,300 individual and 64 corporate customers, 54 staff, and $625K budget. Raised community visibility and established numerous partnerships. Developed new business plan and spun off non-performing assets for $290K debt reduction.

SYCAMORE DISASTER RELIEF, Anytown, CT   1999-2006
Executive Director
Fundraising Director—*Major Gifts and Special Campaigns*
Increased earned, and donation revenue, leading 2 newly merged businesses with 6,300 customers. Raised organization's visibility across all county communities.

- Served as 1 of 8 national disaster fundraisers focusing on securing major gifts of $10K to $100K+. Led initial phase of $80M campaign.
- Increased revenues by 105% in 2 years and lessened dependence on one source from 75% to 32%, while increasing revenue from source. Established major gifts and endowment programs. Increased volunteer staff from 180 to 335.
- Pioneered concept of Industrial Support Committee, building relationships with area CEOs and soliciting advice for continuous improvement initiatives.
- Taught major gifts, planned giving and other workshops to 40+ audiences.

EDUCATION AND TRAINING

BS in Organizational Leadership, MNV College of Management, Anytown, NY

Certified Fund Development Executive, National Board of FDEs, Anytown, VA

The "One Resume" Customized with Two "Core Hiring Motives"

DISTEN DAVIES
22 FIELD DRIVE, BURLINGTON, MA 00000
distendavies@gmail.com | 978.238.9923 | linkedin.com/in/davies5

Delivers sustainable growth, anchored by individual gifts of $10K+, planned giving programs, and operational leadership. Develops effective community relationships, increasing public visibility and service delivery. Hand-on style and commitment to team building. Core strengths:

LEADERSHIP OF CONTINUOUS IMPROVEMENTS
Accomplished leading efforts to continually develop new processes and improve service delivery. Leads cultural changes, mentors and coaches high potential staff, and fosters highly visible and productive partnerships. *Leads positive change from the front.*

FUNDRAISING FROM MAJOR GIFTS
Record of increasing major gifts, capital and annual campaigns, and planned giving revenue. Donor cultivation and solicitation experience; closes major gifts up to $250K and graduates donors to higher levels of giving. *Builds high level of trust quickly.*

EXPERIENCE

ON YOUR WAY UP, Anytown, NY   2006-2013
Executive Director
Led fundraising increases—in annual appeal, major gifts, planned giving—and co-developed capital campaign. Created culture of continuous improvement.

- Increased annual giving by 112% or $67K through major gifts strategy and raising community profile. Efforts at growing service delivery capacity and controlling costs resulted in positive cash flow for only the 3rd time in 17 years.
- Teamed with consultant and volunteers on $424K capital campaign.
- Restructured staffing, operations, and balance sheet for non-profit with 5,300 individual and 64 corporate customers, 54 staff, and $625K budget. Increased community visibility and partnerships. Reduced debt by $290K.

SYCAMORE DISASTER RELIEF, Anytown, CT   1999-2006
Executive Director
Fundraising Director—*Major Gifts and Special Campaigns*
Increased earned, and donation revenue, leading 2 newly merged businesses with 6,300 customers. Raised organization's visibility across all county communities.

- Served as 1 of 8 national disaster fundraisers focusing on securing major gifts of $10K to $100K+. Led initial phase of $80M campaign.
- Increased revenues by 105% in 2 years and lessened dependence on one source from 75% to 32%, while increasing revenue from source. Established major gifts and endowment programs. Increased volunteer staff from 180 to 335.
- Pioneered concept of Industrial Support Committee, building relationships with area CEOs and soliciting advice for continuous improvement initiatives.
- Taught major gifts, planned giving and other workshops to 40+ audiences.

EDUCATION AND TRAINING

BS in Organizational Leadership, MNV College of Management, Anytown, NY
Certified Fund Development Executive, National Board of FDEs, Anytown, VA

Did you notice how the "one resume" version customized with the two "core hiring motives" – placed in the resume's "sweet spot" – <u>forces</u> the reader to notice that this candidate meets their top priorities?

This candidate has dramatically increased their chances at *getting noticed* and being selected for an interview.

And, once in the interview, this candidate can use this customized "one resume" as a platform for addressing the hiring manager's two top priorities with targeted "example stories" (we'll get to that in a later chapter).

Does this candidate have a chance to *close the deal*? Absolutely!

Uncovering "Hidden" Core Hiring Motives

You must speak with networking contacts to make sure you ACCURATELY IDENTIFY the hiring manager's top few priorities. Only then can you truly distance yourself from the other candidates who will be interviewing against you.

I cannot emphasize this point enough.

Certainly, a thorough analysis of the job advertisement is critical to identifying core hiring motives, just as it is with identifying key words and phrases. But, if you limit your resume customization to data collected off of the printed page, your effectiveness at accurately identifying the top 2 to 3 core hiring motives will be stunted.

After all, it is common to have job advertisements written from outdated job descriptions and by recruiters or other human resource professionals who, while well-meaning, do not truly understand the critical hiring criteria for each position. And, since the concept of core hiring motives has importance and reaches far beyond the resume's written words, you must be extremely thorough in your research.

> **"Core Hiring Motives" in Networking and Interviewing**
>
> Choose to use "core hiring motives" when you network and interview for a specific position opening, especially if you started by identifying your "core strengths" and then customized them to align with the top priorities of the hiring manager. You will be perceived as both authentic and credible and may be on the short list of candidates from the beginning.

Let's look at the case of Sarah to better understand the importance of engaging in networking conversations to uncover hidden core hiring motives.

Sarah had utilized the "one resume" format for her resume and had customized it with two core hiring motives she had identified from the job advertisement.

Sarah had also put in calls to several networking contacts connected to the company but chose not to wait for a conversation with those folks prior to submitting her resume.

At first glance, it didn't seem like Sarah really needed their help. This was "only" an individual contributor/hourly wage position, responsible for performing a final quality check on software before products were shipped to customers. And Sarah had relevant experience. Even though there was a very strong field of candidates, the first interview had gone well. Sarah had only one more round of meetings to get through; she had made it to the "final round" of interviewing and was one of only two or three candidates being considered for the position.

That's when an unlikely conversation with one of her networking contacts revealed an additional core hiring motive, *of which the company itself was not even consciously aware.*

It seems that while the former employee had been high-performing, the company's monthly internal audit checks had revealed a surprise in the months after his departure. During the previous several years, the company always seemed to have a software CD or DVD missing each month. Yet, following the departure of the person who previously held the quality test position, the monthly software audit started to come back perfect, with zero discrepancies. And the managers had started to put two and two together.

So, during the second round of interviewing, Sarah continued to use specific example stories to target the two core hiring motives that she had previously uncovered. But when the hiring manager asked Sarah if there was anything else she would like to share about her own background, Sarah seized on the opportunity to deliver a knockout punch. Very matter-of-factly Sarah said: "Well, I was noticing that your website speaks of the importance of honesty and integrity in your culture…and I would just like to add that each of my references can speak directly to the fact that my reputation for integrity is unblemished."

The hiring manager's eyes suddenly widened and he sat back in his chair in silence, taking the measure of Sarah's words for what seemed like an eternity. Then, he excused himself and left the interview room. About 10 minutes later (probably one of the longest 10 minute stretches of Sarah's professional life!), the hiring manager returned with the HR director and made an offer of employment right there in the meeting.

You heard that right.

The interviewers at the hiring company did not even realize exactly what they wanted…until Sarah made them aware of it in the second and final interview…and closed the deal for a job offer on the spot.

A <u>networking conversation</u> gave Sarah the magic words.

It seems that Sarah's networking contact was able to provide insight about a core hiring motive that the job advertisement did not even mention. Insight that connected directly to the company's culture, and which was anchored in honesty and integrity above all else.

You may or may not uncover a gem as valuable as the one Sarah did, but know this:

Networking conversations are <u>essential</u> to uncovering and validating core hiring motives.

Because the job ad may not clearly identify all the top hiring priorities and because the hiring manager and company may not even be fully conscious of what they want!

Chapter 19

Cover Letters

"Either write something worth reading or do something worth writing."
- Benjamin Franklin

I'm with Ben.

After all, cover letters are just not that effective anymore.

I know. I know. You've been told otherwise. In fact, you have probably seen the plethora of books about writing cover letters lining the shelves of bookstores. Lots-o-books. Written specifically about cover letters. About how they can get you noticed. About how they can make the difference in securing an interview. Unfortunately, I just haven't been witness to many instances when a cover letter really did the trick.

If you ask me, cover letters died about 15 years ago.

Let's face it—cover letters were never truly prioritized in the hiring process anyway. Furthermore, *in today's world of speed, speed, and more speed, most recruiters and hiring managers just don't take time to read them.* The resume is the main course, while a cover letter is more often viewed as one of the less-desirable vegetable side dishes.

There are times, however, when you should include a cover letter. If the job advertisement specifically states that you need to submit a cover letter, then you had better send one in and it had better be good. Typically, the more formal the interviewing and hiring process, the more likely it is that a cover letter will be required. Think of the application processes for government and education jobs as examples. So, if you have to write a cover letter…

Play offense, not defense

Cover letters started their rise to prominence in the job search process during the 1940s. Back then the cover letter was viewed almost like a letter of introduction. It telegraphed that you were professional and understood social norms. Even though the cover letters used to give you a slight edge, they were still not read very often. Resumes were main course, even back then. That's because a well written, customized resume plays offense; a cover letter plays defense.

Not convinced?

Consider this case, which I can personally relate to:

Once upon a time, there was a less-than-experienced general manager named Greg. Greg had several open director-level positions, which he was responsible for filling. Since he was committed to interviewing and hiring only candidates with the highest attention to detail and commitment to quality, Greg chose to require a cover letter. Greg intended to screen applicants to exacting standards.

Greg's hiring process was extensive and it was several months before it was complete, with all the key senior-level positions filled. Shortly thereafter, at a human resources advisory team meeting, Greg was complimented on the quality of his new hires.

At the meeting, one VP of HR asked Greg about the elements of his hiring process, including the utility of requiring cover letters. After taking a minute or two to reflect, Greg suddenly realized that four of the seven director level candidates who had been hired had not even submitted the required cover letter!

The VP of HR asked what had caused those four candidates to stand out, to get noticed, and to get interviewed. Again Greg reflected and had an "aha" moment. One of the four candidates was already known to Greg. Another of the candidates had come highly recommended. And the remaining two candidates had been extremely assertive about networking their way into Greg's field of vision. When Greg finished explaining all this, the wise VP of HR leaned back, smiled, and nodded.

I learned a valuable lesson that day, although it was years before my time as an executive recruiter or career coach. And, it was years before I was reading survey data suggesting that cover letters were seldom effective… if they were even read. I learned that:

Cover letters play defense. Resumes play offense.

The "Email Cover Letter" Approach

You need to become a master of the 3- to 4-line email.

Good cover letters take a lot of time to write. And, many of them take a lot of time to read. So, instead of a cover letter, you need to use just a few lines and make sure it is delivered in a form that allows for a quick read: email.

This email should be set up just as a cover letter would be. It has an opening, a body, and a closing. The opening paragraph mentions the specific position opening. The body mentions your two or three core strengths aligned with their hiring motives. The closing paragraph allows you to follow-up.

The "re:" or subject line must grab the reader's attention. It could be as simple as "application for design engineer position." It could be as assertive as "talented design engineer candidate" or "accomplished design engineer meets your requirements." <u>Just don't leave it blank.</u>

Here is what your "email cover letter" might look like:

To: Regina Recruiter
From: Cassius Candidate
RE: *Warehouse Foreman opening – follow-up to phone call*

Regina,

As discussed in our phone call the other day, please find attached a resume to support my interest in the warehouse foreman position.

My strengths are aligned with your requirements and include: five years warehouse experience in lead positions, training in the TRB inventory control system your company uses, and a results-focused attitude.

I will contact you in the next few days to make sure you have received this email and to answer any questions.

Sincerely,

Cassius

If a Cover Letter is Required...

If you are required to submit a cover letter, there are three styles I would recommend you consider using:

- T-style
- Bullet style
- News article style

Each of these styles is highly readable and connects with the company's core hiring motives. The T-style and bullet style were developed more than 50 years ago, are quite concise, and are still two of the most effective styles on the market today. I developed the news article style some years ago for those candidates who want the effectiveness of the first two but also wish to provide a bit more detail about their qualifications.

The three styles have a lot of the basics in common. Each style has a header at the top—including your name and contact information—which looks exactly like the header on your resume and any other attached documents. Each style should be written as a formal letter, using writing conventions that are respectful and demonstrate the ability to effectively communicate in writing. Each style has an opening, a closing, and a body that shows how your core strengths fit with their core hiring motives. The body is always indented from each margin slightly to draw in the reader's attention. And, like the email cover letter, the closing always gives you the opportunity to follow up.

T-Style Cover Letter

The T-style cover letter presents the reader with two short columns in the body of the letter. An oldie-but-goodie, the T-style cover letter is still ranked by many career-coaching gurus as most effective in today's employment market.

The first column simply lists what the company is looking for in a candidate—their 3 to 4 most important requirements.

As previously discussed in the chapter detailing how to customize your resume, these may be primarily determined from your analysis of the job ad and from your networking conversations.

The second column contains several of your qualifications, each of which is aligned with one of the company's top requirements listed in the first column. Each qualification briefly demonstrates how you meet or exceed the corresponding hiring requirement.

The items in each column are often bulleted to promote even quicker intake of the information.

The T-style is succinct and direct.

Bullet Style Cover Letter

The bullet style cover letter is simply the T-style without the first column.

It is assumed that the reader is already aware of their top hiring requirements so they need not be listed.

Therefore, the bullet style simply has one column in the body of the letter that presents a maximum of 3 to 4 qualifications that meet the company's top requirements for the position.

Note: with both the T-style and the bullet style cover letters, it is important to resist the temptation to add more detailed content. They are meant to be Spartan. Their effectiveness emanates from their concise, to-the-point, and targeted advocacy of you as the candidate who meets all of the company's top hiring requirements.

"News Article" Cover Letter

Years ago, many of my clients were struggling with the look of both the T-style and the bullet style cover letters, particularly as related to their rather Spartan nature.

A number of these clients also spoke with experienced hiring managers who appreciated the directness of such cover letters but wanted a bit more content that would demonstrate each of the candidates' qualifications. But, those same hiring managers still liked the quick read afforded by <u>zeroing in on what they wanted—their top hiring requirements</u>. So, I developed the "news article" cover letter.

News articles—whether digital or in print—often have bold titles to begin each group of paragraphs. This technique allows a reader to quickly scan down through the entire article and pick out the key points.

It is this same technique that I utilize in the "news article" cover letter.

The body of this cover letter contains a few short paragraphs, each presenting your qualifications as aligned with one of the company's 2 to 3 top hiring requirements. Each of these paragraphs begins with a bold title, catching the reader's attention during a quick scan. Then, the paragraphs provide more detail to "back up" your assertion that you meet their most important requirements.

Alternatively, you could have the titles reflect your qualifications (you can take your titles from what would have been either column one or two in the T-style cover letter). If you use the exact wording of the top hiring requirements as taken directly from the job ad, you might put those titles in quotes as well as bold. The "news article" cover letter allows you the hard hitting, targeted power of a T-style or bullet style cover letter, while giving you flexibility to provide just a bit more detail about your qualifications. Following are a few sample cover letters.

Sample *T - Style* Cover Letter

SALLY S. SAMPLE
13 WRENS WAY, MOUNTAINHIGH, CO 00000
SSample554@gmail.com | 000.000.0000 | linkedin.com/in/sss554

October 15, 2014

Mr. Ed Example, Global Logistics Manager
First Corporation
444 First Avenue
Anytown, AL 88888

Dear Mr. Example:

Please accept the attached resume for the position opening of International Logistics Specialist posted on your company's website. The position's requirements align well with my qualifications:

Your Requirements	My Qualifications
5+ years international logistics	4 years logistics coordination between 9 locations in Asia, Europe, and the Americas; 3 years inventory distribution in Hong Kong
Excellent attention to detail and follow through	98.7% on-time delivery in 26 months with no lost shipments
Bachelor's Degree	BS in International Business

I would appreciate the opportunity to learn more about your organization and explore the possibility of a fit between the position requirements and my core competencies. I will follow up during the next few days to answer any questions you may have and determine the next steps in the process.

Sincerely,

Sally Sample

Sample *Bullet Style* Cover Letter

SALLY S. SAMPLE
13 WRENS WAY, MOUNTAINHIGH, CO 00000
SSample554@gmail.com | 000.000.0000 | linkedin.com/in/sss554

October 15, 2014

Mr. Ed Example, Global Logistics Manager
First Corporation
444 First Avenue
Anytown, AL 88888

Dear Mr. Example:

Please accept the attached resume for the position opening of International Logistics Specialist posted on your company's website. The position's requirements align well with my core qualifications:

- 4 years logistics coordination between 9 locations in Asia, Europe, and the Americas; 3 years inventory distribution in Hong Kong

- 98.7% on-time delivery in 26 months with no lost shipments

- BS in International Business

I would appreciate the opportunity to learn more about your organization and explore the possibility of a fit between the position requirements and my core competencies. I will follow up during the next few days to answer any questions you may have and determine the next steps in the process.

Sincerely,

Sally Sample

Sample "News Article" Cover Letter

SALLY S. SAMPLE
13 WRENS WAY, MOUNTAINHIGH, CO 00000
SSample554@gmail.com | 000.000.0000 | linkedin.com/in/sss554

November 22, 2014

Horatio Hiring, VP of Wholesale Marketing
KLJ, Ltd.
Undersea Road
Anytown, IN 00000

Dear Mr. Hiring:

Please accept this letter and attached resume toward my interest in the Director of Wholesale opening. After speaking with Norman Networker, your southwest area dealer and my former colleague, I believe my strengths align with your requirements:

> **"Develop and Implement Strategic Plans"**
> Directed development and implementation of comprehensive strategic and rescue plans. Senior level experience delivering brand-aligned results. For last four years, served as Sales and Marketing Manager for NGY, a Consumer-products retailer and wholesaler. Reported directly to owner.

> **"Establish Strong Relationships"**
> Developed key relationships with internal and external partners to open up new channels. For turn-around, teamed with customers and vendors in mutually beneficial relationships. Listened to customer perspectives.

> **"Demonstrate Leadership Qualities"**
> Led by example, with constant people focus and commitment to highest level of integrity. Maximized results by understanding employee motivators. Fostered culture promoting dignity and respect for all.

I would appreciate the opportunity to learn more about your organization and explore the possibility of a fit between the position requirements and my core competencies. I will follow up during the next few days to answer any questions you may have and determine the next steps in the process.

Sincerely,

Sally S. Sample

It is completely up to you which style of cover letter you prefer to use or if you wish to use an alternative style. Just be wary of writing volumes of text in a standard letter format. It will not be read.

Lastly, I would inform you about something I refer to as a "cover memo" that could give you another option for introducing your resume, as long as the job advertisement does not specifically request a cover letter.

Previously, I introduced the concept of an "email cover letter" to utilize in those instances when a cover letter is not requested.

However, if you have cause to drop off a printed copy of your resume, you could choose to print out the "email cover letter," neatly trimming it down to size (say, to 4" x 6" or so) and then attaching it to your resume with a paper clip (remember, never staple resume pages or other application documents together). In this way, you will have created a "cover memo" to accompany the resume.

Part 4: Market

Chapter 20

Using Your Resume

"There are risks and costs to action. But they are far less than the long range risks of comfortable inaction."

— John F. Kennedy

Action always beats inaction.

Now that you have created an effective resume it is time to take it out on the road, time to use it. Of course, the danger is that it is invariably more comfortable to sit behind that computer screen and just wait for your inbox to fill up with offers of interviews. But it won't happen unless you take your resume out on the road. Why?

News Flash: The resume does not magically market itself to recruiters, networking contacts, and hiring managers. The resume does not take action by itself. <u>*You*</u> *have to take action*.

And you're going to do just fine, too. Because all that hard work you put into resume development has prepared you for job search launch or re-launch. "Aha" moment: *the process was as important as the product.*

So…suit up, get on LinkedIn, and buy an unlimited minute plan.

Printed Copies

Of course, with precious few exceptions, gone are the days of mailing your resume to a company. Long gone. But you will need to print some copies. And the details of printing copies still matters.

Whether you are taking a few copies to an interview in your leather portfolio (always take one copy more than the number of people you will be meeting and never staple page one and two together) or you are dropping off a printed copy to a smaller organization in a guerilla marketing campaign, here are the specs you will want to follow:

- Paper Weight: 28–32lb.
- Paper Color: White, Eggshell, or Light Gray.
- Watermarks: not needed; if on the paper, always right side up.
- Cotton Fiber Content: 25% is standard.
- Feel: smooth or rough/porous.
- Envelopes (as uncommon as folded resumes): matching.
- Cover Letter Paper: same as resume paper.
- Brand: less important; I often use Southworth.
- Printer: laser preferred or an extremely high quality ink jet.
- Print: black and white, printing on one side only.
- For Faxing and Scanning: use inexpensive, smooth, 20lb. white copy paper (less porous paper translates to a sharper image).

Just make sure the paper doesn't isn't a pastel color and doesn't have Monet's waterlillies in the background. I love Monet. But that would be so 90s. And unprofessional. And ineffective.

The bottom line? *Your resume needs to look as impressive as it reads.* Presentation matters. It is part of the whole first impressions thing.

24/7 Resume Availability

This is so often overlooked: your resume needs to be 100% available for distribution at any moment. Why? Here's just one story…

Dickie made a holiday trip to Aunt Mable's. As Dickie was unpacking, Aunt Mable said she had to run a homemade pie over to the neighbor, who just happened to be a manager at one of Dickie's target companies.

Dickie had a resume in the car…Aunt Mable put the resume on top of the pie…Dickie had an interview on Monday…and a job on Tuesday.

OK, so you don't want to be carrying your resume with you at soccer games, grocery shopping, and when you are out on-the-town? That's what cell phones are for.

Don't have a cell phone? That's what CDs and USBs are for.

Don't have or want any of the above? That's what attaching your full resume to your LinkedIn profile is for.

Finally…remember Dickie?

A couple years later, the big boss asked him to "just go through the motions" and submit a resume so he might be promoted to manager. Of course, Dickie's computer had long since crashed, but Dickie had emailed a copy to himself and kept it in an inbox folder. Easy update.

Will you please at least email a copy to yourself? Right now? Please?

You just never know when opportunity will knock.

Here is the low-down on five ideas to make your resume 24/7 available:

E-mail Storage
Email a copy of your finished resume to your own inbox. It will be available anywhere, anytime. Even from a library terminal. In case you wish to customize it or send it out. If you're visiting Uncle Bob and he wants to introduce you to a networking contact next door, you can print a copy from his home computer. And, in a pinch, you can even forward it from the email on your smart phone.

LinkedIn
Park your resume on your LinkedIn profile as an attachment. While you might choose to cut and paste portions of your resume to create your LinkedIn profile, did you know that you can also attach a full version of your resume to the summary section?

And, of course, <u>your LinkedIn URL should be printed on your business card and on your signature line for every e-mail</u> so that any recruiter or networking contact can have immediate access to it.

Google Sites
Set up a free web page and attach your resume to it. This allows you a great deal of creative latitude with fewer constraints. You could also choose to share the web page's URL.

Hard Copy To Go
Why not print off a couple copies on fine resume paper, put them in a folder, and place them in the trunk of your car?

It may seem a bit silly…until the first time you need a printed copy on extremely short notice and without access to a printer.

CD/DVD/USB

It is a smart move to make an electronic copy of all your documents, including versions of your resume, and place them on some media other than your hard drive or the web. You could even save a copy to your smart phone's memory chip.

Posting your Resume Online

It's totally up to you.

Years ago, various changes to the online landscape would cause me to either recommend in favor of or recommend against posting your resume online. But for a couple years now, I've felt that this is best left up to the discretion of the individual candidate, largely depending upon their job search strategy.

The advantages, of course, are centered on the concepts of being open and casting a wide net in terms of marketing yourself. Attaching the resume to your LinkedIn profile, creating your own website to place it on, placing it on job boards such as www.monster.com or www.theladders.com, and having it readily available on other social media sites means that you increase your chances of getting noticed. While it shouldn't be relied upon as your only tactic, I have seen its effectiveness. Especially with individual candidates who are just starting out in their careers or requiring, for some specific reason, a high level of visibility in the employment marketplace.

If you do choose to post your full resume online, use your noggin and think critically about where it should appear.

As an example, I've seen some candidates effectively target job boards, related to a particular profession or industry group to which they might belong. This almost has the effect of taking out a tasteful advertisement in an upscale magazine that is read by only a niche group of people.

Just beware of the potential disadvantages, as well.

When you post your resume online, especially to the more popular job boards, you run the risk of losing control of its distribution. Why would you care about such control? Well, for one consideration, your resume should absolutely be customized to target each, unique position opening. Even though you will be using one, foundational resume in most of your networking, posting your resume online means that a number of potential hiring managers may have a first impression of you that is generally favorable but not particularly suited to meet their own hiring needs. First impressions do matter. It's awfully hard to change them. And the more you can customize your marketing material to pique the interest of hiring managers, the more you will increase your chances at *getting noticed* and, later, at *closing the deal* to generate an offer.

A final word on this topic.

I am convinced that anything you post or send digitally will exist in perpetuity somewhere on the web. Forever. Even if you delete it later on.

Don't ask me how or why. That's a question for the tech guys. But some of my clients have been vexed by having older versions of their resume continuing to pop up during their present job search. If such a resume is not particularly well written, has any errors in it, or is targeted to a different audience…you will run the risk of always trying to redefine your brand instead of simply defining it. Be careful what you wish for.

To Mail or Not To Mail?

Should you send your materials in electronic format via e-mail or in hard copy via postal mail?

Or should you hand deliver your materials?

This is a matter of some debate among very knowledgeable career coaches, although many agree that email is the standard today and will limit your risk of standing out for the wrong reasons.

I tend to strongly favor e-mail, but there is a case to be made for alternative methods of delivery.

If you can be reasonably sure that you will be perceived as up-to-date with technology and communication practices, mailing or hand delivering your cover letter and application materials may be a way to increase your chances of getting noticed. We will take a look at some additional, alternative delivery methods a bit later on.

Also, while there is always a risk of coming across as too eager or desperate, I have witnessed some of my clients effectively sending materials by both methods at the same time. This allows quick and easy receipt by e-mail and also delivers a hard copy on fine stationary to emphasize the candidate's polish and professionalism. Be aware, however, that this dual method runs a slight risk of confusing the hiring company, which is most likely used to seeing 99% of all application materials received via e-mail.

And, if you do choose to either mail or hand deliver a hard copy, please remember that you should never to staple pages of a resume or cover materials together nor should you fold them either. A simple paper clip will suffice if you absolutely need to keep materials together.

As you can imagine, the method of delivery matters less than if you have prepared the runway. *The key to getting your resume, cover letter, and materials noticed is networking* – preferably with the hiring manager. You need to have someone at the company primed and on the lookout for your materials. After all, you are investing a significant amount of time and energy in creating customized and effective marketing materials.

Can't you invest just a bit more in making sure they are actually read?

Alternative resume delivery methods

Get your resume to the hiring manager. Any way you can.

That having been said, it's always preferable to operate within business norms whenever possible. You don't want to stand out in the wrong way. But sometimes you're dealing with high castle walls, a moat, and a drawbridge that's closed.

So get creative.

Key to many of the more creative approaches is knowing the hiring manager's name, networking within the company, and having a nothing-else-to-lose mentality. Below are a few thoughts, which have actually been successfully executed. Maybe these ideas will get your creative juices flowing:

Third shift cleaning crew: I referred to this before but I'll state it again to drive the point home. It has just so often worked for my clients. And, it can have the effect of helping out the career of the cleaner as well (assuming you're a great candidate, of course). How does it work?

The cleaner slips your resume under the door of the SVP Operations with a sticky note attached just saying something like: "Know you are looking to fill a purchasing specialist position and happen to have come across this resume." Presto! You are on the hiring manager's radar screen. And, presto! The third shift cleaner is appreciated for going "above and beyond" and for taking an interest in the success of the entire organization.

Impressionable administrative assistant: Convincing the gatekeeper to put your resume on the CFOs desk or chair is a tall order. After all, part of their job is to serve as a gatekeeper. But if you can finesse this one, you're likely to get a response.

FedEx or UPS: Take your pick. The risk, of course, is that no one at the company agrees to sign for a package when they are unsure of the contents or sender. You might print on the outside that it contains a resume for a particular position and that it is for a specific person.

Hand carried: Be very careful here. You risk being branded as someone who doesn't follow the rules. At a minimum, you may be quickly referred to HR. However, with companies of less than 100 or even 50 employees, your bold and direct approach just might do the trick. Be ready for an interview on the spot. Also be ready to take your lickin'.

LinkedIn: If you have a colleague who is directly connected to the hiring manager via LinkedIn, they can send a message directly to the hiring manager suggesting he or she look at your profile, which will have an attached resume. I've also seen unapologetic networkers join LinkedIn or other groups to which the hiring manager belongs, and then let the group as a whole know you're on the market. Again, be very careful here but, if you've got to put bread in the table, don't ever apologize.

Fax or Morse Code: So I've never heard of anyone using Morse Code. But you get the idea. IF the hiring manager's office still has a fax machine and you can get the number, you've still got to figure out how not to come across as either geriatric or desperate. Combine this approach with a call to the administrative assistant to increase your chances.

Professional or social networking event: Perhaps you have intel that the hiring manager goes to professional meetings or their niece's softball games. Again, be extremely careful here. If you risk the intrusion, it's probably not a good idea to whip the resume right out. Instead, try to finesse at brief (1 to 2 minutes maximum) dialog in which you introduce yourself, appear as if attending such an event/meeting is routine for you, and let the hiring manager know you'd appreciate being able to reach out for a conversation at a "more appropriate time." You might want to keep the gorilla mask handy just in case it gets ugly and you need to make a quick and anonymous exit, however.

Text a link: this is also dangerous territory for those of us well into our careers. But I've seen it used effectively in recent years by the Millennial generation in connecting with both recruiters and other Millennials who are hiring managers. Especially at companies with extremely fast paced, entrepreneurial, and technology-based communication orientations.

When not to use a resume

There are exceptions to every rule.

Including the rule of using your resume to *get noticed* and *close the deal*.

DO NOT use your resume in situations like these:

It's a done deal: Infrequently, job search "just happens" without a resume. Perhaps a former employer calls you up and asks if you want to start with them next Wednesday. Maybe your former boss is now working at a new company and calls you up to ask if you want to join her team. In the unlikely event that someone makes you an offer (without a formal interview happening), it's usually not advisable to pull out your resume and start marketing yourself. This would seem to be a no-brainer, but I've witnessed people trying to do just that. Since you've been made an offer, you're into the negotiation phase now. Button down the details and get to work!

The contrarian: Although not a common phenomenon, there are anti-resume people out there. Hopefully you've identified them in your target organization through extensive networking. Especially if they happen to be the hiring manager or in a position of influence, you need to be smart enough not to fight city hall. You can still utilize all the information on your customized resume in discussions about your potential value to the company. Just be careful about whipping out that resume too quickly. You may want to wait until they ask for it.

The owner is in the store: If the business has less than 20 employees and you will be networking directly with the owner, it may be advisable to hold back the resume at first. You want to come across as professional but certainly down-to-earth and unpretentious. In addition, many very small businesses do not tend to have specific position openings, per se. They tend to hire extremely versatile individuals on an as-needed-basis and, often, as they come across talent. Using a resume too early in the process with these individuals may also run the risk of pigeonholing you in their eyes; better to have a conversation first and find out just how you might be able to impact their bottom line.

The gravel pit interview: What do you think happened when my CFO client, who was actually quite adept at running large machinery from previous experience in the family business (and was in need of an additional part-time job for cash), showed up for the 6:00 am interview and offered his resume to the owner of the drilling and blasting company? Exactly. Resumes are not trusted in such a culture. Especially if the interview is a hands-on affair, realize that a resume could make the wrong kind of statement.

Allow a pair of steel toed work boots to substitute in this case.

You are supposed-to-know-everyone already: There are certain networking events and interviews at which you are expected to know every one already. In these instances, offering a resume or a business card may be greeted by a nervous smile and the knowledge that you won't be invited back. How do you know which events these are? Dead giveaways include: cufflinks as standard attire or the guest list includes more than three U.S. senators. But they could also be the pig races at the county fair or Shelley's annual community backyard barbecue. Yes, that's right. My clients have successfully networked or have been hired at all of these.

And their resumes never saw the light of day.

Conformity = Obscurity

The ad says "No phone calls please."

Translation: "Don't call us. We probably won't call you."

Look, it's nothing personal. I have lots of HR friends and they are swamped! Every year, they are required to do more and more with less and less. The days of personalized service concerning your candidacy are long gone. That having been said, from your perspective, the human resources department is not going to pay the rent for you.

So, if you choose to play the "no phone calls please" game, there's only one thing that's going to happen for sure. Eventually, you'll run out of toner ink to print resumes on and your credit card will be maxed out.

As we have already established… **you must get your resume to the hiring manager.** There is no substitute.

Or, you can get a gold star for submitting 100 online applications without any networking. And then get a failing grade for the five phone calls of lukewarm interest you'll receive. The deck is stacked against you. So you gotta get a new deck. And play your own game.

You Were Taught to Follow the Rules

Some of us have been so wired to follow the rules that we will go to any lengths not to network, not to reach around the HR office in a target company, not to bother people who don't already know us. This is especially true for certain segments of the population, including the honorable men and women serving in our armed forces, for whom I have the greatest respect and the privilege of helping with their military-to-civilian transitions. Veterans have been taught to strictly follow the rules…even when the rules keep slapping them in the face.

Take for example, the case of Alice, a veteran who had already made a successful transition out of the military and to a private company by the early 2000s, when the tech sector fell off a cliff.

Alice was a retired Commander in the U.S. Navy and an Annapolis graduate. She was already accomplished in the private sector as a manufacturing and applications engineer. She was widely respected by peers and considered by senior management to be among their star performers at an 850+ employee company, which ended up moving all operations off shore and closing the facility. Bye, bye job.

During her outplacement process, Alice was strongly encouraged to network with anyone and everyone.

But it was terrifying for her.

Alice belonged to a networking group I set up, which was comprised of eight engineers, each of whom was trying to secure a position with a particular target company. Each of the group members held Alice in the absolute highest professional regard and expected her to get hired first at that company.

All eight members of this networking group applied for multiple jobs at the target company, submitting their first-class resumes through the ATS/applicant tracking system. Seven of the eight networked with everyone they could inside and outside the company. And each of these seven was eventually noticed and hired within about 60 days. But not Alice.

Alice also applied for multiple jobs at that company but strictly followed the "no phone calls please" rule, posted on each job advertisement and on the company web site.

After the seventh group member was hired by the company, Alice finally told me she was willing to give networking a chance.

It took just two weeks and three networking contacts before Alice had an interview with the company. Two weeks after that she was hired.

And, can you guess what the hiring manager said to her on her first day as a new employee? Something like: "We've hired a lot of good engineers from your former company, but you are the most outstanding candidate I have come across. I wish you had applied for a position earlier…I would have hired you first!"

"I would have hired you first."

Every single day, you have the choice of whether or not to make the phone calls and send the emails. You get to choose whether or not you are going to follow the rules or network your way out of this mess.

Hey, I don't like networking any more than you do. But I know what's going to get that resume noticed. Be kind to yourself and your career…

Break the rules and pick up the phone.

Business Cards

You won't be keeping a resume folded up in your pocket.

You *should* be keeping business cards with you, however.

You may never need them.

Or, in your entire job search, there may be only a few critical moments when having a business card will be an absolute must.

You had better be ready.

Consider the case of Susan…

Susan was a talented machinist who was in the middle of a job search.

She made a quick run to the hardware store and happened to bump into a former colleague who was a tool and die maker. Although they hadn't seen each other in years, the conversation was easy and they were each reminded how much professional respect they had for each other.

Susan's former colleague asked her to send him her resume but he didn't have any business cards of his own to share with her.

No problem.

Susan, who always kept a couple of her own business cards in her purse, took two out. She gave one to her former colleague to keep and turned the other one over, handing him a pen and asking him to put his e-mail and phone number on the backside so she could email her resume to him.

If Susan hadn't had a couple business cards at the ready, she would have either lost the opportunity or it would have been much more awkward—imagine having to find two pieces of scrap paper to write on at that moment.

The rest of the story?

Susan didn't even have a chance to e-mail her former colleague the resume that evening before she received an e-mail from his boss.

The boss had gone to the LinkedIn address that Susan had listed on her business card, he had reviewed her online professional profile and the resume, which was attached to it, and he was reaching out to her in case she was interested in meeting the next day for an interview!

Just think. That could be you.

If you are ready with a couple of business cards.

So, what should your business card look like?

That's really up to you.

Unlike with resumes, I have no problem if you choose to add a splash of color or be a bit creative in your design. Just make sure it is professional looking. Most places that print business cards have plenty of designs from which you can choose.

What information should be on your business card?

Well, in its most basic form, your business card should include all the contact information that you put on the header of your resume: name address, phone, e-mail, and LinkedIn URL.

It's really up to you whether you choose to add any more or not.

But I would definitely recommend including just a couple words to help remind others of your professional value and/or your area of expertise or skills. It can be quite frustrating to look at a couple business cards you have collected and try to remember details about the people who gave them to you. Make it easy for your new networking contact.

If you do choose to include wording about your professional experience and expertise, try to use functional terminology instead of listing position titles. That will allow you some elbow room to define it further; you will be able to customize the definition on the fly, so it will resonate with particular individuals.

Also, note that you may want to leave some space on the back of the card so that you can write notes or have someone else do so. The way Becky did. So make sure the finish on the back is not glossy or your writing will be limited to a felt tipped marker!

Here a couple sample business cards showing the most critical info:

Sally S. Sample, CPA

Executive and Financial Leadership

13 Wrens Way, Mountainhigh, CO 00000
SSample554@gmail.com | 000.000.0000
www.ssswebsite.com | linkedin.com/in/sss554

SYDNEY S. SAMPLE

linkedin.com/in/sss887

26 Dovetail Court   000.000.0000
Jarville, KY 00000   SSS4@gmail.com

Certified Medical Assistant
Registered Phlebotomy Technician

Chapter 21

LinkedIn & Recruiters

"Start spreading the news..."
                         - Frank Sinatra

This chapter is for everyone…especially introverts!

While you are still going to have to prioritize personal networking via one-on-one meetings and phone conversations, *you must let others know that you are searching.* After all, how will they be able to help you if they are not even aware of your situation? Time to get the word out.

On day one of a job search it's easy to get worked up and anxious about how few people you may know. The task of networking may seem so daunting that you want to put it off until the twelfth of never.

Do not underestimate the power of letting the universe know of your needs.

> **Don't Hide. Get Found!**
>
> Choose to make your newly minted resume easily available to all who might want to find you. Think of yourself as a premier product and, every day, ask yourself how you will spread the word about the real value you offer. You have to advertise yourself or no one will know you are in the market for a new gig. Let the universe know you are ready to get to work!

As an example, your LinkedIn profile and activity helps recruiters and hiring managers find you. It's like taking out a free newspaper ad to let the world know you are job searching.

Certainly, this doesn't mean you're off the hook in terms of networking. It does mean, however, that you get to include a generous portion of what I call "passive marketing" in your activities.

What if you start networking and applying for positions without investing any time in "passive marketing?" Well, how successful do you think a salesperson would be if there was no multi-media advertising campaign to promote their product? What if there was no web site to refer marketing prospects to when those prospects had questions? What if the salesperson offered a product with incredible value but no one had ever heard of it?

If a tree falls in the forest, does it make a sound?

The *discussion* around this question is not really relevant. The *action* around it is critical!

Is your resume done? OK.

Then, get your name out there. Today!

Get the Word Out

While we will explore a couple of these ideas in more detail, here is a list of a few ways you might start letting the universe know you are looking for a new position:

- Create a LinkedIn profile and attach your resume to it.
- Explore and use LinkedIn's many features, including joining groups and identifying companies in which you are interested.
- Send your resume to your entire address book.
- Ask friends and family to send your resume out to their contacts.
- Contact your college's alumni AND career offices to let them know you are looking.
- Pick a topic of interest (learning new skills and best practices within the area of your professional expertise?) and start writing short, daily blog posts in your LinkedIn groups or…create your own blog.
- Send your resume to staffing and recruiting firms.
- Send your resume to your target companies, even if there are no openings.

What is the alternative to taking action? Well, let's take a look at the cases of a couple folks who struggled because of inaction (*and how they finally broke out of their respective ruts*)…

Case 1: The Cowboy

Archie was an accomplished executive, highly regarded by all his peers. He was confident, competent, and polished. But he had also been brought up very conservatively; he had a bit of the quiet, macho, don't-rely-on-anyone-for-help, fiercely independent streak stirred into his personality.

Archie may have also been genuinely embarrassed that he needed a job and that his company had closed after he had been with them for over 20 years (of course, they also took his pension plan with them when they went bankrupt). The combination of all the above was deadly when it came to getting the word out about his availability.

After six months, Archie wouldn't even leave the house and his finances were a wreck. Plywood was about to go up over the windows.

Solution: Once Archie finally created a LinkedIn account and wrote in his profile that he was "seeking employment," he had 25 invitations to connect in his inbox during the first week. And, after he joined nine LinkedIn groups, recruiters began to call. Archie had an interview within a month and was hired weeks later. By the way, on day one, Archie's new boss told Archie that he had been looking for someone like Archie...for six months!

Case 2: Anxiety Through the Roof

Trixie was humankind's gift to customer service on the phone.

Every one of Trixie's former bosses had given her glowing reviews and several said they had to hire 2 to 3 people just to replace Trixie when she had left their company for a promotion or more compensation.

Trixie's career was going great until she came down with a bad case of Lyme disease, which had gone undiagnosed for over a year. Trixie had to leave her job and it took her 24 months out of work to recover to an energy level at which she could consider working again.

By that time, her confidence was shattered and she was uber-nervous that no company would want her. In addition, Trixie didn't have enough energy to hold down a full time job. She started taking in an over-abundance of stray cats (30+) and may have been contemplating starring in the remake of CatLady III. Trixie was in a bunker mentality.

Solution: Although she was still too uncomfortable to actually speak to anyone, Trixie agreed to send her resume out to address book contacts in a mass emailing. She was so nervous that no one would respond that she couldn't even bring herself to check her inbox until five days later. Of course, there they were emails from two former bosses pleading with Trixie to come back to work for them. She negotiated 30 hours a week, flextime, and an increase in her hourly rate so that she was making as much money as working 40 hours previously. And, once Trixie got back to work her recovery really started to speed up.

Which case study can you relate to? Both? Neither?

Would your case study be called "Just Plain Shy," "It Used to be Easy to Get a Job," or "Never Touched a Computer and Never Will?"

If someone were to write a case study about you, how would it read?

This is a key question. Because if you can define your own, unique case study—if you can name your barrier or fear—then you have already started to take away the power of that barrier…and you can start to formulate an answer to a more important question:

What is <u>your</u> unique *solution*?

Hey, someone out there wants to hire you. You just need to get found!

In addition to the priority for more active networking, "passive" strategies are ways you can get the word out to the market that you are available. Think of a "passive" strategy as one that requires some up-front work but then just keeps paying dividends for weeks and months on end. It's like taking out an advertisement that says: "Notice me!"

Placing your professional profile on LinkedIn and letting staffing firms/recruiters know you are looking are two such strategies.

Let's take a look at each.

The Value of LinkedIn

LinkedIn is like a professional Facebook. Except that it's not.

You have complete control of your profile page.

Even if someone writes you a recommendation, it will not be visible on your profile unless you give the OK.

You have the power to search for former colleagues and other networking contacts by fields such as: education, company, and position title.

You have the option of joining professional and industry groups for networking, to learn best practices, and to intellectually engage your professional self during a career transition process that can sometimes take months, and which tries to strip away your sense of professional self-worth.

You are allowing yourself to be "found" easily by company recruiters and hiring managers.

I could go on.

Simply put, LinkedIn has become a necessity in any job search. Whether you like it or not.

Today, if you are not on LinkedIn, with a professional profile filled out and picture attached, many companies will pass you by as a candidate. Their reasoning (whether accurate or not): you are not current with digital/online norms and you might have something to hide.

On the next two pages are my top 10 tips for getting started with your free LinkedIn account:

Top 10 LinkedIn Startup Tips

Here's my top 10 list for getting started with LinkedIn:

1. **Photo:** You need a professional looking head shot with a smile. True, very few people like how they look. With all due respect, however, this is not about how you look to yourself. This is about others' perceptions of you; it is about first impressions and about transparency.

2. **Title:** Consider using a functional instead of position title; use "Electrical and Project Engineering" instead of "Project Engineer." Also, leave out your company name.

3. **Writing the Experience and Other Sections:** You need a minimum of a short description for each section. It isn't necessarily a bad thing to "cut and paste" some truncated portions from your resume — it shows consistency. Remember, though, that LinkedIn has limited formatting options so it is less about bold/underline/italics; if you want to have a few words stand out, consider using all CAPS, fewer words, or a space between those words.

4. **Profile:** While it could simply be the same as your profile/summary section on the resume, ask yourself what your audience wants to know about you, in a nutshell. What are your top 2 to 3 brand differentiators? And make sure you put your email and/or phone in the profile itself. Want to put in a phone but don't want to give out your number? Set up a free Google Voice account and forward texts of the voice mails to your phone.

5. **Most Recent Position/Company:** If you are unemployed or between positions, you have two options: 1. If it is the truth and substantial enough, you could note that you are currently doing some consulting or project/board work for a non-profit. 2. More effective may be to simply let people know that you are looking! Just put something like "Seeking Electrical or Project Engineering Position" for the position title and "Greater Chicago Area Company Preferred" for the company.

6. **Getting a Thumbs Up:** Two thoughts:

   a. Ask for recommendations—they only need to be a couple sentences long and you have control over whether they are posted or not.

   b. List your top competencies/skills under the "Skills and Expertise" section.

   Two tips on the latter. First, when you start typing a skill, LinkedIn will prompt you with its own, related options—it is usually best to choose one of their options. Second, when people "recommend" you for a particular skill, they typically click on the one at the top of the list, so make sure your most important skills are always listed first.

7. **Join Groups:** Join lots of groups (40+ is not too many) so that recruiters can find you, you can keep up on best practices, and you can instantly be connected/see inside group members' profiles.

   However, only make a few groups visible on your profile (more than 10 is too many) so that people won't think you are just joining lots of groups! (which, of course, you are…)

8. **Public Profile Link:** Customize this to something very short and place it on your resume as well as in the signature line of your email address. Tie all your marketing efforts together.

9. **Follow Companies:** Recruiters pay attention to you more if you are following their company. However, if you are already employed, be careful here!

10. **Visibility:** While you can be relatively anonymous, why would you want to be? Wouldn't it be a plus to have others notice that you viewed their profile? After all, this isn't like "stalking" someone on Facebook.

    This is about professional networking on LinkedIn.

    Also, I still don't believe you need to pay a fee for higher visibility—work that free account for all it may be worth first!

Search Firms/Recruiters and Staffing Firms

Given that most job seekers will generate no more than 15% of their interviews through search and staffing firms and given that these firms are the ones doing the seeking (they are paid by client companies to find candidates who are uniquely qualified to fill specific positions), it is advisable to limit your time investment in contacting these firms. That having been said, they may comprise one component of your search efforts and you should have at least some idea of how the process works.

After all, staffing firms and recruiters at search firms can be your best friends…or your worst nightmares.

I used to work for a search firm as a retained executive recruiter. So I should know.

Fortunately, the firm I worked for had an excellent reputation and I was trained by an accomplished retained headhunter whose previous work had been finding executives for such firms as PNC and Mellon Bank.

Companies would enter into an exclusive arrangement with our firm, paying us one third or more of the expected starting salary as a nonrefundable fee upfront to find them top-shelf talent—key contributors, senior managers, and executives.

It was challenging but rewarding work and I was able to get "inside" dozens of companies, walking the floor and developing an intimate understanding of what goes on and who does what.

I had an unobstructed view of the whole landscape.

And, during that time in my career, I became keenly aware that *not all recruiters are created equal*. Reputation is the key.

Ask your friends and colleagues whom they've used.

Conduct a web search and read blog posts to help determine if a firm is thumbs up or thumbs down.

And please realize that, if the company is a large regional or national firm, there can be quality differences depending upon who is managing a local office. Bottom line? Do your homework.

For while recruiters may account for no more than 10 to 15% of all your job search efforts, it is hard to beat the advantage of having somebody open the door for you, prep you for the interview, give you an idea about whom you may be meeting, and explain the company's hiring motives.

> ### NEVER Pay a Fee
> Recruiters are <u>always</u> paid by their client company. Whether you are doing business with a staffing firm, a contingency recruiter/search firm, or a retained recruiter/search firm, you should never be asked to pay a fee. Not even a small one. Never ever. The hiring company pays all fees and related costs to engage the staffing firm or search consultant.

So, how do staffing and search firms differ?

Well, *staffing* firms often recruit for temporary or part-time hourly or non-exempt positions at their client companies.

You will likely interview with the staffing firm and then with their client company, just as with a search firm. But, when you are hired and go to work at the client company, you will actually be an employee of the staffing firm and your paycheck comes directly from them.

Search firms, however, typically focus their recruitment on filling salaried/exempt positions at their client companies.

Nearly 95% of these firms are "contingency" or "commission" based and are paid only if they get the right candidate for the position. Often, their fee to the company will be about 20-25% of the starting salary for the position. So, while it isn't that relevant to you, FYI, their fee on a position with a $60,000/year salary might be $15,000.

Less than 5% of all search firms are "retained" by their client company in an exclusive relationship. These retained firms typically seek to fill key contributor and senior level positions with salaries of $125,000+ and are often paid 30%+ of the entire compensation package.

Their process is involved and their quality guarantee usually reflects it.

Here are a few, sometimes overlooked tips for working with staffing firms and recruiters at search firms:

Staffing Firms
- These firms sometimes also serve as recruiters for lower to mid-level full-time positions with their client companies. Staffing firms are exceptionally well-placed to know what's going on inside their client companies in terms of permanent hiring needs.

  Just because you're not interested in a temporary or part-time position through a staffing firm does not mean that you should overlook their potential value in your search process, especially if they have ties to your target companies.
- Staffing firms fill positions at all professional levels. For instance, there are staffing firms dedicated to filling temporary executive positions. They specialize in placing executives in 4- to 6-month positions in which the candidates will work for venture capitalists, lead turnarounds, or consolidate businesses.

- The "reverse engineering" approach might work for you. *If you are looking for an entry level position with one of your target companies and are having a hard time securing an interview, why not call up the HR department at that company and ask which firm or firms they use to fill their temporary staffing needs?* Then, turnaround and target that staffing firm, letting them know that you are highly interested in positions that relate to that target company. Of course, this tactic is no substitute to networking in your target companies, but might be an alternative if you're unable to break in any other way. And, it sure can be efficient.

- If you turn down the opportunity to interview for one position through a staffing firm, please note that the firm may not prioritize your name the next time a suitable opening presents itself. Don't take it personally. It's simply a matter of volume, efficiency, and availability to the staffing firm. But, you may want to consider each of their calls carefully or they may stop calling you!

Contingency Search Firms and Recruiters

- Remember that these headhunters, often the most highly skilled of sales persons, only get paid if their candidate is gets a job offer from their client company. Therefore, when you interview at one of their client companies, realize that you're probably going up against 4 to 6 other candidates, each of whom may be sent from a different contingency recruiter. Also, make sure you conduct your due diligence when it comes to whether the target company and position are a good fit for you; don't just rely on the recruiter for objective information as they are in the business of selling.

- Keep in mind that contingency- or commission-based recruiters will be selling you to the company and will be selling the company on you, although the best headhunters in this category are genuinely interested in establishing and furthering longer-term relationships with their client companies and candidates.

Again, seek out these firms *based on reputation and referral.*

- It is perfectly acceptable to be working with a couple of these recruiters at the same time, although each firm may prefer that you work exclusively with them. When communicating with each of these firms, however, make sure to give them your utmost attention, respect, and deference. They are in control. While you should always still keep your own counsel on whether a position is a good fit for you or not, never challenge or cross one of these recruiters. I've witnessed the less ethical among them retaliate in ways that could make your job search a living nightmare. Be nice.

- Answer all their questions honestly, leaving no skeletons in the closet. Let the recruiter determine if and when to share information with the hiring company. Remember, they don't get paid unless you are hired! On the other hand, it is also not in their interest to present candidates who may not fit, could be a risk to their reputation, or play games with their client companies.

- Listen to their words carefully; ask for and follow their advice. They can give you a definite interviewing edge.

Retained Search Firms and Recruiters

- While only representing less than 5% of all searches, these firms potentially operate at an even higher ethical and quality benchmark, maintaining longer-term, exclusive relationships with their client companies to search for key contributors, senior managers, and executives.

  As with staffing and contingency search firms, you should not waste their time if you don't fit their profile. And, as with contingency firms, don't expect that you'll have their attention for more than a minute or two unless they're working on a search for which you are well suited.

  Their job is not to get you a job.

  Their job is to provide their client companies with 2 to 3 outstanding candidates for often difficult-to-fill-positions.

> The exception here may be c-suite level executives, who often develop long-term, multi-faceted relationships with retained recruiters. After all, once a CEO is hired, that person often needs a trusted recruiter to help them hire their senior team.

- These search firms will often manage an entire hiring process for a particular position, including consideration of any internal candidates. Realize that they are on retainer and may be paid as much for their advice as for the candidates that they bring to their client companies.

  Their direct contact at the company is often a c-suite executive and, therefore, also be aware that, rightly or wrongly, HR is often less "in the loop" than with the contingency and staffing firms.

Finding Staffing and Recruiting Firms

The *Directory of Executive Recruiters* is published each year by Kennedy Publications and can be found at most larger public libraries. It offers information on thousands of contingency and retained firms, with extensive indices, sorted by industry, profession, and geography.

It might be a useful starting point for you.

Please note, however: just because a firm is national in scope and found in this book does not mean they are reputable and, conversely, just because a firm might be comprised of only one individual and is not found in this book doesn't mean they might not be extremely reputable.

This book is simply a resource for you.

You should prioritize conversations with your network to determine which search firms are reputable and should get your resume.

Of course, asking for search firm recommendations gives you another reason to reach out to your network an additional time!

Staffing firms are often most effectively found by conducting an online search and incorporating keywords related to geography. For instance, you might Google "staffing firms Dallas" to yield a list of those firms doing business in the greater Dallas area.

Pay particular attention to the types of positions for which each staffing firm recruits, as they tend to specialize and you don't want to waste your time or theirs.

And, remember, while you may not hear from the contingency and retained recruiters/search firms for months at a time, once a staffing firm has your resume, you may very well get a call within days.

Be ready. And be nice.

Chapter 22

Online Search

"Pay no attention to the man behind that curtain!"
- Oz, the Great and Powerful

This is primarily a resume book so this chapter will be short and sweet.

My key message?

Your computer could suck the very life out of you. *Don't let it.*

Instead, recognize it as a useful tool...with limitations...and dangers. Take concrete steps NOW so that it doesn't become the biggest distraction and time waster in your search.

You have to get this right.

If you are honest with yourself, you know exactly what I'm talking about. You might hop online to take a quick look at a job advertisement and…fast forward to three hours later…you come up for air feeling exhausted and realizing that all but 15 minutes of your time was wasted.

Don't let the screen control you.

Instead, learn to control it.

Also, ***pay attention to your online reputation***. Because, rightly or wrongly, companies can legally choose not to hire you based on your posts, your social media profiles, the web pages you have visited, and so many other online activities.

Think companies can't get this information? Think that you have a right to online privacy?

Think again.

Ask yourself: did someone with the same name as you just get nabbed for drinking and driving? Get divorced for the sixth time? Have too good of a time at a party where digital pictures or videos were taken? Play the online "Soldiers of CNC" game for a record 27 hours nonstop…during work time?

Once your digital reputation is damaged, it can be difficult to recover.

Once you have typed words into cyber-space, they are there for many years to come.

You can either have the professional you define your brand…or the personal you can define it…or others can define it for you.

Which option will you choose?

No Second Chances Online

Know and protect your digital image when beginning a job search. At an absolute minimum, you should:

- **Google your name** — search for web entries, images, videos.
- **Open a LinkedIn account** — create an online "resume" and positive, professional image.
- **Clean up or close other accounts** — clean up Facebook and delete anything remotely akin to Myspace.
- **Be mindful of your activity** — know what sites you visit and what you do once on them.

Consider that we now live in a world with less privacy and more transparency. And employers are taking advantage of this shift — as well as new technologies — to enforce stricter character guidelines.

Employers Will Check You Out Online

Most companies will plug your name into Google or other search engines. And, as I already mentioned, companies have every legal right not to hire you based on the digital information they find. Whether you agree with this or not, you need to know…

> **As of this writing, companies can legally compel you to give them your passwords to Facebook and any other sites if you want to be a candidate.**

In fact, more and more companies are requiring personal passwords in the hiring process for key contributors. <u>If you choose not to give them your passwords, they can choose not to hire you</u>. Case closed.

Tip: Check yourself out with Google Alert, Tweet Beeps, and Socialmention.com.

Don't Create Digital Dirt

Consider how a potential employer might view your online activity related to religious, political, or polarizing social issues. Even writing too many travel and book reviews or visiting online gambling sites (especially during work) can be dangerous. Certain slang vocabulary or emoticons when texting, blogging, and emailing can tip you up.

Tip: Think before you type and be honest (but don't always share openly).

Develop a Positive Digital Image

- LinkedIn scores high in the search rankings, allows you 100% control of content, and is the "professional" version of Facebook. Companies also frequently use it to find candidates.
- Helpful and considerate blog posts or YouTube "how to" entries can showcase your positive qualities.
- And you could post your resume and/or portfolio on a Google Sites web page you create for free.

Tip: Participate in some aspect of the digital world in a positive way.

Finding Job Openings

Quantity vs. quality. You have a choice to make.

You need to invest a certain quantity of time to conduct the activities and complete the tasks of job searching. You need to put in the hours. But if you find yourself becoming a web-zombie because of all the hours you are putting in every week on these two activities, chances are you've sacrificed quality for quantity and have few, if any, real results to show for it. Your career transition has to be all about quality.

That having been said, let's take a look at some of the opportunities in searching for new job openings online.

24/7 Information Available

The web has certainly provided consumers—including job seekers—with an enormous advantage. Nearly all the information you could ever want is available online, 24/7. It presents a tremendous advantage over the "good old days" when job seekers were forced to subscribe to 5 to 10+ newspapers and move into an apartment next to the library. If you know how to search smart, it will pay big dividends. And, once you've found an opening and/or a company you're interested in, the web also allows you a tremendous advantage in being able to conduct extensive research so that you can customize your resume and attack plan. Access to the web is a must-have tool in today's job search. And even job seekers without two nickels to rub together are afforded its advantages through libraries and other public access.

Meta-Search Sites

In the last few years, the rise of meta-search sites for job openings has further increased the advantage of the web. Meta-search sites are those websites that spider out from your query to search thousands of job boards, company employment web pages, specialty sites, professional and industry association sites, online newspapers, and a variety of other sites with job postings. The power of a meta-search web site allows you access to over 3,000,000 job openings at one time. It's like one-stop shopping!

Arguably, the two most prominent of these meta-search sites are:

www.indeed.com

and

www.simplyhired.com

The search algorithms behind these sites are shifting constantly and, presently, each of these sites will produce about 70% of the same job openings as the other for any particular query. But, I still currently recommend to clients that they start off their search by using both.

Meta-Sites Offer a Second Advantage
The smart job seeker realizes that these sites offer not only the advantage of an efficient way to produce many more results with a single search, but they also offer a view into specialty sites, company sites, and other places on the web that might be of interest to an individual job seeker.

All you need to do to realize this added benefit is to spend a few more minutes reviewing a query's results of job openings. Scan down through the first few pages of results and pay attention to the particular web sites where each job opening was originally listed. Note particular trends or sites that show up more than once. In this way, you'll start to get a sense of additional sites where you may want to spend more time. Some of them may be relatively obscure, some may represent other job boards, and some could be companies that were not previously on your radar screen. Now you are starting to create your own customized list of web sites that could be useful in your search.

Here are just a few meta-search, job board, and career advice web sites you might consider checking out, all of which are preceded by "www." and followed by ".com" :

- indeed
- monster
- dice
- bright
- theladders
- linkedin
- flexjobs
- jibberjobber
- simplyhired
- careerbuilder
- glassdoor
- ziprecruiter
- snagajob
- careerbliss
- fedjobs
- jobcentral
- beyond
- idealist
- salary
- dice
- doostang
- eternships
- insternships
- vault

Federal government position openings, for example, can be found at **www.usajobs.gov** and federal business opportunities can be found at **www.fbo.gov**.

Let's wrap up this chapter with another tip. This is an important one, unless you wish to waste away in front of the screen…

> **Limit Online Searching to Two Hours per Week**
>
> Once you have a list of job search websites and company employment pages organized under the "favorites" tab, you should limit yourself to two hours (or less)/week, as related to uncovering new position openings. After about two hours (unless you are a software engineer), the diminishing returns become exponential. Use your computer, tablet, or smartphone as much as you want to research companies, communicate with networking contacts, polish your resume, and apply for jobs. But don't "hide" behind a screen instead of doing that all-important networking.

Chapter 23

Power Networking

"A consistent soul believes in destiny, a capricious one in chance."
                      - Benjamin Disraeli

You've invested effort in creating an effective resume.

And that effort could all go to waste. In just a few words.

You must be both deliberative and real when you communicate. And your message must be *consistently* communicated across all mediums, including resume, cover letter, email, LinkedIn, social media and, of course, your spoken words! Take some time to think before you speak because, while networking is critical to your search, you cannot afford to make the wrong first impression.

You get one chance. To be both **credible** AND **authentic**.

Your Professional Brand

Remember reading the branding chapter?

Don't think you are done with this branding stuff just because you have your 2 to 3 core strengths or brand differentiators on your resume.

Think of how you will incorporate these 2 to 3 core strengths into your networking conversations…without it coming across like a scripted sales job. If you speak your brand inaccurately, with too many words, in someone else's words, or meekly it won't even get noticed or worse, it will get noticed for all the wrong reasons.

Speak your brand accurately, simply, and powerfully — <u>in your own words</u> — and it will get the attention of decision-makers.

Customize each conversation, but never abandon your brand.

The Shoebox Office

So, your new resume is out there and starting to generate some calls.

Are you ready to take the calls?

First, set up a "shoebox office."

Such a strategy allows you to keep everything you need to take a call in one place. A "mobile" place (you can easily carry something the size of a shoebox). You are ready to take a call…in your house, car, or alternate location.

Make a list of absolutely everything that would be helpful in taking an important phone call. Next, assemble the items on your list and place them in a shoebox-size container, briefcase, or backpack.

Here is a list of items you could include in your mobile shoebox office:

- Your resume, job advertisements, and other job-search materials.
- Pad of paper, clipboard and two pens.
- Hands-free headset that can plug into your home or mobile phone. You can buy a fairly inexpensive one for around $25. Just test it to make sure the sound is OK. This will make it a whole lot easier for you to concentrate on the conversation, especially if you find yourself needing both hands for typing or writing.
- An unopened bottle of water.
- A small package of tissues.
- A couple cough drops (water will not cure a dry cough).
- A calculator.
- A couple Excedrin. If you're 20 minute phone call turns into a three hour marathon, you'll appreciate a little caffeine boost.

What other items can you think of to put in your shoebox?

Your shoebox office can be a lifesaver. It removes ordinary distractions and allows you to focus on the conversation. Don't be without one.

Networking is Job Number One

Do you want to say "yuck" when you think of networking? Well, you are not alone.

But it's your new priority. So identify and overcome your self-imposed barriers. Screw up your courage and dive in.

Because networking is the *fundamental strategy* for strategically distributing your resume, uncovering the best open positions, and connecting with key individuals who are linked to hiring managers.

Some estimates suggest as many as 85% of all "good" jobs are "hidden" from view and only discoverable from networking. You cannot ignore the numbers. Of course, this is a resume book and not a networking book, so please excuse me for not delving into the fundamentals behind the 85% number. Suffice it to say that there is no conspiracy to hide job openings from you. Companies are not just trying to limit their liability by not posting positions, as some advice columnists suggest. It is just a matter of you not looking in the right place at the right time.

You must network to uncover the best-fitting positions.

By the way, if you think of networking as "fake" then think again.

Those who engage in inauthentic networking do so much harm to the concept. You must find your own ways to network and you must always come across as yourself, albeit within a professional context.

> ### Have "Real" Conversations
> Networking is almost always beneficial when it is "real." It is almost always a waste of time when it is "phony." Your effort must be about quality over quantity. Similarly, while maintaining your credibility is key, you must be authentic in your conversations. Your contacts will only appreciate speaking with the "real" you.

Daily Networking Goal

Connect with two new contacts each day. ***And follow up every 4 to 6 weeks.***

That is your goal if you are in a full-time job search.

So, you will be speaking with about 10 new contacts each week.

It may not seem like a lot compared with the admonitions of those who suggest reaching 30+ new contacts each week. But to ensure a QUALITY approach <u>and</u> be able to FOLLOW UP with each contact every 4 to 6 weeks, you must follow my two-a-day rule.

> **Two New Networking Contacts Each Day**
>
> If you want your search to be about quality, this is your number. It translates to just 10 new contacts per work week; a manageable number given that you are going to be researching each contact, preparing to reach out, reaching out, and making notes after each conversation. And, since <u>it is critical to follow up regularly</u> with your contacts every 4 to 6 weeks, once a month or so of time passes you will be contacting two new + two existing contacts each day for a total of four each day or 20 per week. In the month after that, therefore, you will be contacting two new + four existing contacts each day for a total of six each day or 30 per week. See what happens? Don't listen to "experts" who suggest reaching out to 20 to 30 new contacts a week – you would be buried alive! Commit to quality and hold yourself accountable to a daily number. Success will follow.

As the tip above points out, ongoing follow-up is essential.

It is a common rookie mistake to think that it is enough to simply speak with a new contact one time. You are assuming that the new contact will remember you, have you "top of mind" as they come across open positions, and will not lose your resume and contact information.

It won't happen.

That's not how our lives work.

Question: if you met someone today for the first time, could you clearly remember that person's name and some important aspects about them after two weeks had passed? How about after four weeks had passed? Six weeks? No?

Neither could I. That's why, if you can become well-organized about your effort and follow up every 4 to 6 weeks, you will be doing both your contact and you a big favor.

And remember…just because this networking thing is scary and difficult for you DOES NOT mean that it will be scary and difficult for the people you contact!

In fact, while you are networking for your own benefit, you're also doing a favor for each networking contact…*you are giving them the gift of helping you!* This is also critical to understand. Look at it this way…

If someone, professionally and appreciatively, reached out to you for help as part of their job search effort, how would that make you feel?

If someone were just asking you for a few minutes of your time to brainstorm and then politely followed up with you every 4 to 6 weeks (perhaps they even deferentially asked you for "permission" to follow up every once in a while), how would that make you feel?

It would make you feel really good.

If someone really needed just a little helping hand, was evidently already trying hard to help themselves, presented themselves and their core strengths professionally, and had the guts to give you a call, would you even consider turning them down?

No way.

So, to recap this important concept…

> **Give the Gift of Helping**
>
> Every time you ask for help you are giving someone else the gift of helping. The good feeling they will get by just helping you out in a quick 5 to 10-minute conversation will make them feel like a million bucks. Just as it makes you feel when someone asks you, graciously and appreciatively, for help. This out-of-control, fast-paced, externally- and materially-focused world offers so few opportunities for us to really feel good about who we are at our core. When they read your note of thanks, they will feel good for a second time and consider themselves part of your team, feeling vested in your success. Often times, they will even be looking forward to your next call in 4 to 6 weeks. Go on. Make someone else's day!

Organization/Tracking of Networking Contacts

Organize your contacts strategically to maximize your output from networking activities.

Do you prefer a manual, digital, or combination system?

I don't care what you use.

I have witnessed all the possible systems of which you can conceive. Just make sure you set one up. And use it!

I recommend combining all the following methods to organize and track your contacts: master spreadsheet, individual folders, ranking contact importance, and daily outreach.

Only when you truly organize your efforts from top to bottom will you be able to maximize your results.

Let's briefly examine the utility and importance of using all four methodologies…

Master Spreadsheet
Planning and tracking your networking activities are so much simpler with a master spreadsheet, which should include columns for: name, phone, email, date of initial communication, date of thank you note, dates for additional communications, and notes or comments.

My clients have also found it extremely useful to include a column ranking the importance of each contact, with a 1, 2, or 3, and highlighting each row with a color code as a visual reminder to pay attention to those who are most important.

Individual Folders
In addition to the comments section on your master spreadsheet, you will want to set up a larger data storage tool for your most important contacts.

Detailed notes, contact research, information about where they work, and copies of all correspondence should be kept in either a digital form or a manila file folder for each VIP contact.

Consider using a manila folder/paper system because, unless you are adept at splitting your computer screen into 6+ sections, you can't beat the versatility of being able to take out all your information on a particular contact and arrange it before you for a "whole person synthesis." I'm even a big fan of tabbing with colored sticky notes, but you need to find a system that works for you.

Of course, make sure some critical nuggets of information on each person are stored digitally so you can access them on the road at any time. The "notes" function within Google contact should do the trick, or you can rely on another program such as Evernote.

Ranking Contacts

You will definitely want to develop a system for ranking the importance of your contacts. This is all about making an efficient use of your time, maximizing your productivity, and communicating with your contacts in the most appropriate manner.

For instance, you should definitely seek in-person dialog with your top-tier contacts whenever possible.

Middle-tier contacts can be efficiently communicated with via telephone, still affording them a measure of personalized respect.

Lower-tier contacts can be efficiently reached out to through e-mail alone. After all, these lower-tier contacts include folks like the former professional colleague you had lost touch with years ago. And, while they may know of an interesting job opportunity for you, you and they may not want the awkwardness of phone or in-person conversation.

You will be making an initial outreach to each contact by e-mail with your resume attached and, in that e-mail, you will be asking to communicate further with each contact, either in-person, by phone, or by e-mail, depending upon the tier ranking of that contact.

Also, please note that if a lower-tier/email-only contact is open to helping you network into one of your target companies or vouching for you when you apply for an open position, the contact would then move immediately into the top tier.

Daily Outreach

Living by the rule of connecting with two new contacts each day and following up with each contact every 4 to 6 weeks, you should populate your calendar with 2 to 4 names targeted for outreach each day. Then, set up a simple system with just 2 to 3 rules to keep yourself moving in the right direction and making a quality effort day after day.

Some example (self-imposed) rules might include:

- Doubling your outreach the day after you failed to network.

- Performing 20 minutes research on each first- and second-tier contact prior to initial outreach.

- Having a standard five-minute pre-call preparation so that you actually have an idea about the focus of the call and don't waste either your time or the contact's.

Design flexible rules and protocols that make sense for you. Modify them periodically to optimize your networking. Just make sure to follow them when you take action.

Networking Email with Resume Attached

So, how do you get started?

Start by sending out a brief email with your resume attached to each person you know, professionally and personally. Of course, you won't want to send all of them out at once because that would be too many individuals to follow up with at the same time. Networking should always be about the quality of the interaction.

This e-mail should be set up just like a letter. It has an opening, a body, and a closing. The opening gives context and engages; it presents the subject or reason for the email. The body mentions your two or three core strengths. The closing commits you to follow-up. Did you get that? The closing line: *"I will call you (the contact) in the next couple of days…"*

> **Once you have clicked on "send," you have committed to making that phone call!**

Finally, the "re:" or subject line must grab the reader's attention.

If at all possible, it should directly name the mutual acquaintance. Something like "Referral from Lynn Linker."

Just don't leave it blank.

Here is what a sample "networking email" might look like:

Example of Email to Networking Contact

> To: Cary Contact
> From: Norman Networker
> RE: *Referral from Lynn Linker*
>
> Cary,
>
> A mutual colleague, Lynne Linker, suggested I connect with you as part of my current career transition. I previously worked with Lynn at WSD Company where we were both Customer Service Supervisors. As you may have heard, WSD closed its doors last month — hence my current job search.
>
> The attached resume details my background, which includes: eight years in inbound customer service, three years in supervision, PMP certification, and training in the latest RoboCall Global system.
>
> I will contact you within the next couple days to follow up this email and appreciate, in advance, any assistance you might be able to offer.
>
> Sincerely,
>
> Cassius

Create an Elevator Pitch for Conversations

A compelling, 30–60 second "elevator pitch" is an essential part of any successful job search campaign or networking interaction.

Unfortunately, many job seekers are misinformed—not about the content of an elevator pitch but, instead, about how to use it. So let's take a brief look at what an elevator pitch is, why you need an elevator pitch, what its content might look like, and how you should use it.

What an Elevator Pitch Is and Is Not

An elevator pitch is a 30–60 second verbal "infomercial" that introduces and promotes you as a job seeker to people you do not know. It is most typically used in networking. It seeks to answer the question "who are you?" when introducing yourself to an individual or group.

Of course, if you have advance notice that you will be meeting with a particular individual, you will want to customize your elevator pitch. But you also need to be ready with some standard content at any time, with or without notice!

So, an elevator pitch is essentially a marketing tool.

It was developed more than 50 years ago, with the original intent of making a blitz-like introduction during the time to people might find themselves alone together inside an elevator. (Don't try it that way, however!) In theory, if the elevator were slow and you were going to the 49th floor, you might have a shot at limited dialog that could result in exchanging business cards and/or set up of a future conversation.

Fast-forward to the present day digital world, where things have both changed and stayed the same. How so?

The advent of digital communications, including text, actually makes the elevator pitch more important than ever before. Whether in-person or over the phone, job seekers are afforded less and less talk time with networking contacts. So, when you finally do have an opportunity to speak with someone, you had better nail it.

You never know when the gatekeeper to your future job will appear.

While there are many variations on the components and construction of content, I would suggest <u>you think of an elevator pitch as sharing just a bit of information related to your professional **past, present, and future**</u>. Let's take a look at each:

The past might contain information such as a key industry, company, or job that has been important to your career. Since you have limited time and you don't want to come across as pompous or arrogant, it may be advisable not to share too much information related to the past. If you do choose to share additional material, it should be content that distinguishes you, such as a significant accomplishment.

The present should be anchored with few, easily understandable words related to your value proposition and 2 to 3 core strengths. It could also include recent training or certifications, especially if connected to hard skills that are in demand. It allows the listener to get a handle on what you have to offer your next employer. It presents your value proposition.

The future needs to focus on your primary objective, whether it is defined in terms of a specific position, target companies, a geographic area of choice, professional values, or a combination of factors that are guiding your search. The purpose of including information related to the future or direction of your job search is to enable your networking contact to understand how they might be able to help. While sharing such information is not a call to action or direct request for assistance, it sets up the conversation to come.

If you attend a formal networking event at which each person is expected to stand and give their elevator pitch, your elevator pitch might look something like this...

Norman Networker: *Hi, I'm Norman Networker.*

Last month, I was one of 240 employees who lost their jobs when WSG Company closed its doors. I held several positions in my seven years at WSG, including Customer Service Supervisor.

I'm trained in the latest RoboCall Global system, have my PMP certification, and am effective in both key contributor and management roles.

I'm looking for a position in either customer service or project management in the greater Gillamonadnock City, NM area. I would really appreciate any help you might be able to offer.

Now can you understand how an elevator pitch can be a powerful, yet succinct introduction to who you are and where you are going?

However, if you are calling or meeting with an individual networking contact, reeling off such a monologue would be at best awkward for both of you and, at worst, it might doom any further meaningful conversation.

It's just not natural.

People don't speak in monologue. They speak in dialogue.

Back and forth.

People share information, ask questions, and listen to each other's answers.

So, a more appropriate and realistic use of the past, present, and future related information in at elevator pitch might look something like…

Norman Networker:	*Hi, I'm Norman Networker.*
Cary Contact:	*Nice to meet you, Norman. What can I do for you?*
Norman Networker:	*Well, I don't know if you heard but WSG Company closed its doors last month.*
Cary Contact:	*I wasn't aware of that. Did you know Lynne Linker? I believe she was a Customer Service Supervisor.*
	I have always thought highly of Lynne.
Norman Networker:	*Lynne and I were peers! In fact, she mentioned that you might be a good contact to reach out to.*
Cary Contact:	*Well, I'm happy to help, but I don't know of any customer service positions currently.*
Norman Networker:	*No problem.*
	I appreciate your willingness to help. Just so you know, I'm looking at both customer service and project management positions. I passed my PMP exam last month.
Cary Contact:	*Really? A former colleague of mine at TXC Company is actually looking for a couple project coordinators right now. I'd be happy to forward your resume to her.*
Norman Networker:	*That would be fantastic! Should I give her a call as well or would you suggest another kind of follow up?*
Cary Contact:	*Why don't you let me reach out first with an email and your resume, Norman? But if you don't hear from her within four or five days, I would indeed give her a call.*
	And feel free to use my name. If you worked with Lynne, you must be excellent.
Norman Networker:	*Great. You are going above and beyond for me, Cary. I really appreciate it…*

Did you notice the difference? **Use elements of your elevator pitch in 2-way conversations for best results.**

Practice Makes Perfect

Practicing an elevator pitch so that you have a <u>command of the content material</u> is absolutely essential.

On the other hand, practicing an elevator pitch just so you can deliver a smooth monologue is nonsense.

Each time you meet a new networking contact and have that initial dialog, you might be constructing slightly different sentences. That's OK. That's normal. The key is to **use similar content each time** you open a conversation with a networking contact. That way you will be presenting a consistent message across the market.

And, remember, consistency in messaging is critical to a successful job search. So, you elevator pitch needs to connect with key elements of your resume, LinkedIn profile, and so forth.

Another reason I suggest using a past/present/future template for the elevator pitch relates to versatility.

Perhaps you are networking with someone who is familiar with your background. There would be no need to use that content; it would be more appropriate just to focus on the present and future.

Or maybe you come across someone you used to work with when applying for a position at one of your target companies. In that case, the past- and future-related information becomes less relevant and, once you are done sharing stories about the "good old days," you can focus your initial comments almost exclusively on the present.

Not sure how to go about practicing? Well, I bet your mobile phone has an audio recording device built in to the function which allows you to record audio or video...

Collaborating with Competitors

It's easy to become a job search lone ranger, especially if you are in competition with those around you.

Yet, a complete search strategy includes a component of collaborating with your potential competition. I know this concept may be pushing the envelope for some of you but you've got to take calculated risks if you want your career karma to soar.

Now I'm not asking you to blindly trust everyone with whom you come into contact.

That would be madness.

I am asking you to open up your thinking about how you can trade competition for collaboration.

That almost always makes sense.

*So, while making smart decisions about whom you can trust…*consider joining forces with the very people you are going up against.

Why?

Because job search is not about survival of the fittest. It is about finding that best fit. Even if your competitors have similar experience and skill sets, they have different personalities, motivators, wants and needs, and other characteristics that make each person unique. You and they "fit" in different positions and with different companies. So, you are not really in that much competition after all.

And how many other job seekers are willing to collaborate with their competitors? This tactic can really give you an edge.

I could cite many examples in which competitors looked out for each other to the benefit of all involved, but just consider the case of Flo, Harry, and Burly…

Some years ago, Flo, Harry, and Burly were laid off from their jobs… along with about 700 other individuals…when their company closed the doors for good.

Now, while they were certainly not close friends in a company which once boasted over 3,500 employees (they worked in different departments), they knew of and respected each other. Let's consider them professional acquaintances of a sort.

They were each working both hard and smart at their job search when Flo finally secured an interview for a mid-level position with one of her target companies.

I customized Flo's resume and advised her on interviewing strategy. She went into the interview with measured confidence.

A few days later my phone rang.

"Greg, this is Flo. I have a question for you. The interview went well and they want me to come back for the second round next week. It looks as if I'm their leading candidate. I'm interested in the job and know I could do well at it but I know someone who would be a better fit: Harry. What is your advice about also letting Harry know of the position opening?"

"I think that's fine," I said, "but it's really not my decision, Flo. That's very much up to you."

Flo thanked me for listening and hung up the phone.

About a week later my phone rang again.

"Coach, this is Harry. I have a question for you. Flo told me about this really great job opening, which she applied for. She encourage me to apply as well. I did and now they've asked me to come back for a second interview. I'm so thankful for Flo's call. It looks like I may be their new leading candidate. Now, I think I'd be really good in his job, but one of my coworkers named Burly would be an even better fit. So, what do you think I should do? Should I tell Burly or not?"

"Well, I really think that is your decision," I offered, "but, since Flo was the one who let you know about it, I would certainly counsel you to check with her first in that case."

Harry thanked me and hung up the phone.

So, you know who got the job, don't you?

It was Burly, of course. He was the best fit for the position.

But, can you guess how the rest of the story played out?

Well, after Burly started his new gig, he spent every non-working hour helping out Flo and Harry with their searches.

He made it his mission to get them hired.

Within a matter of weeks, Flo had been hired by one of Burly's former employers, in a similar position but with 20% more pay!

Within a couple more weeks, Harry ended up at the same company where Burly was working but in a position that was even more aligned with his strengths and that had more potential for advancement!

So, what's your excuse for not joining forces with your competition? Why not give them a call?

It's time to be open to new approaches, to challenge accepted norms, and to take action.

That is, unless you want that masterpiece of a resume you just created to go to waste. That would be a shame.

> ### *Identify People You Can Trust*
> You must be able to trust those closest to you. Or you'll end up like Caesar just after he crossed the Rubicon. Negative and less ethical people can be a big barrier to job search progress. The people you surround yourself with—in a job search and in life—must want an open, honest, mutually beneficial, and high-quality relationship. The alternative is drama, negativity, distraction, and a lack of job-search progress. Choose your relationships wisely.

Now, about the business of creating a list of networking contacts with which to populate your master spreadsheet…

In this digital age, you probably have most of the names right on your phone!

But I bet you don't have as many of the third-tier contact names in there. Remember those? People you lost contact with 3 to 5+ years ago? They could pay dividends in your networking effort.

You don't even have to speak to most of them. After you have researched what company they are working at, just send them an email with you resume.

So, do your best to write down the names of those folks right now on the next page…

Names of potential third-tier networking contacts:

Chapter 24

Interview Success

"One chance is all you need."
- Jesse Owens

It's show time!

You've worked hard to *get noticed*: writing and customizing your resume, conducting extensive research, networking into target companies, and getting your resume in front of the hiring manager.

Finally, you've secured an interview. Now it's time to *close the deal*.

To do that, however, you can't leave anything on the table.

There are no second chances.

You need to nail each meeting with company representatives…whether the hiring process consists of one interview or six. You can't score a "B" on any single interview and expect to move on in the process.

Make sure "you, in person" equals the quality of "you, on paper."

So, you need to understand some fundamentals about interviewing.

First, let's examine the link between the resume and the interview:

- The interviewer probably will refer to your resume's content when developing questions so *you need to be ready with detailed <u>example stories</u> that relate to all the information on your resume*.

- You need to bring copies of your resume to the interview. As previously noted, these copies should be top-quality and printed on 28- to 32-pound fine stationery, not be folded, not be stapled together, and should number at least one more then the number of people you expect to be meeting.

- You should be prepared to pay attention to certain key points your resume makes. Don't wait for the interviewer to bring up the content of your resume. In answering the interviewers' questions, take the initiative at least a couple times during the interview to link your answer with compelling resume content.

- Since you have customized your resume for that particular position, you must review it carefully prior to the interview.
    - First, review how you have customized your resume, as you may have reordered bullets, added content, and modified wording to target the particular position.
    - Second, review the key words and phrases, as well as the key hiring motives, that your resume speaks to.

- You need your verbal language to match the written language of the resume.

Don't assume that each interviewer has read your resume thoroughly or, if they have, that they remember your key points.

Consider these possibilities:

- Some interviewers will indeed have read and reread your resume, marked it up, and have detailed questions for you about its content.

- Other interviewers may have had their interest piqued by several key points on your resume, but have not read additional information, instead preferring to speak with you directly first.

- Still others may have been pulled into the interviewing process with little or no preparation and may be completely unaware of your resume's very existence or, if they have a copy, they may not have reviewed your resume at all.

  Note: With this last group, be very careful not to force them back to your resume as they will have their own priorities and agenda items to discuss and you need to speak directly to those.

Remember…

The interviewer's perception is their reality.

So, while you need to let them be in control of the interview, you also need to convince them that you should be their first choice.

And you need to do it from the moment you meet them. Whether or not your resume has captured their attention. It is up to you.

Also, you need to understand that different interviews seek to accomplish different things. While this is a resume-writing book and not an interviewing book, I think it is important to spend just a bit of time discussing a few of the more common types of interviews and how you might prepare for each.

Consider these common types of interviews...

Five-Minute Phone Screen

Recruiters, whether working as an employee of your target company or for a staffing or search firm, often find themselves with at least 10–15+ initial candidates who seem, on paper, to be potential fits for a particular position. Thus, they need to pre-screen the candidates to identify a more manageable 3- to 6-person group for interviewing.

Understand that a phone screen does not typically include much two-way dialog.

It is often comprised of no more than five questions to which you need to offer a direct and succinct response. Your correct response to five out of five questions will get you over that hurdle and onto the next stage in the interviewing process. Your correct response to four out of five will not.

<u>The interviewer is looking to determine both your competence and your confidence</u>.

For instance, if an interviewer asks you to rate yourself on a scale from 1 (lowest) to 10 (highest) in a number of areas, you will not move on to the next stage in the process without giving yourself ratings that are all 9s and 10s with perhaps one 8 allowed as an outlier. Giving yourself a 7 usually means an end to the process.

Let me repeat that...*rating yourself a 7 will mean you crash and burn.*

I know. Sickening. But you must play the game if you want to move on.

So, what if you have limited knowledge or experience in one of those areas, however? What should you do then?

Well, while you should typically not offer any explanation for your numerical self ratings, if there is one weaker area, consider rating yourself an 8 and then offer a quick and brief explanation: honestly disclose that you have less experience or knowledge in that area and that your rating of 8 represents your *high level of confidence* that you will be up to speed before day one on the job.

The above example of rating yourself illustrates the basic psychology of the five-minute phone screen that, again, is just a very quick pre-qualification to move onto a more thorough interview. If your interviewer doesn't check off all of the boxes on their list, your candidacy is going nowhere fast.

30-Minute Phone or Skype Interview

It is critical that you practice the phone or Skype interview.

You must *understand how you come across* within these communication mediums. Recording yourself and playing back the tape will be an eye-opener. I guarantee it.

A laptop's web cam or smartphone's recorder should do the trick.

And you may want to involve a trusted friend as the mock interviewer to make it seem more real. Simply come up with some sample questions derived from the job ad and any other research you have completed. Then, roll those cameras!

You should prepare for this type of interview just as you would for an in-person interview, including dress, posture, facial expressions, and tone. Otherwise, even on the phone, you will not convey optimum nonverbal messaging. Think of it this way:

You need to pass the security check or you aren't going to board the plane.

In-Person Interview

The in-person interview may take many forms. It could be a panel interview, one-on-one interview, fish bowl interview, conversation over a meal, or any one of a number of other forms. Remember that both <u>tone</u> and <u>content</u> are important, as are being authentic and credible.

Speaking of combining credibility and authenticity, my advice for your foundational interview preparation strategy really deserves its own tip:

> ### Prepare 10—15+ Targeted Example Stories
>
> It is once again time to apply the concept of "core hiring motives." Critical to your success in the interview is preparing 10—15+ example stories that are aligned with the company's core hiring motives for the position. Create at least 5 to 6 stories for each core hiring motive. Practice saying each out loud. This is a key strategy in linking what got you noticed with what's going to close the deal for you. The example stories allow interviewers to develop an image of you as being successful in their open position. And that will be key to their hiring decision.

Key elements of in-person interview preparation include:

Research, Research, Research

Don't let this go until the last minute. Yeah, you. I hear you chuckling.

As with customizing your resume, you must conduct extensive research on position and company—well ahead of time so that you can then target your example stories. Don't forget researching the background of your interviewers as well. And it can't be just online.

You have to make the calls and reach out to your network as well as any "spies" you might have in the target company.

You can't do too much research.

Your Questions Must Be Dynamite

Prepare five to ten thoughtful questions. They need to demonstrate that you've done your research. They need to be specific to the position.

The most powerful and useful questions are often those that inquire about what the company expects the successful candidate to accomplish in the position. Ask what "success" might look like at the 30-, 60-, and 90-day milestones; determine what they want you to accomplish. Perhaps another couple questions might relate to "fit" within the company's and/or department's culture. Is coming up with super questions a tall order? Not if you really want to work there. *The quality of your questions speaks volumes about your quality as a candidate.*

While the priority is convincing them to hire you, this is a two-way street. You need to make sure this opportunity is right for you, too. Don't blow the interview or make a foolish decision to join the wrong company because you didn't have the right questions ready.

Verbal and Nonverbal Messaging

Content is king but in terms of spoken communication, messages received are about 10% verbal (word content) and 90% nonverbal.

Our body language and facial expressions, the way we use our hands, and our posture all need to be right on when it comes to an interview. Practice makes perfect—so make sure you're über-aware of the signals that you're about to give off. Practice with a trusted friend for maximum effect.

Dress for Success

It is almost always the best bet to be on the conservative side here. Also, if faced with a choice, it is always better to be a tad overdressed instead of underdressed.

Follow the basics here.

Slacks and a silk blouse are foundational for women in professional interview settings, while navy or charcoal gray slacks or suit is a must for men.

Shoes are always polished to a shine, with women always having toes covered and, usually, a slight heel.

Of course, belt and shoes match, men's shirts are starched and have a t-shirt under them, legs are always covered over the calf, perfume and jewelry are kept to a minimum, a watch with two "hands" is a must…I could go on.

Just make sure you dress appropriately. If you're interviewing for a construction job and the interview is comprised of you getting up into a backhoe or dozer and demonstrating your proficiency as an operator…know that they won't even let you in the machine if you are all suited up or without steel-toed work boots. Also, especially for women, be aware of geographic and cultural differences. If you are interviewing for a position with a small, "local" company, your dress could certainly be different in Atlanta versus Savannah.

Don't be shy about admitting that you need some guidance.

Let's tell it like it is: women usually know how to dress while men often would be best served by seeking another's counsel. Of course, there exceptions to this gender gap.

No long discussions here, just make sure you consult someone who understands the finer points if you are unsure.

You must invest in a look that will say confidence and professionalism.

Remember, *there are no second chances*.

That Car

Yeah, you know the one…yours.

At a minimum, it needs to be immaculate inside and out, including under the seats and in the trunk. Those of you who are chuckling right now know who you are. Even if you plan to park in the back of the company's parking lot…the interviewer may follow you out and end up getting a peek at the inside of your auto.

Boy, could I tell you stories. Please don't become one of them.

Written Directions

So your car is a newer model with a built in navigation system.

And, you're going to drive the route on the day before your interview.

Believe it or not, I've seen both fail.

So, make it your mission to visit www.mapquest.com and print out the directions as well.

Also, a smart move is to know where the nearest Starbucks or Dunkin' Donuts is located in relation to your destination. That way you'll have a place to spruce up and take care of any other business before you walk through their door.

When to Arrive

This has changed from a few years ago. Know that <u>10 minutes early is just about right and 20+ minutes early shows desperation</u>. Of course, you need to plan to be 45 minutes early just in case the unexpected happens. Which it always does, if you don't plan for it. So plan for it and hang out at the near-by Starbucks until your interview time.

Finally, if you have to fill out paperwork or take a pre-employment test, you had better factor that in…

Pre-Employment Testing

According to one American Management Association survey, over 40% of responding members (i.e. hiring managers) utilized some type of employment test(s) in hiring. Similar statistics have been garnered by the Society for Human Resource Management. Testing is on the rise. Although employers cannot legally make hiring decisions based solely on test results, they are often used as a double-check for "fit."

The chances of you spending a day with a psychologist or taking the Minnesota Multiphase—in order to check for that "fit"—are growing increasingly remote. There are, however, plenty of 15- to 30-minute online tests that an employer can have you take in order to better evaluate that "fit." So, you need to be prepared…

<u>Identify the Test</u>: Find out what assessment this organization uses. Then, go online to become familiar with the test.

<u>Take the Test</u>: Why not? Once you have identified the test type, contact an independent practitioner and take the exact same test!

<u>Research</u>: Go to the test's website, try to obtain a copy of a sample test report and/or sample questions, read blog posts, speak with your career coach, call your HR contacts, and access relevant journal articles.

Read Articles on Test Taking: There is a bevy of information out there on test taking, from online articles to books. Consult the experts.

Visualize: Return to what has worked for you in the past related to picturing your own future success. How do you remain positive in situations of impending stress? Don't recreate the wheel.

Now, a few possible test-taking strategies…

Test Early: If you have a choice, take assessments early, when you are alert, well hydrated, and at your maximum cognitive ability.

Be honest: If the purpose is to determine your "fit" with the organization's culture, try not to over-think your answers or you may come across as having a different personality. And most reputable tests have hidden inconsistency and lie-scales built in anyway.

Be honest, but…: What!? I know I just said "be honest"… but *be honest from a professional perspective.* Your answers should reflect your thoughts and behaviors *as they are on the job*—not as they are at home. Answering personally is not always appropriate and may not lead to a hire.

Consider the employer's perspective: This is key when shifting into a new role that requires slightly different behaviors. Ask yourself: "What is the standard of excellence that this employer is trying to measure?"

Take your time: You may be told to answer quickly. Forget this advice (unless the test is timed). But don't overthink your answers either.

Read the instructions for each section: Sometimes a test will have several sections with several different sets of instructions. Carefully read and consider each before answering questions.

Control your environment and minimize distractions: Especially if you are taking these tests online and at home, be sure to control your environment to the maximum, including privacy.

Relax — be easy on yourself: Some of these tests can be buggers! Do your best overall, don't spend too much time on any one question, and remember that the test is only one piece of the process. Remain calm.

Guess: When you are at a complete loss on how to answer a question, eliminate any obviously incorrect choices and then guess.

Move on: Once the test is over, move on. Remind yourself that there are other pieces to the process and you cannot control the test results or even influence them anymore. Don't let negative thoughts linger.

Power Posing

Stop giggling! Yes, it really does work.

A couple minutes right before your interview should do the trick. Whether it's hands on hips with head up and chest out or arms in the air, don't go against the science. Get yourself physically prepared to go in with every advantage. "Feeling" more confident is one of the bigger advantages you can give yourself.

Find your own method for getting "pumped up" for the interview.

Example Stories

I can't overstate their importance.

More about these in a couple pages but, as mentioned in the tip a few pages back, it's a must that you have 10–15+ example stories ready.

Each must show one of your core strengths as aligned with one of the company's 2 to 3 core hiring motives for the position.

Your examples need to be in *story* form for optimum impact.

Your integrated and targeted marketing effort will stand out in comparison to the rest of the pack of candidates. You'll be making key points with the interviewer while your competition flails about with a scattered approach, trying to satisfy every minute requirement listed on the job advertisement.

Live and die by Pareto's 80/20 Rule to set yourself up to *close the deal*.

The Close

Have your close pre-prepared.

No messing around here. Strong, succinct, and clear.

Either ask for the job or, at the very least, consider incorporating these phrases into your close:

> **"I have the highest level of interest in the position…"**

> **"I'm looking forward to the next steps in the process…"**

A strong handshake with eye contact should complement your close.

Survival Kit

Someone reading this is going to thank me.

I don't want to see your pockets or your purse bulging, but you better be prepared for the unexpected.

Huh? What am I talking about?

For example, a cup of water won't placate a dried throat cough; you need a cough drop ready in your pocket.

And that 90-minute interview that suddenly turns into 4+ hours? It will require the caffeine jolt that only an Excedrin can give.

A power bar in your suit pocket can also satisfy hunger so that you don't suffer from a gurgling stomach distractor. As with the Excedrin, the power bar can be ingested during a quick bathroom break. I'm not going to go on and on because you get the idea.

Hey, this is a resume writing book and not an interviewing book so I'm not going to dive into detail here. Just know that others have torched their own chances so you can learn…Don't sneeze your way into second place just because you are without a pocket sized packet of tissues.

By the way, save your red handkerchiefs for that camping trip.

The Three Types of Questions

Be ready for behavioral, situational, and motivation-based questions.

Prepare for each type by developing those 10–15 example stories, each aligned with one of the company's 2 to 3 core hiring motives.

Let's review each of these three types of questions briefly…

Behavioral

Behavioral interviewing has been around for several decades now. It is foundational to most professional interviews. Googling "behavioral interviewing" or looking it up on YouTube will offer you more information than you ever wanted to know.

The premise of behavioral interviewing is that <u>your past behavior will predict your future performance</u>.

Therefore, be ready to be asked for examples to back up the assertions on your resume, as well as to shed more light on certain interview answers. You can often catapult yourself ahead of the competition by offering powerful example stories during the interview.

Examples told in a story format will boost your credibility and allow the interviewer to picture you as someone who will be successful in the open position.

Situational

These questions are extremely similar to behavioral questions except that an interviewer will be asking about what you would do in a certain hypothetical situation. Which, by the way, is probably what you are really going to be facing when you're on the job.

Take your time and be thoughtful about your answer.

After you tell the interviewer what you would do in a situation, <u>be sure to back up your answer with an example story that you have developed</u>.

Situational interviews can be exceptionally good at testing critical thinking, decision-making, and leadership.

Motivation

Not to be confused with a counseling technique called "motivation**al** interviewing," this is a relatively new but powerful interviewing format that explores what really motivates you and what de-motivates you.

Be ready with some examples of work tasks that motivate you, as well as how you deal with assigned tasks that most people would consider to be drudgery.

The company is looking to make sure that you will be fired up and genuinely interested in performing *all* the tasks of the position, not just a few of them.

Of course, everyone is excited and fired up in the first few weeks but, sooner or later, the honeymoon period will expire.

And, just think about it for a minute.

It is in your best interest to explore whether the day-to-day tasks of the position would motivate or de-motivate you as well. You don't want to end up in a position in which 80% of the duties are a real grind.

Share with the interviewer what you are really passionate about, what your true interests are, and what makes you tick.

Hopefully your authentic self fits well with the daily duties of the position. If not, you didn't want the job anyway.

Even if the company does not ask you any motivation-interviewing type questions, you can use this concept to your advantage.

Set yourself ahead of the competition by sharing with the interviewer how the duties of the position are similar to those which have motivated you in the past. Tell them how you really enjoy all those tasks that others might dread.

Once a company has hired a high potential candidate and starts investing in that new employee, the organization has a vested interest in retaining that person. Show them that you are motivated to perform the tasks of the job, as well as grow with the company.

Core Hiring Motives

You are already a master at this concept. It has been beaten into you.

In customizing your resume (especially if you are using a "one resume" format), you've utilized the concept of core hiring motives to determine the company's top 2 to 3 hiring priorities—as related to the position—and you are showing that your strengths match with these priorities. You've used Pareto's 80/20 Rule to identify the 20% of their requirements that will translate into 80% of the position's effectiveness.

All right. So, if you have a blank look on your face right now, you need to go back and review some material from earlier chapters. It's kind of important. Otherwise, you'll risk wasting your time in trying to prepare to speak to every one of the 10−20+ requirement and qualification bullets listed on their job advertisement and/or job description.

You must be targeted about your approach in order to boost your credibility and show them that you are the best hire they could make.

Once you have identified the company's 2 to 3 core hiring motives for a particular position, you must develop at least 4 to 6 examples from your past work experience to speak to each hiring motive. That will allow you a repository of 10−15+ total examples as ammunition for any question they might ask.

Some career coaches believe you only need five really good examples, because each example has so many facets that it can be used multiple times to answer different questions. The weakness with this idea relates to human memory. I would agree with their premise if the human mind, during the battle conditions of interviewing, had 100% recall. I've field tested this premise and found that most people need 2 to 3 times the availability of the examples they will utilize. Because most people only have quick recall of about a third of what they have learned.

Therefore, <u>in order to recall and utilize 5 to 6 good examples, you'll probably need at least 10–15 prepared</u>.

Of course, a few of these examples can be taken right from the resume, as you may already have described them in bullets and have customized the document for this position.

Then, once you have your examples ready, you need to turn each into a 30–60-second story for maximum effect.

> ### Limit Each Interview Answer to 30–60 Seconds
> Every answer you give must be no more than 30–60 seconds in length, even if it is in response to a question like: "Tell me about yourself." Even just 2 to 3 minutes in length and you will have the interviewer mentally snoozing. Don't worry about being too brief. The interviewer will ask follow ups if they need to. And the 30–60-second format will actually lend itself to creating a back-and-forth dialog, which are the best kind of interviews!

Certainly, one of the most utilized interview formats in the history of professional interviewing is "behavioral interviewing" in which the interviewer asks you to provide specific examples of your work, skills, or traits to help predict how likely you are to be successful in the open position.

For years now, I have suggested my clients come up with numerous 30–60 second examples aligned what I have called the 2 or 3 "core hiring motives" of the position and/or company. This sets the stage for a powerful and targeted interview in which you give the interviewer exactly what they are looking for while staying honest, authentic, and true to the "core strengths" in your professional brand.

Turbo-Charge Your Examples

Now, imagine taking each example and turning it into a story.

The result?

Your credibility soars as the listener is engaged and actually takes in the content of your example.

You don't have to be a master storyteller or be a colorful personality to deliver the goods; the story will take care of itself.

Just make sure that when you refer to each example it connects to:

- **an individual…**
- **who says something specific…**
- **at a particular moment in time.**

And…presto!

Instant story!

I refer to the interviews in which a candidate utilizes these stories as "storytelling interviews."

They can be your best friend when it comes to *closing the deal* in a highly competitive job interview process.

On the next page, consider the following difference between an "example" and an "example story"—each given in response to a behavioral interviewing question…

"BEHAVIORAL" QUESTION asked by Interviewer

Interviewer: *You say that one of your core strengths is being a "hard worker," so please tell me about a specific example that demonstrates your work ethic.*

"EXAMPLE" ANSWER given by Candidate

Candidate: *Absolutely. Work ethic is deep-rooted with me – all the way back to my school days. I was on a fixed allowance and found that, if I wanted extra money, I would have to earn it. So, I spent hours and hours one summer planning, opening up, and running a home-made lemonade stand on our front lawn. It was hard work for little pay, but I persevered and made a success of it.* (Interviewer nods and jots down positive comments)

"EXAMPLE STORY" ANSWER given by Candidate

Candidate: *Absolutely. Work ethic is deep-rooted with me – all the way back to my school days. I was on a fixed allowance and remember asking my dad for money to start a lemonade stand. He responded "Don't you already get an allowance?" Later, I asked him for a ride to the store to buy the lemons and he chuckled and asked: "Do you still have that bike we gave you for your birthday?" Finally, after several days, I had my stand all set up and who should walk by but my dad. I held up the first glass of lemonade I had ever poured and after he drank it down he thanked me and commented on how tasty it was. I felt like a million dollars. But when I said "That will be $1 please" my dad responded "Not unless you want me to charge you rent for setting up on my front lawn" and, instead, he gave me a hug and told me what a great worker I was. I'll never forget his pride at my initiative and hard work. It still drives me today.* (Interviewer chuckling and fully engaged with the candidate)

So...which candidate would you hire?

"Personal" Example Stories Create Chemistry

Nearly all of your example stories should come from your work experience.

After all, you are applying for a work position!

Often, however, the trigger to *closing the deal* rests on chemistry.

FYI...*chemistry can be created*.

So many job-search books suggest that you practice fake smiles and less-than-genuine gestures. While a fake smile is certainly better than no smile it all, it doesn't lend itself to chemistry. Only an authentic smile can do that.

And the most authentic of smiles comes from showing your true self.

That's why developing just a couple of personal example stories should be a top priority for you.

Each of these personal examples stories needs to relate to some aspect of your character or personality — something about you that speaks to your core and will suggest a good fit with the position.

Often, it is useful to choose an example from childhood (such as the example on the previous page), to demonstrate how deeply rooted a certain character or personality trait is in you. It's easy and safe to smile or chuckle at yourself when recalling a childhood memory.

If you're not sure what I'm talking about here, just look at the example a couple pages ago.

The lemonade stand example story above is actually a personal example story!

The interviewing process can often be somewhat formal, professional, and sterile. So, your ability to *humanize* yourself in front of the interviewer can become a huge advantage. And, if for some reason your personal example story doesn't resonate, did you really fit with the culture of that company? Boosting your credibility in the interview takes top priority. But revealing your authentic, true self is also a must if you want to close the deal.

Think of it this way...

Delivering examples in the form of 30–60 second stories allows you to connect on a "feeling" AND "thinking" level.

This is key because, while hiring decisions are probably 90% based on objective analysis, <u>what clinches the decision are often the intangibles that deal with "fit" or "chemistry."</u> And you can't count on the interviewer to create the chemistry. That's your job, as tough as it might seem. So, reach back into your formative years and find an example story that will show a deep-rooted character trait. Who knows?

Your own unique "lemonade stand" story just may *close the deal*.

Wait until Tomorrow to Send a Thank You Email

A short, genuine, and professional thank you note is a must. Handwritten is preferred. But, sometimes given the timing of the interview process, e-mail becomes more effective.

Just don't follow the advice of many well-meaning folks and send it the same day you have interviewed.

What, on earth, might I be talking about?

Let's think tactically.

In today's marketing-driven world, if a company with a powerful brand had the choice, over a week's time, of you noticing seven advertisements in one day and none for the rest of the week or having you notice one advertisement each day throughout the week, which would they choose? It's elementary. Because the more points of contact a brand has with you over a period of time, the better-positioned that brand is to convince you to buy. It becomes top-of-mind.

Well, we can apply the same rationale effectively if we have an option about when to have multiple points of contact with a company or hiring manager.

One contact a day for several days in a row wins every time.

Therefore, you may prepare a thank you e-mail to each of the individuals with which you interviewed, but don't have the email hit their inboxes until first thing the next morning.

Give yourself the gift of a multitude of minor tactical advantages, and you just may find they will add up to an offer.

Chapter 25

Confident Negotiating

"He who speaks first loses."
— Author unknown

Yuck. You knew it was coming.

But, really, it's just a natural next step after they make you an offer. Which is what you have been wanting all along.

OK. Now for the fundamentals. Negotiations begin when an *offer is made and not before*. An offer relates to specific compensation for performing the duties of a specific position and, often, for realizing a specific result. An offer *is not* someone asking you how much money you would want if you were to come to work for them.

You need to know the difference.

An offer is not: "We really like you and, if your references check out, we want you to work with us."

An offer is: "We are offering you the position of customer service representative for $14.50/hour, plus benefits."

In almost all cases, it is wise to **avoid any discussion of compensation or benefits prior to an offer being made.**

Sometimes, of course, there is no choice in the matter.

Filling out an online application will often force you to fill in the blank from a drop down menu offering choices for your desired salary. But if somebody asks you what your salary range is, you need to become a master of the finesse and put off answering the question.

Pre-Negotiations

What should your response be if someone asks you *"How much will you be looking to make?"* during a networking or interviewing dialog?

It is important to know you answer in advance.

Because, most probably, you will be asked that very question a number of times during your search for the right position.

Well, while you should never state that compensation is unimportant to you, you might respond that you are **prioritizing the right "fit"** with the position and company as your most important criteria.

Another response to hold them off might focus on either the fact that you would **expect to be competitively compensated** to the market (you just don't know what that amount would be, if you are asked, because you've been focusing on finding the right "fit").

Or, you could say that you are **somewhat open in terms of compensation** *depending upon the position and its job duties*. The idea with this response is that you would need to interview to learn more about the specifics of the position. Just make sure to include the "depending upon…" part, because to simply say you are "open" in terms of compensation makes you appear very weak.

Don't blow it by responding with a number or range if they pressure you.

That number or range you give them could be too high and so you'll be excluded from the interview process.

That number or range you give them could be too low and so they'll write that number down and it will be the exact offer in the future… even if you later find out that the specific duties of the position will take 5 years off your life.

That's right, this is akin to another Goldilocks analogy.

If you were, say, making a big purchasing decision in your life, would you enter into negotiations before having seen the product or service?

Absolutely not.

Hold the line until an offer is on the table. **He who speaks first loses.**

1-2-3 Negotiating

I know, I know…you just want a simple way to get the money!

I don't blame you.

But there's a little more you need to know about negotiating.

Here's my standard, simple, three-step negotiating framework (*once an offer is made*)...

> *Step One*: Show **ENTHUSIASM** for joining their team.

> *Step Two*: Ask any and all **QUESTIONS** you may have.

> *Step Three*: **NEGOTIATE** for either a little or a lot more money.

Now, let's examine these three steps in more detail...

Step One: *Show ENTHUSIASM for joining their team.*

Showing your enthusiasm seals the deal.

It is all well and good to acknowledge the offer and say "thank you," expressing sincere appreciation. But "thank you" won't really matter much to the company. So, if you need to do it for yourself, go ahead. But a "thank you" has minimal impact. And it could even backfire.

Hey, the offer is NOT a gift they just gave you. It is an option to work your fanny off for some greenbacks. A trade. Hopefully, a fair trade.

But showing enthusiasm *validates* their choice to make you an offer by telling them you are eager to join the team and get started. It signals to them that they made the right decision in picking you.

Your enthusiasm matters to them. A lot.

This concept runs counter-intuitive to most life negotiations, of course.

After all, you wouldn't walk right into a car dealership and simply tell the salesperson of your enthusiasm to purchase a certain car, would you?

But, in response to a job offer, if you choose to stiffen up and simply give them a formal thank you for the offer, you run the risk of deflating their interest and placing your own negotiating leverage in jeopardy.

Tell the hiring manager that you are "excited at the prospect of working for the company"..."because of the fit" and "because you know that you will get results for them" and "because you can also see yourself developing professionally."

Note: while you don't want to go overboard here, it can also be useful to reiterate your enthusiasm for joining the company a couple times throughout a longer, more drawn out negotiation process. Essentially, you would be reminding them that they still want you!

Step Two: *Ask any and all QUESTIONS you may have.*

This is your chance, your one-and-only chance, to ask any and all questions you may have. About benefits—how much they will cost, when they are available, specifics about the plans, and so forth. About the particulars of the compensation structure. About flextime. About workspace, the normal workday, or other details of the job. About resources—including cell phone, travel, laptop, and reimbursement.

And about anything else of importance to you.

<u>I repeat, this is your one-and-only chance.</u>

You need and deserve to know the full details of the offer in order to consider it purposefully and then negotiate with all the information at your disposal. *After all, you are never worth more than the moment before you say "yes" to an offer.*

I strongly recommend you <u>make a list of all the potential QUESTIONS</u> you might have for a company and stick in a folder. Do it right now.

Step Three: *NEGOTIATE for either a little or a lot more money.*

Here you have a choice between the purple pill and the green pill.

Notice that I did not say you had a choice to simply accept their offer. Notice that. Of course, you can just accept the offer. I'm not going to scold you for accepting a job offer! But hear me out first…

One of the most important concepts to remember here is:

Negotiating shows confidence.

I almost always recommend to clients that they *try* to negotiate.

Even if they are satisfied with an offer, pushing gently and respectfully for just a bit more shows their confidence and sets the stage for a strong start on day one of the new job. Even if the hiring company doesn't budge on its offer.

After all, a key to the whole networking and interviewing process is showing your confidence. So, of course, confidence is also crucial to transitioning into the job.

I could recount story after story. Suffice it to say that making an attempt at negotiating almost always gives you an advantage.

Do you believe in yourself or not?

Show your professional confidence, stand on your own two feet, and let them know that you're worth it.

Just like when you show enthusiasm, showing your confidence by negotiating will validate their decision to make you an offer.

The Purple Pill — Asking for *just a little more...*

In this option, you are just going to push back, gently.

For most of you, this probably amounts to hoping for another $1-2K per year or $.50-1.00 per hour. If the offer was in excess of $100K per year, then you might be hoping for $2-4K extra. Essentially, you are prepared to accept their offer, "as is." But you have confidence in yourself and your value (and want them to know you do) so you are going to take a low risk approach and counter offer by saying something like:

> "I am genuinely excited about the position and your company; I want to make this work. In that spirit, I would really appreciate it if you would take this offer back and just see whatever else the company might be able to do."

Of course, your tone in delivering this message needs to be just right. And, please note that you will not be asking a close-ended question, but will be using an OPEN-END STATEMENT. Always.

In using an open-ended approach, you are not really making a counter offer but instead asking them to put more money on the table. Who knows? Instead of thinking that you would accept another $1-2K, maybe they'll just come back with another $4K! Or, in the very least, they should appreciate you standing up for yourself.

By the way, what is the *compounded* value of another $2K per year now, considering raises built upon that base, over the next 25 years? A lot.

Of course, I suppose there is always the risk in negotiating that the company could withdraw the offer. I have never seen it happen, but there is always the risk. But, if you took this gentle, respectful approach and they did rescind the offer, what would that tell you about how they treat employees? Would you want to work there anyway?

The Green Pill—Needing another 5-10%+ to accept the offer...

In this option, you have a red line. You need additional money or benefits to be able to accept an offer. It might be another $1.50 per hour or another $5K. But you need the money to meet your financial obligations. Otherwise, you will have to walk.

So, in this option, you need to make a counter-offer.

The counter offer will be in terms of a range. But you would NOT say something like "I would need your offer of $50K per year to be increased to somewhere in the range of $55K—$60K per year in order to accept.

Why not?

Because you are always hoping for the high end of the range...and *they will always hear the low end of the range*. If they are willing to agree to a figure within your range, your hopes of getting anything other than $55K just went out the window. So, just as with the Purple Pill option, we want to leave things a bit open to their interpretation. You might say something like:

> "I am genuinely excited about the position and your company; I want to make this work. But, I will need an annual salary well into the 50s."

or

> "I am genuinely excited about the position and your company; I want to make this work. But, I will need an annual salary in the mid-50s to low 60s."

You are leaving it somewhat up to their interpretation, which could only advantage your position in this scenario.

Again, of course, your tone in delivering this message needs to be just right. Additionally, you better know when to be quiet. Let me repeat that key tenet of any negotiation: **he who speaks first loses.**

When the company comes back with their next number, 95% of the time, that will be your signal to either accept or reject. Negotiation complete. With the exception of senior manager and executive positions in this day and age, there are few negotiations that continue beyond this point. The candidate pool is just too deep and strong.

I could go on and on about negotiation strategy but, hopefully, you now have a template that will provide a foundation for success.

I know—you still have doubts. So, you have me down on my knees, as I do everything I can to look out for your interests. If you just can't seem to stomach any kind of negotiating on your own behalf, then…

Do it for Tiny Tim

Hey, look, I despise negotiation as much as any of you.

So the only way I will convince myself to do it is if I have the strongest of motivators. Like feeding the family.

If you can't negotiate for your own benefit, do it for someone else's.

Dig deep and remind yourself that you work not only to make a difference in the world but also to provide food, clothing, and shelter for those you love (if you are single, do it so someone else doesn't have to pay your rent). Don't let them down. Screw up your courage, think of your loved ones, and stand up for your professional value. If it's not a matter of honor and dignity, make it a matter of love.

Now, go get the cash!

Post-Negotiations

After you have *closed the deal* and have an agreement to start work for a new employer, don't take your foot off the accelerator.

While organizations bear responsibility for orienting you and for giving you the physical tools to do the job, you are responsible for your own "onboarding," which is: making sure you hit the ground running, establishing a high level of credibility from day one, building key relationships quickly, avoiding any missteps, and identifying how to get some "quick wins" early. Especially if you are entering an unfamiliar organization or position, onboarding needs to be well-planned and executed. Invest some time considering these tips:

Research the Culture: You started doing this before the interview but now it's time to go deeper. Ask current employees, past employees, customers, and key stakeholders about culture and unwritten rules/norms. Determine unspoken ways of communicating, how to build relationships, and common methodologies. Identify potential mentors and support team.

Research the Company: Know the business cycle and where you are entering into it. Know who your customers are—internal and external—and know their perspectives.

Keep the Emotional Support Team in Place: You had this during the career transition or job search. Even though a new role is exciting and positive, it is not time to cut your lifelines.

"Sharpen the Saw": Embrace the 7th habit in Stephen Covey's *7 Habits of Highly Effective People*: identify skills to turbo-charge or update. Close any training, knowledge, or skills gaps. Do this before your first day.

Welcome Yourself: They will welcome you, but you need to be proactive. It is your responsibility to make useful professional bonds.

Get Your Messaging Right: You get one chance at this. What message do you want to send? How are you going to do it? It must be clear, consistent, and congruent with why you have been hired. Make it easy for people to size you up and safe for them to approach you.

Develop a Plan: Common frameworks for onboarding plans are: "research-engage-produce," "acquisition-accommodation-assimilation-acceleration," and "30-60-90." Research these templates or make up your own but be sure to set daily objectives and execute them.

Immerse Yourself: Avail yourself of all resources: company directories, organizational charts, blogs, mentoring programs, and the like. Go to/participate in events, in-house talks and professional development programs, voluntary committees and task forces. Make time.

Be Ready to have Less (or More) Power: One big stumbling block can be a change in the amount of control or power you have, as compared to previous roles. Accept feelings of vulnerability.

Be Ready for Shifting Roles: You were hired into one role. However, within 60-90 days, even though your title may not change, your role may already start to shift. Be aware of and open to change.

Get the Quick Wins: Focusing on a six-month objective in the first 30 days is one strategy, but you might not last much longer than 30 days without results. Or you might not build enough momentum to achieve credibility. Identify and pick the low hanging fruit in the first few weeks. A couple quick wins will assure credibility for bigger projects and any unexpected rough seas. Build trust ASAP.

Be Open to Learning: Remain open to and seek out constructive feedback from day one, as long as it comes from a trusted source. Ask for help when needed. Look for ways to learn more effectively.

Appendix

Sample Resumes

This appendix is not why you bought the book.

If this was a book about sample resumes, I would have provided significantly more samples representing a wide variety of formats. Indeed, there are many effective formats available. Instead, this book is about the detailed process of writing and using an effective resume, with my preference for the "one resume" format I have developed.

Think of the samples as "assists" to help you visualize the end product.

On the following pages, you will find 27 sample resumes - each created in my "one resume" format and each, with the exception of only a couple of the samples, representing an actual client who has engaged my services. Among the samples are 6 resumes from senior managers, 4 from recent college graduates, and 5 from individuals transitioning from military to civilian employment. These resumes helped my clients get noticed. May the resume you create do the same for you.

SYDNEY S. SAMPLE

56 GARRAND COURT
ANYTOWN, CA 00000
      WWW.LINKEDIN.COM/IN/SSAMPLE
      000-000-0000
SSAMPLE@QQQEMAIL.COM

Leadership of advertising production efforts for $1M+ accounts in fast-paced, competitive market environments. Warm, accepting, and energetic style engenders immediate trust and a feeling of connection at all levels of an organization, building a platform for productive change and growth. Balanced account management approach highlighted by cost containment, internal process efficiencies, and highest levels of client trust and confidence. Areas of core competency:

- **Account Management**
- **Television Commercial Production**
- **Advertising Analysis**

EXPERIENCE

NVQ WORLDWIDE, Anytown, CA   2009-present
   Production Lead - KLL Account
   Managed television commercial production department on KLL advertising account.

- Saved $120K annually in production overages by design of internal systems and processes.
- Oversaw $7M+ production budget's financial tracking and money management.
- Created efficient contractor RFP process, tripling the number of proposals generated and increasing saving $280K per year for client company while maintaining service quality.
- Managed all related live meeting and media projects. Held full responsibility for client satisfaction, budget, schedule, and final product.
- Led 8 person team in increasing account's overall customer service rating from 2.8 to 3.6 on a 4.0 client service satisfaction scale. Re-wrote scale to be utilized on a bi-monthly basis.

JFR PRODUCTIONS, Anytown, NY   2006-2009
   Producer / Owner
   Co-created production company, serving as producer of corporate films and television commercials. Brought clarity and order to all project and production challenges while maintaining highest level of client satisfaction. Served as consultant and sub-contractor to larger production companies.

- Teamed with partner to grow company to 6 employees and 14 clients, with $2M in billings annually.
- Developed team and related infrastructure to yield more effective client business practices.
- Managed all aspects of production, including client relations, budgeting, scheduling, talent casting, hiring and leading crews, booking equipment, location scouting, set building, post-production activities, negotiation with vendors, and problem resolution.

HGR ADVERTISING AGENCY, Anytown, NY   2005-2006
   Production Business Specialist
   Supported television commercial production on GTH Automotive and VCD Fast Food accounts, each with $10M+ advertising budgets. Partnered with producers at all stages of process.

- Created and tracked detailed budgets. Saved $120K by negotiating with vendors and production companies. Involved with talent casting and scheduling as needed.
- Served as key liaison between VCD Company, account management, and production department.

EDUCATION

24 credits towards MS in Multi-Media Advertising, YTR University, Anytown, CA
Advanced Research Project on "Effects of Integrated Social Media-Television Advertising Campaigns on Y-Generation Consumers"

BS in Communications, JGT College, Anytown, NY
Minor in Accounting

SABRINA S. SAMPLE

57 GREENLAWN LANE　　　　　　　　　　　　　　　　　　　　　　　　　　　　000.000.0000
ANYTOWN, RI 00000　　　　　　　　　　　　　　　　　　　　　　　　　ssample@qqqemail.com

---

Versatile and highly productive with experience in operating many types of commercial vehicles and machinery, as well as performing functions requiring precision and safety. Proven work ethic, team orientation, and ability to learn new techniques and tools quickly and easily. Takes pride in exceeding efficiency and quality standards. Core strengths:

RESULTS MOTIVATED
Achieves objectives related to both quality and productivity of work. Continually seeks to improve, remaining open to feedback and challenging self to exceed standards. Solves problems efficiently.

TEAM ORIENTED
Commits to team success, always mindful of personal performance and of helping group effort. Builds relationships at all levels in an organization, helping everyone to remain focused on tasks.

LEARNING FOCUSED
Seeks opportunities to learn new skills and processes, develop to a level of mastery, and assist others to promote team success. Eager and fast learner. Committed to excellence.

EXPERIENCE

ECD PRINTING COMPANY, Anytown, RI　　　　　　　　　　　　　　　　　　　　　　　　2012 - present
Printing Press Operator III
Responsible for setting up and running offset presses for top custom stationary producer.

- Exceeded productivity goals consistently, with 2011 and 2012 results at 111.72% and 122.56%, respectively. Maintained spoilage rate below the 5% goal and remained committed to quality.
- Recognized for team attitude and ability to remain open to feedback via promotions to higher levels of proficiency each year. Troubleshot machinery.

CXB GYPSUM, Anytown, MA　　　　　　　　　　　　　　　　　　　　　　　　　　　　　2006 - 2012
Warehousing Specialist - *Gypsum Wallboard*
Served in versatile warehousing role, operating fork lifts and other machinery to move yard material.

- Operated different types of machinery, including CAT, Toyota, and Hyster fork trucks, CAT and Volvo front end loaders, and Kubota and John Deere backhoes. Ran Marklift, Varsalift and Aerial Lift hydraulic lifts. Focused on safety while maintaining high rate of productivity.
- Stacked 50,000 lb. loads 50' high with ¼" variance. Traveled safely at speeds up to 20 mph.
- Performed welding, used oxygen/acetylene torches. Operated various power and hand tools.

ZWS TREE EXPERTS, Anytown, CT　　　　　　　　　　　　　　　　　　　　　　　　　　2000 - 2006
Foreman - *Utility Bucket*
Utilized critical thinking and supervisory skills in versatile, front-line role.

- Provided hands-on supervision to small crews which removed tree-related obstructions and performed other tasks. Adjusted to a unique situation on each job, utilizing critical thinking skills and operating various types of machinery, including 150' high crane, wood chippers, bulldozers, lifts and fork trucks, and class B vehicles / trucks. Maintained safety at all times.
- Responded to emergency situations, including ice storm of 2002 which was marked by 67 days without power. Cleared Great Lake right-of- ways, involving 208 of 210 poles being down.
- Held various licenses and certifications, including: Maine State Arborist, R.O.W. Pesticide Applicator, and Certified Tree Climber.

EDUCATION

Certificate - Professional Photography, intensive 10 month curriculum, ECD Institute
Certificate - Black and White Program, 10 month curriculum, KLJ School of Photography
Certificate - Graphic Arts, Anytown Regional Technical Center
Diploma - Anytown High School

SOPHIA S. SAMPLE

904 LILLYWAFFLE AVENUE WWW.LINKEDIN.COM/IN/SSAMPLE 000.000.0000
ANYTOWN, CT 00000 SSAMPLE@QQQEMAIL.COM

Customer satisfaction focused with accomplished background in marketing coordination, sales, and project management. Expertise includes conducting market research, understanding motivators, and solving problems. Proven ability to open new accounts and close business. Builds trust quickly and easily at all levels of an organization through positive energy, helpfulness, and initiative. Effective in individual contributor, team member, or project lead roles. Core strengths in:

- MARKETING AND SALES
- NEW PRODUCT SUPPORT
- CUSTOMER SERVICE

EXPERIENCE

UUW COMPANY, Anytown, CT 2011-2014
Sales and Marketing Coordinator
Coordinated residential project sales for 160+ employee manufacturer of windows and patio doors.

- Supported 30 independent sales representatives across the country, with average of 6-8 in-person and 35-45 telephone conversations per representative per year. Also responsible for relationships with 2 major distributors of patio doors and windows. Traveled 75%.
- Served on 5 member team for new product development to expand offering from 1 to 6 products, targeting higher-end residential market. Conducted research, analyzed data, coordinated elements of design, coordinated with engineering in prototyping, assisted in building campaigns, and scheduled launches.
- Redesigned and helped deliver product training sessions for dealers nationally.
- Teamed with representatives to attend 5 major account sales calls per month. Proposed program of bringing representatives to plant for residential side product training.
- Coordinated with advertising firm to developed new product literature, including residential book, 5 product sheets, commercial literature, trade show materials, and new website.

HXG CONTEMPORARY INTERIORS, Anytown, OR 2009-2011
Sales Specialist
Member of national sales team for 20+ employee company producing paneling systems.

- Grew account revenue through expansion of multiple-channel customer base. Supported efforts of internal and external sales forces as needed.
- Co-redesigned trade show booth and presence – attending 2 regional shows and 5 customer-based area shows – transitioning from 10 x 10 to 20 x 20 space allocation.
- Learned and implemented process to capitalize on 300+ inquires/month. Trained on new networked sales automation system, call center, literature fulfillment, and field follow-up.
- Assisted marketing with development of high quality merchandising and sales tools.

MQP ENTERPRISES, Anytown, OR 2007-2009
Account Representative
Executed marketing strategies for 1,200 employee manufacturer of windows and patio doors for nationwide network of dealers and distributors. Promoted from contract position.

- Marketed 3 brands and 20 lines to architectural design community on the corporate level.
- Redesigned database to provide insights into needs, changing conditions, and future products.
- Co-created inter-departmental support group to provide internal backup to field sales team.
- Selected as 1st non-employee/contract member of President's Sales Group. Realized results by clearly defining architectural channel sales process and developing related tools.

EDUCATION

BS in Business Administration, University of PLV, Anytown, WA

SIENNA S. SAMPLE   000.000.0000
984 WINDY WAY   SSAMPLE@QQQEMAIL.COM
ANYTOWN, CT 00000   WWW.LINKEDIN.COM/IN/SSAMPLE

Conscientious and talented in CNC programming and machining processes, with versatile manufacturing supervision and project background. Effective in team and independent roles. Productive and calm when under deadline. Easy going style relates well to all levels and fosters winning-as-a-team environment. Serves as a technical resource. Core strengths:

CONTINUOUS IMPROVEMENT INITIATIVES: Takes initiative to explore, suggest, and implement process improvements throughout the floor. Assisted on R&D and projects, such as new heat sinks.

CNC PROGRAMMING AND MACHINING EXPERTISE: Recognized as SME / subject matter expert in CNC programming and troubleshooting. Improves efficiency through programming, setup time reduction, new tooling, cycle time reduction, and coaching other machine operators.

PRODUCTION SUPERVISION AND LAYOUT: Serves as supervisor for all 3 shifts on an as-needed basis. Big picture and tactical understanding of production organization and processes.

EXPERIENCE

WFG MANUFACTURING, *formerly known as MCQ Tool and Die*, Anytown, CT   1991-present

Engineering Technician / CNC Programmer / Supervisor
Served in versatile supervisor/lead, CNC, project, and production roles for manufacturer of commercial fuses with site employment ranging from 250-800+.

- Improved Mazak cell by adding conveyor system. Result was savings of 3 fte positions and reduced footprint in lights out mode during weekend. Recognized with Responsibility award.
- Saved $20K+ per year by replacing shop's metal cutting coolant with MQL / Minimum Quantity Lubrication system. Actions also led to decrease in waste material and became big step in going green. Recognized with 2nd Responsibility Award. Efforts over 14 month period included:
    - Testing products for 2 months to determine best replacement option for water soluble oil coolant. Recommended change to Accu-Lube lubricant and Spider Cool dispensing units.
    - Converting all machines to MQL during the next year.
    - Reclaiming floor space from coolant recovery, storage, and transport equipment.
- Maximized production by completing entirely new floor layout for 50,000 square foot plant and approximately 100 assemblers and machine operators. 3 month project included:
    - Utilizing Cadra to design the layout, updating drawings as needed.
    - Diagramming for safety - exits, fire extinguishers, safety glasses, and safety shoe zones.
    - Coordinated individual machine and resource needs across 6 departments.
    - Teamed with consultant and 4 person group to work out material flow throughout plant.
- Setup reduction in primary machine department, standardizing tooling and fixtures.
- Programmed and proofed part programs on all CNC equipment for production floor. Edited and proofed robot programs for machine tending operations.
- Designed new manufacturing tooling and fixtures, enhanced processes, and analyzed job methods Held numerous previous positions, including CNC Programmer and Machine Operator.

EDUCATION

Diploma, Anytown High School, Anytown, NY

SELECT MACHINING EXPERTISE

Mazak Integrex 200-IV ST with Mazatrol Matrix controller, Haas Super VF 2 mill, Mori Seiki MVJR mill, Mori Seiki Partner M-300 mill x2, Matsuura RA-1F mill, Cincinnati Sabre 500 mill, Mori Seiki SL-00 Lathe, Mori Seiki SH-400 horizontal mill x2, Cincinnati Avenger lathe x2, and Mori Seiki SL25 and ZL 25 lathes.

SOLOMON S. SAMPLE, FNP-BC

45 LEAF LIMIT LANE
ANYTOWN, MT 00000

000.000.0000
ssample@qqqemail.com

Guides patients to care for their own health through education, empowerment, and empathy.

PATIENT - PROVIDER RELATIONSHIP
Utilizes patient centered approach in developing mutually agreed upon healthcare goals. Clearly outlines provider and patient responsibilities. Reputation for providing exceptional, well rounded care. Known for genuine caring and warmth.

HEALTH PROMOTION
Maximizes individual wellness potential via current evidence-based practice guidelines addressing disease management, illness prevention, and screening. Explores alternative therapies as part of holistic approach. Maintains focus on quality of life within framework of culturally competent care.

APRN INTERNSHIP EXPERIENCE

DEVON D. DOCTOR, MD, Anytown, MT   2012-2014
   Family Practice

   Completed 950 hours of direct care working 1-on-1 with board certified physician in internal medicine and pediatrics. Employed humanistic approach while utilizing evidence-based practice and screening guidelines. Managed complex patients with comorbid conditions.

CLINIC AGAINST FAMILY VIOLENCE, Anytown, MT   2011-2013
   Pediatrics

   Volunteered 10 hours/week to help establish APRN pediatric clinic serving 25+ shelter families. Administered well child exams for infants to 18 year olds. Provided wellness education for parents and children utilizing State's Medicaid preventive child health service model.

RN EXPERIENCE

ANYTOWN VALLEY ELEMENTARY SCHOOL, Anytown, MS   2005-2011
   School Nurse

   Provided family centered care in title one school with culturally diverse population. Created and implemented individualized care plans for children with insulin dependent diabetes, hemophilia, and asthma. Educated staff and families on health topics, disease processes, and confidentiality. Planned and implemented student education on hand washing, hygiene, nutrition, and puberty.

ANYTOWN REGIONAL HOSPITAL, Anytown, MS   2002-2005
   Medical/Surgical Nurse

   Employed patient centered approach in caring for variety of patients: post-operative, wound care, drug and alcohol detox, and hospice. Coordinated care with team of providers to improve patient outcomes, minimize hospital stays, and transition to outpatient care.

EDUCATION

MSN, UNIVERSITY OF MNT, Anytown, MT
Family Practice Concentration

BSN, UNIVERSITY OF MSS, Anytown, MS

LICENSING/CERTIFICATIONS

Nurse Practitioner, State of Montana	Pending
FNP-Board Certified, American Nurses Credentialing Center	2013-2018
RN, State of Mississippi – RN 00000	2002-2011

SCOUT S. SAMPLE

217 CEDAR VILLAGE ROAD   000.000.0000
ANYTOWN, VT 00000   LINKEDIN.COM/IN/SSAMPLE   SSAMPLE@QQQEMAIL.COM

Builds trust quickly and easily with customers and at all levels within an organization through positive energy, helpfulness, and initiative. Analyzes business situations and develops plans for both short term tactical and longer term strategic growth. Effective management, training, coaching, and mentoring of staff at all levels. Collaborative style. Proven ability to open new accounts. Competencies include:

GENERAL MANAGEMENT: Leads B2B and B2C development and internal change to impact margins while controlling costs. Maximizes growth opportunities. *Creates value through change.*

MARKETING AND SALES: Develops strategies to identify high potential prospects and retain existing customers. Skilled at digital research, trend analysis, and product introduction. *Closes new business.*

INDUSTRY RELATIONSHIPS: Builds relationships in all sectors: retail, commercial, factory direct to business, architect partners, and green building projects. *Leverages broad industry experience.*

EXPERIENCE

TRADITIONAL INTERIORS, Anytown, VT   2010-2014

National Sales Manager

Grew sales and infrastructure at 3 year-old start-up on 3rd round of financing. Hired to focus on major account development/retention and marketing initiatives. Built internal marketing/customer service infrastructure and external sales force from scratch.

- Closed 2 new key accounts worth $400K+ and rejuvenated relationship with 2 others.
- Designed and implemented process to capitalize on 3,000+ inquires/month. Introduced networked sales automation system, call center, literature fulfillment, and field follow-up.

DUCK STONE MILLWORK, Anytown, VT   2006-2010

Founder and CEO

Started and grew business to $1.4M with 25+ commercial customers and 10 lines.
Led management, finance, marketing, and sales of 14 employee semi-custom job shop.

- Invested up to 50% of time in marketing and major accounts calls. Created brochures, mailings, catalog, pricing guide, programs for dealers and for customers. Exhibited at NRLA show and developed annual open house which attracted 75-125+ dealers.
- Led 45 day start up effort with 3 person team to secure capital, facility, distribution agreements, and logistics. Responsible for all financial management following launch.

VCF AND COMPANY, Anytown, NY   2004-2006

General Manager

Led 90 day turnaround, restoring customer confidence and staff accountability.
Met with 60+ commercial customers in 1st 3 months. Improved reputation and built high performing culture while fighting declining market and product line constraints.

- Cut losses by up to 50% or $150K+ in 1st year. Reduced inventories, dropped non-performing lines, reduced staff, eliminated truck leases, and changed manufacturer.

GRD MILLWORK, Anytown, NY and Anytown, VT   1998-2004

General Manager – *new location*

Opened new site and grew sales to $6M with 15% margins.
Opened new warehouse in Anytown, NY, growing space from 3,000 to 12,000 square feet in 18 months with 10 employees. Promoted from territory sales position. Led project to build new 30K sq. ft. distribution and millwork facility. Grew to 20 employees and 100+ customers.

EDUCATION

BS, Business Administration, University of NYX, Anytown, NY

SCARLETT S. SAMPLE

7 SEASIDE LANE　　　　　　　　　　　　　　　　　　　　　　　　　　　　　　000.000.0000
ANYTOWN, SC 00000　　　　　　　　　　　　　　　　　　　　　　　SSAMPLE@QQQEMAIL.COM

Recent Writing Samples at: http://scarlett.writersgbxm.com. Password: ssscopy#33

Accomplished and authentic with experience producing compelling copy for financial services, technology, and health care industries. Translates strategy into messaging to drive growth. Quickly establishes smooth working relationships; prioritizes professional respect, active listening, and collaboration. Delivers high quality work in fast paced environments. Core strengths:

COPYWRITING AND STORYTELLING

Persuasive storytelling and writing talent for creating content to stimulate particular B2B and B2C consumer behavior. Produced promos and 2-30+ page samples for financial newsletter niche market. Researches and listens to target audiences to gain complete understanding of consumers. Skilled at generating appealing headlines and direct response copy. Understands SEO and SERP content indexing. Training in: Glazer-Kennedy, CeM, web, and autoresponder copywriting. *Zeros in on consumer motivation by situation immersion.*

CONTENT EDITING AND DEVELOPMENT

Highest level of expertise in writing, editing, and managing content related to blogs, news feeds, press releases, and e-newsletters. Conceptualizes new ways to market familiar products and services and develop new offerings. Helped launch microsite for mobile health IT industry to become sponsored site. Experience also includes leading a monthly business IT publication to #1 market position, with circulation of 32,000. Proficient at audio and video editing. *Manages, edits, and creates content for sustained audience attention.*

EXPERIENCE

PHV NONPROFIT, Anytown, SC　　　　　　　　　　　　　　　　　　　　　　　　　　2012-2014
Communications & Media Relations
Created and edited marketing communications for 700+ employee mental health nonprofit. Highlights:

Copywriting

- Developed ad copy and customized marketing materials across all distribution channels, including traditional display, direct mail, email, radio, TV, and online/SEO. Also completed 16+ ads per year for placement in professional journals.
- Created two-year weekly ad campaign with Anytown Media. Wrote full-page ad copy for 108 consecutive weeks, saving organization $2.5K+ by completing writing in-house. Ads attracted 3 year matching grant and matching funds totaling $300K.
- Provided art direction on photo/video shoots as needed.

Content Development and PR/Marketing

- Wrote and produced original video for promo DVDs, website, and branded YouTube channel.
- Co-develop long-term marketing campaigns based on organizational imperatives identified by the board of directors and senior management team.
- Interview industry experts to support content requirements.
- Managed public relations, responding to 24+ media inquiries per year, producing average of 2-3 public service announcements per month, and developed media relationships.

SCARLETT S. SAMPLE

SCARLETT MEDIA, Anytown, SC　　　　　　　　　　　　　　　　　　　　　　　　　　　2006-2012
Editor and Content Creator
Created and edited specialty marketing content, SEO copy, special reports, white papers, and case studies for B2C and B2B publications in healthcare, technology, and financial services industries. Highlights:

Lead Health IT Correspondent – JNV Computer Chip Manufacturer

- Identified, wrote, and edited online content for hospital administrators, HIT professionals, clinicians and healthcare consultants with readership of 35,000. Contributed blog posts.
- Aggregated industry news content relevant to interests of mobile point-of-care professionals.

Editor, NFGHealthITWatch.com - MNB Media *formerly LKJ Associated Media*

- Helped launch and manage B2B web presence for international health IT industry. Grew website's voice and identity through regular blogging and social networking activity.
- Identified and managed aggregated news content across 6 vendor channels.
- Produced and edited podcast interviews for monthly subscriber-based newsletter.

CXW MEDIA GROUP, Anytown, GA　　　　　　　　　　　　　　　　　　　　　　　　　　　2003-2006
Editor - *CXW Tech News and CXW Media Business News*
Launched monthly business technology news publication with circulation of 32,000, creating vision, voice, and content. Interviewed CEOs to define market niche. Led publication to #1 market position. Highlights:

- Managed development and content of a related website. Site received GeorgiaITSite's annual award for "most recommended" by business leaders.
- Supervised 10 direct reports under tight deadlines to develop publication from market evaluation to first distribution within 2 months. Led phase of rapid readership growth.
- Appeared regularly on The IT Live Hour, a live call-in talk radio show with 75,000 listeners.

ADDITIONAL EXPERIENCE

Associate Editor – *Home Medical Supply News*, CBE Publications, Anytown, GA

Registered Financial Representative, LJU Investment Bank, Anytown, NY

EDUCATION

Graduate Coursework in Creative Writing, CDP University, Anytown, SC

BA in English, HFF University, Anytown, GA

SELECTED COPYWRITING TRAINING

All programs through American Writers & Artists, excepting CeM through eMarketing Association.

Glazer-Kennedy Certified Direct Response Copywriter

Certified eMarketer / CeM

Accelerated Copywriting, Autoresponder Apprentice, Web and B2B Copywriting

TECHNICAL COMPETENCIES

Fosters productive and easy collaborations with graphic designers, leveraging skills in:

Proficiency: Scrivener, InDesign, Drupal, Expression Engine, Celtx, Final Draft CMS, Mac & PC
Familiarity: Photoshop, Gimp, Final Cut, Sony Vegas
Social Media Experience: YouTube, Twitter, Facebook, LinkedIn, Tumbler, Pinterest

SELICIA S. SAMPLE
347 BOULDER HIGHWAY
ANYTOWN, IN 00000

000.000.0000
ssample@qqqemail.com
www.linkedin.com/in/ssample

Accomplished and hardworking B2B sales representative with record of success across multiple lines. Relationship building approach emphasizes listening to individual needs, customizing sales approach, and fitting product features to requirements. Meets marketing goals while maintaining highest ethical and professional standards. Effective in both individual and team sales roles. Competencies include:

BUILDS RELATIONSHIPS
Practices integrity in relating across all functions and range of cultures. Develops connections and closes sales in business units of any size. Leverages experience marketing to primary care physicians in AZ and IN, as well as selling injectables and vaccines for 6 years in hospitals and nursing homes. *Builds authentic relationships based on mutual trust and respect.*

ADAPTS TO MARKET CHANGES
Provides leadership in managing sales cycles marked by shifting standards. Utilizes versatile background which includes having introduced 5 new indications and 10 new products to health care providers through total office call approach. Stays current on all HIPPA requirements and remains sensitive to cross-generational confidentiality. *Learns and masters new techniques easily.*

TRAINS AND MENTORS
Assists new representatives in learning customer accounts, routing, and software. Seeks to support development of high potential individuals and share technical expertise with any team member who can benefit. Creates and leads workshops on new products and competition at POA meetings. Engages in ongoing and collaborative learning with peers. *Believes in "winning as a team."*

EXPERIENCE

MNB LAB CHEMICALS, Anytown, IN   2012 – 2014

Account Executive – IN and southern IL
Sold 200-300 standards of liquid/chemical elements which are used to calibrate lab instruments. Utilized proprietary CRM and completed average of 35 calls per day.

- Sold 16+ new accounts, including State of IN. Targeted corporate and government accounts of all sizes, from 5 employee labs to 500+ employee corporate divisions. Sales ranged in size from $700 to those with potential of $40K+.
- Teamed with 2 others working out of small office to support limited customer service and marketing efforts. Attended trade shows in Clearwater, Galveston, and Edmonton.

GVF PHARMA, Anytown, IL   2009 – 2012

Sales Specialist - Neurology Subsidiary for IN and IL
Sold pharmaceuticals FDX, CGF, and UTY to federal, teaching, and community hospitals.

- Developed thought leaders and advocates to support products. Trained new field reps.
- Ranked in top 20 in the President's Club regional neurology sales force, 2011.
- Received President's Club Regional Silver Level Award for placing 5th out of 55 in zone and 19th out of 207 in nation, 2010.

Sales Representative - Primary Care for IN, IL, and OH
Managed territory for partner company in NH and VT. Sold pharmaceuticals FDX, CGF, KJJ, and UTY to specialists and primary care physicians. Launched OPX.

- Gained OPX formulary status in 3 hospitals.
- Ranked 6th of 65 in region for total revenue and won regional CGF contest, 2009.

SELICIA S. SAMPLE

KJJ STATE HOSPICE, Anytown, IL   2008 – 2009
   Account Executive – eastern IL
   Promoted hospice to physicians, hospitals, assisted-living and nursing care facilities.
- Converted 5 high-end assisted living facilities from competitor services, teaming with nurses, social workers, chaplains, and home health aides to plan conversions.

REM PHARMA VACCINES, Anytown, IN   2006 – 2008
   Territory Manager – IN and southern IL
   Sold pharmaceutical EES vaccine to pediatricians, primary care physicians, and pharmacists. Created new accounts, checked inventory, and ordered vaccine in 140 offices. Informed staff of CDC guidelines.
- Received Mid-West Region Award for achieving 118% cumulative public catch-up sales through February, 2008, ranking in top 35%.
- Received Pharma Star Award for creating step-by-step training for accessing new sales POA slide deck so 40+ sales force could study prior to national meeting.
- Ranked 6th in region of 85 for public catch-up sales, April 2007.

ADDITIONAL EXPERIENCE

KJH LABORATORIES - **Medical Representative** - IL
LMN PHARMA - **Sales Representative** - IN and IL
MBB LABORATORIES - **Territory Specialist** - OH

EDUCATION

BA, Art History, University of VCQ, Anytown, OH

PROFESSIONAL DEVELOPMENT

Dale Carnegie Course in Effective Speaking and Human Relations
LJK College of Cardiac Physicians' Neurology Specialty Training
REM Pharma Territory Specialist Training Program
XCD University Cardiology Preceptorship
LMN Specialty Sales Skill Builder Course

SYDNEY S. SAMPLE

71 SYCAMORE DRIVE
ANYTOWN, IA 00000

000.000.0000
ssample@qqqemail.com

Leads efforts to achieve customer service excellence, market leadership, and smooth running operations. Proven ability to break down processes, analyze business practices, develop strategies, and implement detailed plans for continuous improvement of systems to support profitable revenue growth, brand development, and market penetration. Trains, coaches, develops, and supports team to integrate efforts and exceed objectives. Committed to helping others make good decisions. Competencies in:

CUSTOMER SERVICE DISTINCTION
Develops, integrates, and implements unique customer service programs designed to make already satisfied customers feel "delighted" about their personal experiences. Converts transactional businesses into relationship-based ones focused on brand loyalty, ongoing interactions, and future sales. Fosters highest sense of appreciation and trust by customers.

MARKETING ANALYSIS AND DIFFERENTIATION
Creates systematic and ongoing efforts to analyze both competition and customer trends, allowing customization of marketing efforts to target multiple groups with efficient programs. Provides both strategic and tactical direction in leading customer acquisition and retention.

ACCOUNTING AND BUSINESS MANAGEMENT
Focuses on designing efficient and team-oriented operations to support integrated customer service and marketing. Trains, coaches, and develops staff. Considers tax, risk management, and corporate structure implications. Promotes culture of continuous improvement.

EXPERIENCE

HDF AND SONS ACCOUNTING SERVICES, Anytown, IA   2013 - present
Vice President
Engaged as small business advisor and accountant, focused on growing business consulting and tax preparation business with 5 staff completing 4,000+ returns per year.

- Analyzed business and proposed various growth strategies throughout IA and WI market areas. Increased billings by $7,000 and tax services revenue by $6,000 in IA.
- Assisted clients with corporate structuring, tax advantages, competitive analysis, budgeting, planning, marketing and brand development strategies, internal organizational development, and customer retention.

GHB REALTY, Anytown, IA   2005 - 2013
Realtor – The Sydney Sample Team
Built and sold one of most successful real estate brands in state, with $400-550K of annual gross revenues and 50-68 sales per year. Realized numerous sales accomplishments, including growing to 15% regional market share by 2008 and negotiation of 15 of 17 short sales in 2009.

Marketing and Customer Retention

- Developed print advertising strategy, contrary to industry trend, including targeted postcards to 50+ individual neighbors and past clients for each new listing. 3-4,000 postcards sent annually realized triple effect of: generating new clients, keeping existing clients engaged, and rejuvenating interest of past clients.
- Offered professionally certified stager to increase days on market by 50% and list-to-sell ratio from 96% to 98%, allowing streamlined negotiations. Created educational packages about the process of selling or buying a home.
- Implemented customer survey service to track customer "happiness."
- Designed internal office systems for tracking, communicating with, and seeking regular feedback from customers. Integrated efforts of building referral business with other brokers.
- Developed communication system to constantly touch clients with information. Included feedback interpretation sheet revealing "what they meant" v. "what they understood," 2 week contact, 30 day review, and comprehensive package with "what happens next" timeline.

SYDNEY S. SAMPLE

GHB REALTY *continued*

Business Operations and Management
- Grew and developed unique team concept - emphasizing role of closing coordinator, specialization of buyer agents, and collective winning philosophy. Team concept allowed increase from 30 to 65 annual transactions, improved service, and new marketing strategies.
- Trained and coached team in use of DISC behavioral styles to maximize ability to communicate with clients, present information, and utilize in marketing.
- Recruited to train brokers outside of team and serve in other professional development and coaching roles as "go to" industry sales and marketing expert.
- Implemented pre-list inspection system to reduce liability / ensure no lawsuits.
- Developed office communication systems to increase quality, consistency, and accountability.

WDF AGENCY, Anytown, IA   2002 - 2005
Realtor
Developed brand differentiators and professional team, allowing expansion from 9 to 33 transactions per year, with outstanding customer service. Developed and marketed brand through targeted networking. Invested in significant professional and sales training – courses, conferences, and mentoring. Adopted strategy of continual analysis of competition and customer requests.

PLK AGENCY, Anytown, IA   1999 - 2002
Real Estate Sales Agent
Grew sales from 0 to 9 in first year. Still communicate with all 9 clients 15 years later.

VBR FAMILY BRICK COMPANY, Anytown, IA   1997 - 1999
Cost Accountant – temporary position
Advised family owners concerning product being sold for less than cost of production; discovered via manufacturing cost analysis. Managed A/P and secured health insurance for employees.

JKL CONSTRUCTION / LAKE TALL TREE CAMPS, Anytown, IA   1995 - 1997
Bookkeeper / Office Manager / Summer Camp Staff
Managed A/P, A/R, and general office. Performed fly fishing camp duties. Developed brochures and marketing materials. Assisted in establishing automated customer service system. Efforts to fill 18 cabins for summer resulted in 50% occupancy in year one and 70% occupancy in year two.

EDUCATION AND SELECTED TRAINING

BS Business, *Accounting and Finance Concentrations* – LHN University

DISC Personality Profiles, Leadership University, and Teams & Systems – PRW Training

Win-Win Negotiations, Foreclosures & Short Sales, and Deeds – GHB School of Real Estate

Certified Distressed Property Expert – DPI

SELECTED ACHIEVEMENTS AND AFFILIATIONS

Platinum Club Award Winner, 2007-2009, 2011
Top 25 Team in Midwest, 2004-2007, 2009
#3 GHB Team in Iowa and #12 in Midwest Region, 2011
Board Member – NYH Pavilion House, 2007-2011
Member – Anytown Economic Development Committee, 1999-2004

SEBASTIAN S. SAMPLE

9 LUCERNE LANE
ANYTOWN, CA 00000

ssample@qqqemail.com
000.000.0000

Results focused professional with versatile skills, positive energy, and initiative.

Motivated to achieve organizational objectives. Demonstrates self-direction in overcoming challenges, addressing conflict, and fostering team involvement. Builds trust relationships quickly and easily at all levels. Follows through on details to ensure tasks completed on time and to key performance metrics. Proficient in Excel, Word, PowerPoint, Kronos Payroll, Empower Scheduling, and other software programs. Appreciates an employment culture which prioritizes accountability, ethics, and continuous learning. Effective in key contributor, team, and supervisory roles. Competencies include:

OPERATIONS

Demonstrates high levels of motivation, dedication, and work ethic in meeting business demands through hands-on management of operations. Exercises good judgment and fairness when supervising front line staff. Creates procedures, schedules work flow for 150+ employees, and coordinates administrative functions. Additional experience with purchasing, inventory, A/R and A/P, contracts, brochures, and vendors. *Keeps daily operations running smoothly.*

HUMAN RESOURCES

Performs wide variety of HR functions, including those related to: recruitment / staffing for up to 50 openings at a time, employee involvement and recognition, employee development plans, payroll, personnel record keeping, performance reviews, compliance, safety, training, and employee committee projects. *Diffuses conflict and focuses employees on achieving results.*

CUSTOMER SATISFACTION

Takes initiative to develop positive interpersonal relations with both internal stakeholders and customers. Creates and leads efforts to achieve customer service metrics. Models commitment to the customer and seeks out honest feedback to adjust efforts. Engages with professionalism and respect. *Meets or exceeds expectations of both internal and external customers.*

EXPERIENCE

KLF BUILDING AND SUPPLY DEPOT, Anytown, CA   2005 - present

Associate Support and Human Resources
Scheduler
Supervisor – *Customer Service Desk and Front End / Cashiers*

Selected to serve in various roles in order to focus on significant business priorities of store with 150-200 employees and $30M revenue. Tasks included: advising senior management, scheduling, writing procedures, creating newsletters and other materials, planning events, leading teams, and improving employee engagement. Representative accomplishments in several areas include:

Business Operations

- Met coverage guidelines of 98-101% through digital scheduling of 150-200 employees 2-3 weeks in advance. Interpreted complex forecasts which accounted for differing priorities in 22 separate departments. Served as lead scheduler for 9 store district over 10 year period.
- Created and distributed 6-8+ page monthly district newsletter. Tasks included researching events and news, securing content, inserting visuals, writing to recognize 30-50 associates.
- Realized satisfied customers via supervision of 50+ customer service and front end associates.
- Performed administrative and other tasks as needed.

SEBASTIAN S. SAMPLE

KLF BUILDING AND SUPPLY DEPOT - *continued*

Staffing and Scheduling

- Realized adequate staffing, overcoming significant internal corporate constraints and external competition. Maintained full coverage for 100+ store operating hours/week. Efforts included:
    - Producing detailed annual staffing forecast with monthly variances, following analysis of year-over-year history, market demand, seasonal demand, and sales goals.
    - Coordinating 2 in-store hiring events and 15+ job fairs each year, emailing DOL and local colleges twice each month, and overseeing project and temp hiring for up to 120 days during seasonal demand.
    - Prescreening and coordinating interviews with hiring managers.
    - Preparing all paperwork and compensation rate material for offer.
    - Setting up initial training and orientation of new staff.
- Maintained 160+ employee files, ensuring confidentiality and accuracy.
- Evaluated performance reviews, oversaw individual development plans, and coordinated awards for 40-80 employees annually, utilizing Kronos database.

Employee Engagement

- Managed the 7-10 person "Employer of Choice Committee" which managed annual survey with 60-100 total questions across 15+ categories to identify action plans. Spearheaded or coordinated nearly weekly events and employee promotions to boost morale, including 10-15 fundraisers and 7-12 employee events each year.
- Managed $23K district-wide project in which 40-60+ volunteers each day renovated the DFC Nonprofit offices and warehouse at Anytown Food Distribution Center. Total transformation of facility included: new windows, new kitchen, remodeled rooms, new flooring, interior and exterior painting, and landscaping.

CDS RETAIL, Anytown, CA   2003 - 2005

Business Operations and Administration

Managed custom orders work flow for 30-40 weekly orders and secured payments from up to 12 delinquent accounts each month. Completed weekly payroll for 12 person staff and performed all other HR related functions, including training and reviews.

XFD COMPANY, Anytown, AZ   1998 - 2003

Buyer / Department Manager

Purchased all merchandise for department in excess of $3M, building 20-30 vendor relationships. Managed all contract sales. Scheduled 8-12 subcontractors and staff of 20.

EDUCATION AND TRAINING

AS – History, KJV Community College, Anytown, AZ
Selected Courses – Accounting, LKN University, Anytown, AZ
Microsoft Office Applications, KBN Continuing Education, Anytown, AZ

RECOGNITION

Regional Quarterly HGF Southwestern Territory
District Trainer for Forecasting and Scheduling Tool
District Associate Coordinator of the Year

SKIPPER S. SAMPLE
155 LIGHTHOUSE LANE, ANYTOWN, ME 00000
ssample@qqqemail.com | 000.000.0000 | LinkedIn.com/in/ssample

---

Dynamic HR leadership and innovation to maximize employee engagement.

Energetic and hands-on, with proven business acumen, HR expertise, and trust building at all levels of an organization. Provides counsel to senior management. Takes initiative to analyze opportunities and threats, develop and implement creative solutions, and follow-up for impact. Approachable, professional, caring, and adaptable style. Natural mentor and developer of high potentials. Experience spans various business environments – from slow to rapid growth.

PROCESS INNOVATION

Leads change initiatives and Lean concepts, as appropriate, to break out of constraining paradigms and invest in human capacity. Collaborates across functions to determine areas of greatest need and potential gain. Leads creation of training and coaching programs to support front line and upper level management. Fosters forward and right-minded thinking. *Reduces costs and creates efficiencies.*

HR EXPERTISE HR PROGRAMS SERVICE

Drives continuous improvement through hands-on management of all HR functions, from talent acquisition and employee relations to benefits and compensation negotiations. Implements health and safety initiatives. Builds culture to align with values, while maintaining strict legal compliance. Designs and delivers training programs. Resolves cultural and individual conflicts by tactfully yet directly addressing root problems. Creates handbooks and policies. *Lowers risk and develops talent.*

STRATEGIC LEADERSHIP AND COACHING

Applies business and market understanding to determine how HR can impact strategic goals. Analyzes financial and operational realities. Advises and collaborates with leadership to develop strategic concepts. Coaches and mentors managers and supervisors to increase resilience, develop emotional intelligence, improve critical thinking, and improve decision making. *Turns ideas into action.*

EXPERIENCE

WXD MANUFACTURER, Anytown, ME   2010 - 2014

Senior Director, Human Resources

Created high performance HR team to overcome challenging business conditions.
Led HR with hands-on approach at $470M, 870 employee manufacturing subsidiary serving medical instrumentation, defense/homeland security, and commercial aviation markets.

- Led continuous improvement within non-production group. Utilized Lean concepts with 14 member HR team, implementing Kwick Kaizen goals and quarterly check-ins. Led team to achieve 28 Kwick Kaizens in 2012, increasing to 64 in 2013.
- Managed recruiting/onboarding for 175+ yearly hires. Hired recruiter to save $310K+ in fees.
- Teamed with HR peers on numerous uniformity initiatives, taking lead on writing new 30+ page employee handbook and vacation policy. Assisted with global HR presentation in Israel.
- Initiated consultant-assisted creation of modular supervisory and management training. Program organized into 8 – 6+ hour modules with 25 to 40 attendees/session. Efforts:
  - Improved 220 managers' supervision, coaching, and team leadership skills. Program adopted by corporate and expanded across entire US enterprise.
  - Wrote curriculum and led rollout to all business units.
  - Taught "Emotional Intelligence" and "Conflict Resolution" modules.
- Provided direct and proactive employee relations support. Conducted 25+ investigations.
- Exceeded required 14% cut of $3.9M HR budget by $275K, while maintaining service quality.

SKIPPER S. SAMPLE

PMN COMPANY, Anytown, CT   2005 - 2010
Director, North America Human Resources
Controlled employment costs while maintaining a positive work environment.
Provided hands-on management of all HR services for 400+ employees in US and French locations of world's leading manufacturer of thermal management solutions.

- Supervised US and French HR managers. Interfaced with HR professionals in Europe and Asia to support global organizational initiatives.
- Established efficient processes for expense analysis and developed cost reduction strategies, reducing annual benefits cost increases from 22% to 7%.
- Became 1st of EDS Benefits' customers to design and implement HRA health plan.
- Performed wide range of employee relations activities and managerial coaching. Wrote employee handbook from scratch.
- Saved $240K through research and discovery of medical insurance invoicing errors.
- Facilitated closing of 2 Colorado plants with 200+ employees each. Led 4 CT plant layoffs.
- Reversed double digit premium increases in workers' compensation to annual credits.

TBH HANDYMAN'S DEPOT, Anytown, VA   1999 - 2005
Assistant Store Manager
Drove business results and culture continuity during period of explosive growth.
Exceeded aggressive revenue targets and customer centric measures in fast-paced merchandising environment. Held various roles at 9 different 350+ employee locations, each with 250+M in sales.

Human Resources
- Provided employee relations support for approximately 300 managers, supervisors, and employees, including: monitoring performance, resolving conflicts, conducting training, counseling employees, overseeing terminations, and coaching managers.
- Mentored and trained newly promoted operations managers for VA/MD region.
- Supported safety & health programs. Managed workers' compensation program.
- Involved with all recruitment, on-boarding, retention, and benefits administration.

Operations, Merchandising, and Inventory Control
- Led department teams to achieve $12M annual revenue through creative sales techniques.
- Achieved 98% on-time vendor-to-store deliveries by developing relationships and improving communication. Fostered and modeled excellence in customer service.
- Held P&L accountability. Responsible for $1.6M in inventory at highest volume location.
- Completed 2 year management fast-track training in 21 months, serving in operations, merchandising, and management roles with 13 to 22 direct reports/role.

EDUCATION

RDK UNIVERSITY OF VIRGINIA, Anytown, VA
MBA, *Human Resources Management*
Graduate Certificate, *Personnel Administration/Industrial Relations*

CDP COLLEGE, Anytown, NC
BA, *Business Management*

SLOAN S. SAMPLE

59 SEVEN TOWERS STREET 000.000.0000
ANYTOWN, TX SSAMPLE@QQQEMAIL.COM

Accomplishment and lean focused with ability to lead a team, work independently, or initiate and complete projects. Direct supervision style shows respect for and seeks to remove distractions from high performers. Continually seeking new ways to improve efficiencies and adjust to changing business demands. Manages internal and external relationships with an ongoing focus on productivity, delivering quality results on time, maintaining safety, and minimizing scrap. Core strengths:

MACHINE DESIGN AND BUILDING PROJECTS
Initiates projects to improve efficiency and flexibility of equipment. Researches and analyzes options, engages with engineers and production to make best decisions, designs machines, and manages custom builds. Manages vendor relationships, including quoting and negotiating.

PRODUCTION AND TOOL ROOM SUPERVISION
Prioritizes cooperation and productivity, managing with a direct and respectful style allowing highly skilled employees to remain focused with fewer interruptions. Schedules longer term requirements and immediate needs. Understands managing a union workforce. Supervisory experience includes filling in for 6 months as interim plant manager for operation with 70+ assemblers.

TECHNICAL EXPERTISE
Utilizes versatile machining and tooling background, with high level of expertise in die making and grinding, as well as experience on numerous other lathes and milling machines. Manages the relocation and setup of tool rooms, as well as training new hires in US and Mexico plants.

EXPERIENCE

XJR INTERNATIONAL, Anytown, TX

Tool Room / Production Supervisor
Provided hands-on management of tool rooms ranging from 5,000 sq. ft. and 6 employees to 10,000 sq. ft. and 13 employees. Provided as-needed shift supervision and, at times, led up to 5 departments at manufacturer of commercial fuses with site employment ranging from 250-700+.

SUPERVISION and TOOL ROOM

- Led continuous improvement efforts to meet or exceed quality and productivity metrics. For example, in 2011, improved tool room throughput from 4 to 2.5 days on average, reduced scrap below target to .67%, reduced tin overlay stockouts, achieved cycle count goal of 98%, and came close to achieving component availability of 98% at Juarez plant, In 2012, continued to improve productivity and further lowered scrap to .44% while coming in under budget by $47K. In 2013, continued to lower scrap to .382% and improved WIP, prior to staff reductions.
- Forecasts accurately and takes action to support shifts in business, while containing costs. For example, repairs dies when identified as "high risk" and monitors stock levels for critical parts and blanks. Even with unexpected die rebuilds and other factors, typically controls spending at 5-7% below budget. Maintains vendor relationships for quick turnarounds when needed.
- Assisted in implementation of 5S, including audits and value stream mapping. Served on related teams, including the Element Lean Project. Conducted 5S training for production supervision.
- Created Excel based die tracking system with updates and distribution 3-4 times each week.

SELECT RELOCATION PROJECTS

- Coordinated project to move tooling from acquired plant in Honduras to TX. Supervised moving of 6 presses. Evaluated condition of tooling and teamed with co-worker to set up.
- Managed move of tooling functions, including move of 6 machines to Juarez, Mexico, 15+ machines to Mexico City, and 7 to JRZ Company, a vendor in El Paso. Traveled to Mexico multiple weeks to assure smooth transition.

SLOAN S. SAMPLE

XJR INTERNATIONAL *continued*

CHANGE MANAGEMENT

- Turned around tool room in 6 months; proved competitiveness with outside sources by managing the build of highest quality dies and managing vendors. Production management turned to prioritizing tool room as 1st source for meeting needs. Established accountability, getting team to keep track of their time and activities.
- Took over all outside quoting with engineering and managed relationships with 48 machine shops. Utilized spreadsheets to develop comparison quotes for accounting and senior management. Segmented projects to drive down subcontracting costs and assure quality, save $2-5K/month, and improved delivery dates by 2-4 weeks. Led cultural shift so that tool room takes pride in supporting new product development projects and is responsive to engineering.
- Reorganized ordering and supply for all operations consumables, from cutting tools to paper towels. Created pull sheets to expedite ordering with clear vendor numbers and information. Brought vendors in and renegotiated a lower price and more favorable terms, saving about $10K in 1st year. Works towards goal of "zero" stock outs.

SELECT MACHINE BUILD PROJECTS

- Built cut-to-width machine with resolver technology, allowing set up sensors to talk to feeder, which was also self-correcting. 3 month project realized significant savings by eliminating 3 ftes and cutting down from 3 shifts to 1.
- Duplicated and improved French line, replacing $160K - 20 strokes/minute press machine by purchasing $2.5K Perkins press with $9K of modifications. Increased efficiency to 80 strokes/minute, with 1 machine to make all 63 products.
- Managed 3 day design project to improve machine flexibility, cutting down on idle press time and allowing work on any product. Oversaw J&M machine building feeder mounted on container and mounted side loading bottle jack, with press talking to feeder with 1 pigtail.
- Implemented 20 Ton Perkins indexing system to save $80K+ over alternative and improved operator efficiency on the first shift during a number of months as acting supervisor, simultaneously maintaining tool room supervisor duties. When returned solely to managing tool room, continued to fill-in as needed for production supervision on all shifts.

Previous positions held included: Maintenance Machinist, Toolmaker A and B, and Die Maker.

EDUCATION

STATE VOCATIONAL TECHNICAL COLLEGE, Anytown, TX

Completed 12+ courses toward AS in Machine Tool Processing

SELECT TRAINING

- 5S
- Lean Manufacturing
- Problem Solving
- Access and Excel
- Leadership Development
- SPC Principles
- ISO 14001
- JD Edwards
- QPC
- Set-Up Time Reduction
- Safety Leadership
- Managing Priorities
- Team Dynamics
- Pull Signal System
- Value Stream Mapping

SIDNEY S. SAMPLE

5 FEATHER LIGHT DRIVE
ANYTOWN, OK 00000

000.000.0000
SSAMPLE@QQQEMAIL.COM

Achieves customer service excellence - leading improvements, solving problems, and engaging others at all levels. Drives P&L gains by constant analysis of metrics, strategy development, team leadership, and uniform execution with sense of urgency. Earns trust and respect quickly and easily. Balances proven self-motivation and confidence with belief in success or failure as a team. Core strengths:

REALIZES CUSTOMER SATISFACTION

Focuses on meeting or exceeding customer expectations in a timely manner. Listens actively and genuinely strives to appreciate alternative perspectives. Follows up to receive feedback and continually improve whenever possible. *Always puts the customer 1st.*

DEMONSTRATES SUPERIOR WORK ETHIC

Achieves goals irrespective of extra effort required or environmental stressors present. Operates with consistently high levels of energy and tenacity for getting the job done right. Chooses a positive and professional attitude at all times. *Completes 100% of tasks.*

PROMOTES TEAM INVOLVEMENT

Balances individual initiative with respect for others and preference for succeeding as part of a team. Practices positive regard for peers, subordinates, and supervisors. Seeks to be helpful, communicate clearly, and collaborate in building team spirit. *Energizes teams.*

EXPERIENCE

KRV SUPERMARKETS, West Anytown, TX
Drove customer service excellence and profitability through projects and operations. Analyzed all aspects of store and led efforts in continuous improvement, efficiency, and profitability within increasingly competitive market.

Assistant Store Director – Anytown, OK   2012 - present
Launched customer service initiative which raised CSI / Customer Service Index from a score of 61 to 72 over 4 month period, during which time the store goal was 70 and the district average ranged from 68 to 70.

- Exceeded customer service goals with efforts such as: selection of 8 "Customer Service Champions" as mentors; multi-channel communication with all 110 associates; and 3-4 brief "Huddle" floor meetings each day to celebrate success and brainstorm best practices.

Assistant Store Director – Anytown, TX   2008 - 2012
Led operations and customer service improvements at Biddeford store while contributing to district-wide improvements, teaming with peers to research and execute best practices. Selected accomplishments:

- Led store to #1 ranking in district and teamed with 3 peers to lead district to #1 ranking in company via leadership of customer service initiatives. Improved district Medallia score by nearly 20%. Corporate asked team to share strategies with all 165 stores.
- Teamed with 3 peers in year-long effort to increase stock availability company-wide, realizing improved customer service scores by 1% and $800K in additional sales for territory. Audited and advised territory stores. Established best practices for fresh freight and back stock.
- Reduced perishable in-store shrink to 2.80%, subsequently leading efforts which reduced territory shrink from 3.25% to 2.90% over 3 months. Conducted analysis and created strategy which focused on sales v. shipments, cooler and freezer organization, rotation, coding, merchandising. Trained, developed, and mentored associates across Southwest Region.
- Turned around safety / risk record within 1 year, from worst accident rate to #1 in district and top 10 in company, saving $125K. Location named "Model Safety Store" of the year.
- Championed sales contests and merchandising initiatives, improving store sales. Teamed with peers to incentivize sales and merchandising displays, resulting in $150K district increase.

SIDNEY S. SAMPLE

KRV SUPERMARKETS *continued*

Store Operations Manager – Anytown, OK   2004 - 2008
Managed operations and customer service projects for 100+ employee store with emphasis on SWOT-type analysis, collaborative action, and follow through. Led project to close old store. Selected accomplishments:

- Earned recognition for leading a smooth and efficient transition out of old store location during opening of new location. Maintained high customer service levels, managed inventory run down, coordinated facility cleaning, shut down systems, and transitioned employees.
- Reduced labor costs by about $20K per year per store and minimized shrink across all stores in territory by leading organization and streamlining grocery back rooms and implementing best practices in role as 1 of 12 grocery efficiency trainers company-wide.
- Selected as 1 of 6 Store Operations Managers to test all aspects of a Case Ready Meat Program. Realized most successful implementation but recommended against adoption across company due to unfavorable margin results more than offsetting the 8% labor savings.
- Teamed with 12 others selected from a diversified strata across the company on deli Six Sigma project which reduced annual store labor costs by about $5K and annual shrink costs by another $5K. Analyzed tasks, schedules, physical set up, product mix, and work flow.
- Teamed with 3 peers on company-wide pricing auditor initiative which resulted in customer service score increase of .5% and margin-to-baseline increase of .5%. Audited, counseled, and mentored territory stores concerning pricing accuracy/integrity.

Assistant Store Manager – Anytown, TX   2002 - 2004
Managed store operations after serving in previous Bakery Manager position. Selected accomplishments:

- Served on cross-sectional team in Anytown, NM which developed system to automate bakery production process for all 100+ stores, using captured sales data to optimize floor product mix and minimize stale product. Assisted in rolling out system in various stores. Drove bakery in Anytown, TX to growth of 3% in 1st year and 6% in 2nd year.
- Teamed with peer on district-wide Halloween candy sales effort which resulted in 55% increased sales and 8% increased margin across the district.
- Increased hardy mum sales by 400% and won nation-wide award for "merchandising nirvana" picture through team effort with Floral Manager.

EDUCATION

BS Anthropology, University of TXA, Anytown, TX

AS Business Services, NMX College, Anytown, NM

SELECTED SYSTEMS AND SOFTWARE

Inventory: Inventory Management System with Cycle Reporting used with $1M+ physical inventory, Smart Ops Forecasting, SRO and PRO / Supervised & Perishable Re-order, Excel use for projects.

Human Resources: SWS / KRONOS Workforce Solution: scheduling, payroll, and benefits tracking.

Research: WEBSAS / Web Security Administration System: daily and weekly analysis of sales, billing, and other areas, especially as compared with other stores.

Financials: Microstrategy – business intelligence reporting related to financials, store comparisons, and P&L; Cycle Inventory Reporting – Purchase, distribution, sales, and other reports reconciled weekly.

SADIE S. SAMPLE
122 ANY ROAD, ANYTOWN, MN 00000
ssample@qqqemail.com | 000.000.0000 | LinkedIn.com/in/ssample

---

Collaborative and innovative leadership in enterprise architecture and IT strategy.

Accomplished at applying the right technology to address business challenges across the enterprise, while containing costs and leveraging multiple internal and external resources. Team leadership style includes: communicating a clear vision, promoting cross-functional cooperation, providing clear goals / accountabilities, and offering positive encouragement. Strategic decision-maker.

ENTERPRISE ARCHITECTURE
Leads from a breadth and depth of experience in platform architecture, including mainframe, UNIX, and Windows. Proficiencies: disaster recovery, IT security, identity management, and concepts such as Active Directory. Additional knowledge: networks, firewalls, databases, business intelligence, and data centers. *Drives cost-effective architectural improvements.*

STRATEGIC IT PLANNING AND INNOVATION
Innovates within the business and industry through team efforts and partnerships. Leverages deep understanding of multiple technologies and business challenges across the enterprise to discover areas for improvement, consider the big picture, set priorities, and create solutions for internal business users. *Leads technology innovation for strategic business impact.*

TECHNICAL TEAM LEADERSHIP
Develops, resources, and supports high performing teams in pursuit of IT and client service excellence. Leads followership known for open collaboration, mutual positive regard, and focus on meeting stretch goals. Instills sense of team sacrifice to achieve objectives. *Coaches and mentors high potentials.*

EXPERIENCE

GBH COMPANY, Anytown, TN   2011 - present
Primary Enterprise Architect
Collaborates with IT leadership and the business to ensure consistency of technical direction with overall IT strategy, consults on complex IT solutions and project teams, conducts system reviews, offers architectural guidance, and defines target direction of IT infrastructure.

- Performed in-depth architecture reviews on 140+ projects, resulting in technology or process changes to nearly 50% and information security improvements to nearly 50%.
- Served as technical lead on POS replacement project containing 14 tracks, including customer loyalty, electronic payments, and business reporting.
- Cultivated and teamed with KLL Company eCommerce VP and his direct reports to influence recreation of their product line, leading to substantial improvement of KLL product capabilities in online ordering and curbside pickup in North America and Canada.

Director, Platforms Engineering – *JJH Subsidiary and NHF Subsidiary*
Led 5 teams of level 3 engineers in development, implementation, and support of: 4 mainframes/ 95TB storage, 2,100+ Wintel servers, 379+ UNIX servers, and 9,000+ PC/client platforms with 134,000+ users at 1,100+ locations. $9M capital and $8M expense budgets. Up to 40% travel.

- Teamed with IT executive and peer level leadership to create entirely new IT structure for newly merged organization, including transitioning 100% of managers into new roles.
- Organized teams to create common Active Directory identity across North America and Canada, reducing security exposure and risk through mishandling of AD domains.
- Saved $1.3M+ by avoiding data center expansion. Virtualized 415+ Wintel servers into fewer than 120 physical servers and 65 UNIX servers into 2 large-frame virtualized servers.
- Eliminated 1 of 4 data centers, improved continuity, and reduced electrical costs by 50%+ via team effort. Led move of 4 mainframes, 65 UNIX servers, and 250+ Wintel platforms.

SADIE S. SAMPLE

JJH COMPANY, Anytown, IL — 1993 - 2011

Manager, Systems Services

Led teams of 3-9 engineers each, servicing: 2 mainframes, 200+ UNIX servers, 400+ Windows servers, 170 Blackberries, and 1,950+ PCs. Managed support for 3,400 users of enterprise services, such as Websphere, MQSeries, Lotus Notes, Patching, and Antivirus.

- Created 1st Center for Excellence team to serve as shared IT resource between 2 companies. Result was lower overall cost, improved understanding, and efficient collaboration.
- Teamed with KLL Company to lead design effort for sister company's Active Directory project. During development, test, and implementation, shared staff with sister company for 1 year.
- Advocated for and led "Mobility" project which enabled laptops or logon IDs to function for any employee sitting at any banner at every location. Built trust across the 3 companies and completed on-site testing in TN, IL, KY, OH, Toronto, Montreal, and Mexico City.
- Advocated for and partnered with KLL to lead conversion from SGI based data warehouse system to KLL's X7000 system. Tested and compared potential new system by benchmarking own data on-site with minimal risk and cost prior to committing to 2X version. Creative testing partnership with KLL noted in National Computing Quarterly's centerfold.
- Contributed to Open Source UNIX as panel member for 2 years. Shared examples of how, as an enterprise, it created difficulty and risk to manage and use such an environment as 3rd largest KLL customer of OL configuration.
- Led change to IT team providing 24x7 support to each other, resulting in decreased incident resolution times, creation of email-based trouble reporting, and proactive improvements to server services. Change was accomplished by tiered transition to Blackberries being used by all 28 team members, during time when culture only supported use by executives.

Team Lead Distributed Systems

Created new team to support Windows and Unix platforms, in data center and retail locations. Migrated Network Operating Systems and collaboration platforms.

Senior Technical Analyst

Supported Honeywell retail automation platform and piloted next-generation replacement.

TECHNICAL EXPERTISE

Operating Systems: UNIX – AIX; LINUX; MS Windows Server; VMWare; Citrix.

Systems Design: High Availability, Disaster Recovery, Storage, Backup, and Active Directory.

Identity Management: Reduced or single sign on, access provisioning, and Active Directory.

Information Security: PCI, SOX, and HIPAA.

SELECT CERTIFICATIONS

MCSE / Microsoft Certified Systems Engineer + I
A+ Service Technician

Certified Lotus Professional: Notes & Domino
KLL Certified Specialist XG 7.1

RELEVANT TRAINING

NTL Human Interaction Laboratory
ITSM Foundations
Silicon Advanced System Administration
HACMP/6000 Operating System Principles

Tivoli Identity Manager V2.1.1
12+ Workshops on KLL Campuses
1561 Designing Directory Services Infrastructure
HGF StorageData Implementation

SUMNER S. SAMPLE

5 FULCARO COURT, ANYTOWN, TX

SSAMPLE@QQQEMAIL.COM | 000.000.0000 | linkedin.com/in/ssample123

Operations excellence at the intersection of ideas, people, and systems.

Leads global programs, manufacturing operations and engineering projects, with competencies in product development and quality control. Develops ideas and solutions in lean manufacturing and workforce involvement to achieve continuous improvement, lower costs, improved morale, and customer satisfaction. Motivated by concepts, challenges, and a positive, can-do environment.

INNOVATES PROCESS IMPROVEMENTS
Engages entire workforce to achieve reduced inventory and lead times, improved quality, and lower costs. Integrates value stream mapping, Kaizen, waste elimination, and other lean tools. Analyses and simplifies complex systems, develops KPIs, and drives innovative solutions.

LEADS NEW PRODUCT DEVELOPMENT
Introduces profitable new products on time and within budget. Guides 'concept to launch' process, including product selection and revenue projections. Delivers new product on time through constant communication, milestone tracking, and potential problem analysis.

ENGINEERS HUMAN RELATIONSHIPS AND SYSTEMS
Solves problems and creates new synergies through employee engagement. Relates to others in their own preferred style when possible. Develops motivation and reward initiatives. Approach:

> *Fosters Collaboration*: Creates project partnerships and team efforts through positive engagement of key stakeholders, raised expectations, group objectives, and clear roles.
>
> *Develops High Potentials*: Increases impact of high potentials by removing interferences, offering encouragement, developing core strengths, and teaching self-motivation.
>
> *Coaches to Corporate Goals*: Aligns individual performance with overall business goals, coaching others to overcome obstacles, share achievements, and see the big picture.

EXPERIENCE

JKL COMPANY, *a division of URR Corporation*, Anytown, TX   2005 – present
VP Operations
Led 220 employee operation and served on senior team which turned around company, realizing 30% growth and best-in-industry lead times in declining market. Select accomplishments:

- Created and led senior manager forum and detailed feedback method which systematically collected and shared employee perspectives based on core competencies for the business.
  Result: Noticeable improvement in managers' behavior.

- Introduced lean manufacturing methods and made more effective use of technology in order processing. Initiatives included: coaching department manager to quantify problem, brainstorm alternate solutions, and reach out for IT assistance; involving employees and other internal customers for input and buy-in; upgrading technology; and adjusting the plan.
  Result: 35% labor savings and reduced order processing time by 75%.

- Created 1st truly aligned quality system, with 21 sets of separate departmental goals aligned with overall business goals. Implemented stretch goals for all 44 business processes.
  Result: 10%+ quality improvement in departments with most quality issues.

- Led strategy development process with customer service targets and plans to meet revenue goals for all 14 departments and 270 employees. Created simple, single page document highlighting path to greater profitability while preserving 100% guarantee to customers.
  Result: 5%+ increase in total order volume over 3 month period.

JKL COMPANY *continued*

Director of Production
Led 90 employee production and fulfillment operation, consistently delivering new product programs and improvement projects on-time and within budget. Established multi-brand system within single production flow. Managed NPIs from concept to launch. Select accomplishments:

- Refocused operations on 4 key customer satisfaction priorities and PCE.
  Result: Achieved shortest ever lead-time at highest ever-outgoing product quality.
- Created new value-added metrics and implemented tiered performance-based comp. system.
  Result: Significant improvement in production efficiency through employee motivation.
- Implemented value stream mapping and reengineered inventory allocation process.
  Result: 45% reduction of in-process waste.

OOP COMPANY – Personal Care Products, Anytown, CT   2002 – 2005

Program Manager
Led transition of several product lines to new global supplier in accelerated timeframe by promoting collaboration across different parts of the organization. Implemented brand upgrade across 11 manufacturing centers and global markets. Select accomplishments:

- Proved that fewer items could be tested without increased business risk. Held collaborative meetings between R&D, manufacturing, and suppliers to reduce overall testing burden.
  Result: Completed changeover in 40% of time, while maintaining production supply.
- Pioneered rapid deployment process.
  Result: 8 new products launched in 1/3 of standard time.
- Delivered cost saving program.
  Result: $10MM+ in annual savings realized.

OOP COMPANY – Razor Systems Manufacturing, London, UK   1996 – 2002

Production Services Manager
Managed factory materials planning group, IT and materials control function. Promoted from position as Total Quality Manager. Previous positions held included: Production Manager, Shift Manager, Quality Control Superintendent, and Quality Engineer. Select accomplishments:

- Utilized TOC / Theory of Constraints as methodology to impact planning efficiency.
  Result: Planning horizon reduced from 4 weeks to 1 shift.
- Created dynamic process flow map and simulated potential peak demand scenarios. Utilized critical chain problem solving and DBR concept to eliminate barriers to effective flow.
  Result: 75% reduction in WIP, with 10% increase in schedule adherence.
- Implemented lean manufacturing system.
  Result: 80% reduction in factory inventories.
- Introduced initiatives to increase flexibility to market demand.
  Result: 75% reduction in schedule commitment window.

EDUCATION

LHF UNIVERSITY, Anytown, England
Master's Coursework in Quality Improvement & System Reliability
With exception of thesis, completed all required coursework and exams, with overall distinction.

VVN UNIVERSITY, Anytown, England
Bachelor's Degree (Hons) in Production Technology and Production Management

CEOP / CENTER FOR OPERATIONS DEVELOPMENT, Anytown, France
Certificate in Operations Management

SIEGFRIED S. SAMPLE
4 PHILLIPS COURT, ANYTOWN, PA 00000
ssample@qqqemail.com | 000.000.0000 | LinkedIn.com/in/ssample

---

Results catalyst via objective analysis, detailed planning, and employee engagement.

Action-oriented leadership of productivity and quality advances in both service and manufacturing industries by performing roles related to customer service, call centers, HR, training, organizational change, cross functional teams, and workforce management systems. Balances hands-on project management with talent development through delegating and coaching. Provides strategic counsel and leads with energy and integrity. Motivated by challenge. Core strengths:

PROCESS IMPROVEMENT DRIVE
Influences and teams with leaders at all levels to develop and execute continuous improvement initiatives which impact the bottom line. Focuses on employee productivity, cost containment, and morale as keys to moving forward. *Directs organizational energy toward positive change.*

HUMAN RESOURCES EXPERTISE
Develops and implements sustainable solutions by examining root problems, integrating best practices, and managing change within existing organizational frameworks. Grounds decisions in accurate understanding of all perspectives. *Champions employee engagement initiatives.*

CUSTOMER SERVICE FOCUS
Manages teams and projects designed to achieve customer satisfaction. Listens to customer and employee input, communicates goals and action steps clearly, and follows up on feedback. Motivated by customer challenges. *Seeks excellence in serving external and internal customers.*

EXPERIENCE

CFD COMPANY, *JKL Company subsidiary*, Anytown, PA　　　　　　　　　　　　2008 - 2014
VP HR / Employee Services and Customer Service

Led both internal HR and external customer service functions during tenure, serving as organizational and cultural change agent for market leading manufacturer of custom stationery and wedding invitations. Teamed closely with executive leadership and senior management team in continuous improvement efforts. Select accomplishments:

- Created job grades to bring people in to alignment with market, promoting salary equity and improving ability to hire high performers and high potentials. Utilized Hay philosophy and ensured that compensation and performance improvement plans were congruent, with impact of saving $100K+year and establishing higher levels of accountability.

- Reduced employee attrition from 150% to 9%, significantly improving productivity and morale to position company to compete for "Best Places to Work" status.
    - Designed and delivered training programs focused on team building, securing buy-in and involvement from direct supervisors as well as senior management.
    - Launched retention team, comprised of 20 non-exempt employees, which developed list of 30 recommendations, 20 of which were adopted. Representative recommendations involved changes to compensation, benefits, communications, and recognition.
    - Established a 10 member "Best Places to Work" team which met weekly and brought about additional modifications, including wifi, more schedule flexibility, BRAVO awards, and review changes. Synchronized efforts with corporate assessments.

- Championed wellness initiatives and standing employee team which assisted with adopting many best practices, including tobacco-free workplace, on-site wellness coach, and enhanced stretching. Significantly impacted both attendance and benefits costs.

- Improved company quality by 20%+/- on annual basis through via training, coaching, and interdepartmental cooperation. Typically exceeded 97%+ quality and 96%+ reliability goals, with standards raised higher each year and results approaching 99% for both.

SIEGFRIED S. SAMPLE

VWS CORPORATE GROUP, Anytown, PA and Anytown, CO 2000 - 2008
Director of Call Center Operations - VWS Automotive Services Business Unit

Managed all aspects of call center operations for 2 centers with up to 1,000 associates handling 500,000 monthly calls. Led planning and analysis group responsible for $20M budget. Responsible for multi-site training. Promoted from Manager. Select accomplishments:

- Developed and implemented plans and systems for: enhanced performance management, quality reward recognition / compensation, quality, universal training, and force planning.
- Presented and spoke at numerous events, including ICMI World Conference, ICSA meetings and events, and American Teleservices Association Seminar.
- Led task force efforts resulting in over 20% reduction in attrition for 400+ person call center.
- Set goals, standards and benchmarks for entire operations division resulting in significant service quality improvement and cost reductions.
- Develop and implement associate training plan for exempt workforce.

YG&H, Anytown, OH and Anytown, IN 1994 - 2000
Call Servicing Manager - Consumer Services Division

Provided leadership to 6 customer service centers with over 630 associates handling 250,000 daily customer contacts, while administering $23M budget. Developed and implemented processes and guidelines around a team centered management environment. This included bringing together 4 autonomous unions/labor business units with traditional method of support. Received the National Quality Award, Spirit of Leadership Nomination and Hall of Fame Award. Coordinated and facilitated a "Changing Role of Manager" workshop to over 200 managers.

EDUCATION

BS Finance, University of SRD State, Anytown, OH

SELECT HONORS AND INVOLVEMENTS

Leadership Continuity Program, YG&H
Malcolm Baldridge Award
AT&T Sales Assessment Certification
ICSA National Member – Anytown, PA Chapter Vice President and President
HRASM - SHRM Chapter Vice President

SUSAN S. SAMPLE
4452 SILVER BULLET BOULEVARD
ANYTOWN, NC 00000

000.000.0000
ssample@qqqemail.com
LinkedIn.com/in/ssample

Executive impact involves creating a smooth running, highly accountable, and customer-centric organization through leading and executing strategic initiatives, as well as maintaining operational excellence. Successful track record in analyzing situations, devising response strategies, and implementing programs in an expeditious, cost-effective manner. Partners with key stakeholders and fosters employee engagement and development to sustain growth in the market. Core strengths include:

STRATEGIC INITIATIVES

Administration and Compliance
Develops key relationships and designs detailed action plans to maintain high regulatory trust, resolving findings, anticipating challenges, and heading off potential issues. Led two banks to improved regulatory standing, with stronger internal controls. *Analyzes and solves complex challenges.*

Financial Innovation and Brand Development
Counsels stakeholders and leads brand development strategies to capitalize on market changes. Innovates by listening to and delivering on the experience customers want. Improved balance sheets and financials at several banks and organizations. *Identifies and leads growth opportunities.*

COMMUNITY BUILDING

Builds credibility by promoting and modeling core values, seeking community input, and prioritizing local, sustainable initiatives. Encourages local investing. Partners with and develops products for small business and community organizations. *Motivated by local impact.*

RELATIONSHIP DEVELOPMENT

Engages with Board, stakeholders, and staff to achieve business objectives. Consultative and collaborative style builds trust, encourages initiative, and appreciates alternative viewpoints. Mentors and challenges high potential employees. *Engages easily with respect and trust.*

EXPERIENCE

RKR BANK OF ANYTOWN, Anytown, NC   2010 - present
President and **Chief Executive Officer**
Retained by Board of Directors and Principal Owners to manage overhaul of operations for this struggling de novo bank facing significant regulatory issues in all areas of operation.

- Designed and implemented strategic plan to respond to regulatory issues. Reorganized operations leading to successful elimination of Consent Order and satisfactory regulatory standing.
- Re-energized disconsolate employee base, prioritizing mentoring and development.
- Realized 25+% growth annually in loans and deposits. Tripled total assets in 4 years.
- Reduced Efficiency Ratio from over 192% to 67% in 4 years.
- Eliminated significant operating loss and established Core Operating Profit.

BCV BANK, Anytown, VA   2003 - 2010
President
Executive Vice President and **Chief Administrative Officer**
Recruited to assist in addressing immediate regulatory compliance needs for this publicly traded $270 million commercial bank holding company. Positions also related concurrently to BCV Bancorp.

- Realigned struggling commercial bank to achieve core profitability and satisfactory regulatory compliance. Hired or promoted entire senior management team.
- Created marketing campaign to re-direct and re-focus the image of the bank in the marketplace. Led senior team to join community organizations which covered strategic centers of influence.

SUSAN S. SAMPLE

BCV BANK *continued*

- Managed corporate communications and shareholder relations. Represented bank in dealing with a variety of shareholder issues and SEC compliance.
- Reviewed, analyzed and formulated response strategy to address substantial volume of regulatory violations and non-compliance issues. Successfully improved regulatory relations and ratings from less-than-satisfactory to satisfactory across all areas of the bank, including safety and soundness, information technology and compliance.
- Managed overhaul of policies to improve operational efficiency and regulatory compliance.

SSSAMPLE CAPITAL, Anytown, VA 2002 - 2003
Independent Investor
Managed personal assets, including stock and real estate investments.

RWD INVESTMENT BANK, Anytown, VA 1999 - 2002
Director - Investment Banking
Served as national business development officer, advising broad range of corporate, financial services clients.

- Advised boards of directors and senior management, ranging from international diversified financial services companies to community banks.
- Involved directly in dozens of successful transactions with banks and thrifts, as well as with equity and debt financings. Developed mergers and acquisitions expertise.

XQS INVESTMENT BANK, Anytown, PA 1998 - 1999
Vice President - Investment Banking
Served as business development officer advising depository institutions in the Mid-Atlantic. Completed debt and equity financings, as well as M&As, for regional institutions.

BOL SECURITIES, Anytown, MD 1996 - 1998
Vice President
Created capital markets division of this NASD broker dealer with 35 registered representatives. Efforts included leading successful equity offering for a RI-based manufacturing concern and advising in sale to JMN Savings Bank. Compensation financed law school education expenses.

WRD INVESTMENT BANK, Anytown, NY 1993 - 1996
Associate
Analyst
Specialized in financial institutions supporting dozens of successful transactions, including equity offerings for banks, insurance companies and specialty finance companies. Promoted directly to associate from MBA level, analyst position.

EDUCATION

JD, University of KLN School of Law, Anytown, MD, 1998

Coursework in Business and Corporate Law, Secured Transactions, Bankruptcy, and Corporate, Personal and Estate Taxation.

BA in Physics, XCD University, Anytown, MD, 1993

SANDY S. SAMPLE
22 ANY DRIVE, ANYTOWN, CT 00000
SSAMPLE@QQQEMAIL.COM | 000.000.0000 | LINKEDIN.COM/IN/SSAMPLE

Achieves sustainable, profitable growth through marketing and finance initiatives.

Executive and financial leadership of small and mid-sized private or subsidiary companies. Experience in both domestic and international consumer goods markets and at both ends of the retail price spectrum. Develops key partnerships based on trust. Leverages global finance and strategic planning expertise. Understands power of motivated employees. Core competencies:

STRATEGIC BUSINESS LEADERSHIP

Marketing
Examines customer perspectives and market trends, engaging senior leadership team and key stakeholders to establish strategic plans for change. Communicates clear and concise goals. Leads product development and marketing initiatives. *Aligns efforts with market demand.*

Turnarounds
Leverages finance background and understanding of business success factors to develop and execute comprehensive recovery plans. Improves operational and financial performance, customer satisfaction, and market position. *Directs changes toward sustainable growth.*

FINANCIAL MANAGEMENT
Analyzes complex financial and market data to identify areas for growth and savings in both CFO / VP Finance and CEO roles. Integrates business planning, forecasting, and reporting with corporate strategies. *Creates culture of operational and cost efficiencies.*

RELATIONSHIP DEVELOPMENT
Develops key relationships with both internal and external partners to maximize results. Prioritizes motivation and development of employees to ensure effective decision making. Listens and appreciates alternative viewpoints. *Engages with respect and trust.*

EXPERIENCE

GHH COMPANY | JKL DIVISION, Anytown, CT   2008 - 2014
President and CEO

Repositioned company for post-recession growth and profitability.
Led change at 275 employee manufacturer of luxury stationery products. Advanced new growth category, developed comprehensive digital strategy, and opened up D2C sales.

Strategic Realignment of Business

- Led creation and implementation of 3 Year Strategic Plan with focus on wedding category to achieve sustainable growth in mature recessionary market. Recession took 30% to 40% of the fine stationery market, with some competitors losing up to 60% of their business.
  - Lowered break-even point for "new reality" through business wide cost reductions, including RIFs which impacted 50+ positions and saved $1M+.
  - Implemented and adjusted plan, including development of new product categories and expansion of existing lines.
  - Launched 1st new products 4th quarter, 2010.
  - Realized both growth and profitability by 1st quarter, 2012.
- Changed traditional market focus of company to capitalize on "recession-beating" wedding category, developing new product lines, including wedding favor boxes and personalized napkins. Aligned all aspects of business with new vision and brand attributes.

SANDY S. SAMPLE

GHH COMPANY *continued*

- Developed and implemented first ever digital strategy. This strategy grew to account for 12%+ of gross revenue and 20%+ of profit.
  - *Product* – Developed and launched new products, including digital photo cards.
  - *Manufacturing* – Added digital production capability, including improved pre-press and large scale digital printing and also incorporating new formats, such as witness posters and decals. Total investment exceeded $500K capital value.
  - *Marketing* – Adopted social media strategy into limited marketing budget, including Blog, Facebook, Twitter, and Flickr.
  - *Distribution* –Launched D2C website. New digital asset base: assisted retailers in reaching their customers online, established industry leadership via an in-store digital ordering system, and realized annual double digit sales growth after 1st year.
- Managed top level relationships with all key retailers personally, during business change period. Efforts resulted in high levels of loyalty and customer satisfaction.

New Product Introduction through Partnerships

- Implemented strategic partnership with Vera Wang, licensing and launching new line of wedding products which generated 10% increase in market share. Re-negotiated additional 4 year term, with 25% cost savings.
- Realized incremental wholesale revenue exceeding $1M through "previously unimaginable" partnership with Tiny Prints, a leader in on-line personalization.

Growth Anchored by Employee Engagement

- Generated 3 years of record growth and profits in mature market due to culture of employee engagement. Claimed place as market leader in fine stationery personalization with a combination of product, service and relationship development.
- Realized improved employee engagement and better decision making by partnering with VP Employee Services to introduce "wellness and empowerment" culture.
- Teamed with VP Employee Services to encourage collaboration at all levels. Retained consultants to deliver customized "From Me to We" and "Stepping Stones" programs.
- Championed 3 Six Sigma initiatives, saving a total of $100K annually. Engaged workforce in reconfiguring press stations, streamlining order preparation, and automating pre-press.

JNM COMPANY | SDF BUSINESS, Anytown, NY   2003 - 2008
CFO and COO

Reduced costs through relocating production and creating "lowest cost" culture. Served as CFO and COO of this wholly owned greeting card subsidiary of JNM, specializing in the sale and distribution of greeting cards to the mass channel. Responsible for the finance, MIS, operations and retail services functions. Promoted from CFO position.

- Partnered with leadership team to produce years of growth with strong EBIT and ROA.
- Realized 10 year transformation of unprofitable $15M company into highly profitable $92M company by introducing low cost culture and marketing and sales initiatives.
- Developed 2 cost reduction projects, moving production of boxed greeting cards from the UK to the Far East and moving production of single greeting cards from the UK to the US and Canada. Improved competitiveness in the discount and "dollar" greeting card markets.

SANDY S. SAMPLE

JNM Company *continued*
- Served in key leadership role in transition from subsidiary of a UK plc to subsidiary of JNM. This included the production changes, full systems, warehousing and distribution integration.
- Enhanced working capital levels, including 38% improvement in A/R days outstanding and doubling of inventory turns.
- Improved order turns from 2-3 days to 12-24 hours through operational efficiencies.
- Partnered with CEO, during tenure as CFO, to develop "Low Cost Operator" environment essential for profitable growth in discount greeting card market. Simplified order process for major customers, instituted same day order turn time, created multi-tasking assignments for key functions, and introduced low cost culture.

DWR CONSORTIUM, Anytown, England   1999 - 2003
US Group Vice President, Finance - Anytown, MA
Sold off 3 entities with revenues of $3-8M each, allowing focus on core products.
Served as Group Vice President, Finance for a US holding company responsible for 4 US based subsidiaries of $500M UK public company specializing in the personal expression, greeting card, and gift industry. Promoted from Group Financial Controller.

BXDS CHARTERED ACCOUNTANTS, Anytown, England   1995 - 1999
Audit Manager
Served in role as Chartered Accountant - CPA equivalent - performing various functions, with final position leading external audits of public corporations.

EDUCATION

KRE UNIVERSITY, London, England
BA (Hons), Accounting & Financial Control - 1st Class honors degree

CERTIFICATION

Association of Chartered Accountants - Institute of Chartered Accountants of England & Wales.

SYBIL S. SAMPLE
1296 GEMRADLE COURT
ANYTOWN, NY 00000

000.000.0000
ssample@qqqsampleemail.com
LinkedIn.com/in/ssample

Dedicated law enforcement professional with versatile military police background and interest in local public safety career. Demonstrates excellent on-the-spot judgment and significant stress tolerance. Earns trust of peer team members easily. Follows procedures and functions with the highest integrity and unimpeachable character. Eager to learn new skills.

LAW ENFORCEMENT: Experienced with wide range of police functions, including: patrol, investigations, domestic disputes, traffic control, public de-escalations, apprehending suspects, dispatch, reports, and analysis. Expert level marksman. Recognized for correctly following detailed procedures and extensive knowledge of applicable laws.

EMERGENCY RESPONSE: Trained as EMT and experienced in coordinating with fire, rescue, ambulance, emergency management, and other police forces. Qualified in advanced HAZMAT compliance and crisis response. Acts instinctively to secure public safety.

EXPERIENCE

UNITED STATES MARINE CORPS — 2010 - present

Law Enforcement – Anytown, VA and Anytown, FL

Provided police protection and armed security for communications and training facilities. Deployed on several combat and non-combat missions. Additional duties: performing traffic control and reporting, conducting investigations, and transporting sensitive documents.

- Selected to co-lead weekly night law enforcement readiness audit, examining 45 procedures to be followed by 13 on-duty security staff in protecting base with 29 buildings. Suggested changes in Excel spreadsheet reporting which streamlined audit protocol and increased individual accountability.
- Conducted early morning patrols of 112 housing units and adjacent 450+ acre wooded training area 2-3 times weekly. Interrupted 10+ burglaries, responded to 32 domestic disputes, and assisted in saving the life of 1 heart attack victim.
- Awarded 2nd place small arms marksmanship honors on base for 2 consecutive years. Chosen to serve on panel to review marginal scores of new recruits.
- Received additional training in emergency first response and advanced HAZMAT.

BVN SECURE LOGISTICS — 2009 - 2010

Transportation Security – *Mid-Atlantic Logistics Division*, Anytown, PA

Served in armed security role, transporting valuable documents and cash from retail financial institutions' head offices to and from Federal Reserve, insurance companies, and investment banks.

- Completed average of 3 transports per day in armored cars, without incident. Followed detailed, restrictive procedures and completed all daily reports.
- Cross-trained as backup dispatcher / traffic coordinator.

EDUCATION AND TRAINING

13 of 16 courses completed - **AS Law Enforcement**, SDR Community College, Anytown, MA
Courses included: Investigation I and II, Advanced Negotiation, and Crisis De-Escalation

Emergency Medical Technician

Tier III Elite Marksman Certification

SIMEON S. SAMPLE
62 DEER RUN STREET
ANYTOWN, NY 00000

000.000.0000
ssample@qqqsampleemail.com
LinkedIn.com/in/ssample

IT Security and Systems Architecture

Achieves optimum levels of IT security, consults and builds system architecture to best practice standards, and develops technical proficiency in high potential team members. Seeks to partner with other highly accountable and motivated technology professionals in an environment which promotes continual learning and growth. Energized by solving complex problems to the root and implementing systems to identify and mitigate future challenges. Strengths include:

IT SECURITY MANAGEMENT

Drives improvements in safety of information and integrity of systems to provide uninterrupted usability, even during catastrophic events. Prioritizes achieving triple redundant backups via simple, easy to configure processes. Utilizes six sigma philosophy to promote continuous accountability checking and process improvements. **Secret clearance.**

SYSTEMS PLANNING

Focused on strategic systems planning anchored by proven expertise in platform architecture, with competencies in: identity administration, IT security, Active Directory, Level 3A firewalls, databases, and data centers. Leverages deep network of colleagues and vendors to identify best practices. Leads needs analyses, customizes solutions, and executes changes.

TECHNICAL COMPETENCIES

SECURITY DESIGN	SYSTEMS ARCHITECTURE	NETWORK ENGINEERING
• Selected Access	• Catastrophic Planning	• CISCO Wireless
• Ti67 Restrictions	• Disaster Recovery	• Remote Access
• PCI and HiPPA	• Active Directory	• WAN Accelerators
• Power Systems	• Mainframe, UNIX, & GFD	• VLAN Layout
• Checked Firewalls	• Vendor Management	• Topology Discovery

EXPERIENCE

UNITED STATES ARMY 1987 - present

IT Security Instructor / *Captain* - NHG Military Academy, Anytown, NY
Senior Systems Architect / *Lieutenant* - Combined European Task Force, Anytown, Germany

Served in information security, IT training/instruction, and system architecture roles following rare promotion / field commission to officer grade for performance of duties in Afghanistan. Transitioned from network administration and security background via USC and MIT online education. Core achievements:

- Improved IT security for Combined European Task Force to 99.997% from previous 99.894% rating over 18 month period by: researching best practices, creating inter-departmental Technology Security Team, and implementing new accountabilities.
- Spearheaded effort to achieve double redundancy at 4 secret 3+TB data centers.
- Completed 4 six sigma projects, including $6M upgrade of firewalls on 10 servers linked to 17,000+ PCs and terminals across Europe and North Africa.
- Facilitated 141 student IT security capstone projects over 3 year period, resulting in 11 patent filings and 4 projects selected by Defense Intelligence Agency for further study.
- Co-wrote overhaul of IT security curriculum, including 3 core courses, 6 grant applications, and successful proposal for $35K capital equipment upgrade to 2 classrooms. Taught new curriculum to average of 77 students per semester.

SIMEON S. SAMPLE

US ARMY *continued*

IT and Communications Field Support / *Sergeant Major* – G2 Province Task Group, Afghanistan
Senior Systems Architect / *First Sergeant* – Command HQ, Afghanistan
Communications Technology Team Lead / *First Sergeant* – Ft. NBV, El Paso, TX
Special Forces Technology Training Supervisor / *Master Sergeant* – numerous locations

Provided hands-on network administration, IT security, systems architecture planning, and technical training. Specialized in field support and systems. Recognized for taking initiative to tie all efforts with IT security and readiness to volunteer for critical field missions. Core achievements:

- Created 1st-ever disaster planning protocol for 100% small device reliability in field operations. Tested and re-tested protocol across 3 provinces in Afghanistan and 1 in Iraq, involving total of 12,500 individuals and 42 units. Protocol used as model for similar DOD-wide efforts underway. Served on DOD SDA Reliability Sub-Committee.
- Re-designed network enhancement, involving 24 gigabit uplinks to redundant main from 1,600 desktops. Realized collapsed, high-density data-center network, increasing transfer speed by 30%+ while building space for future revisions.
- Performed in excess of 242 field tests for IT device security protocol, including nearly 40% conducted in combat zones. Findings contributed to 24% increase in mobile device security.
- Accomplished 98.8% average availability of LAN and WAN links during crisis operation and 99.96% average availability during non-crisis operation at the battalion level during 2 different deployments. Simplified test methods and trained specialists.
- Increased remote device performance by 140%+ via installation of HFD WAN accelerators at 5 bases over 7 month period. Conducted ongoing testing to maximize performance.
- Recognized with 3 Silver Stars for distinguished service in combat situations on 3 separate occasions. In one situation, assisted with improvised rescue of captured squad by holding off 20+ enemy combatants for 4 hours single-handedly.

EDUCATION

BS Computer Science, KIT Institute of Technology, Anytown, MA
Concentration in IT Security Configurations

SELECT CERTIFICATIONS

CompTIA Security+

MS Systems Engineer

Information Technology Architect Certification

SOLOMON S. SAMPLE
933 TRISDELL DRIVE, ANYTOWN, VA 00000
ssample@qqqsampleemail.com | 000.000.0000 | LinkedIn.com/in/ssample

---

Achieves emergency preparedness solutions by improving processes and fostering collaboration.

Manages development and implementation of emergency plans, remaining flexible to adapt to shifting priorities and realities. Leads with energy and conveys clear sense of direction and purpose. Seeks ongoing input from across all functions and levels within an organization. Highly skilled in running complex operations which require close collaboration with public and private sector resources. Demonstrates continuous improvement mindset and initiative. *Top Secret clearance.* Proven in various roles:

ARCHITECT OF EMERGENCY PREPAREDNESS STRATEGY

Creates detailed and user-friendly action plans integrated with larger strategies to realize highest levels of readiness for small to catastrophic events. Researches and applies best practices. Involves other departments and organizations in planning and drills. Proven ability to "see" and analyze potential threats and unknown variables. Aligns emergency planning with resource allocation. *Factors in total landscape of variables when designing strategies.*

CHAMPION OF CONTINUOUS IMPROVEMENT INITIATIVES

Increases efficiencies and promotes smooth running operations via critical review and enhancement of existing systems and processes. Bridges gap between expected and actual results by creating simple solutions to complex problems and developing tools to measure effectiveness. Incorporates lean and Six Sigma methodologies right down to the work and project group levels. *Realizes new efficiencies via system improvements.*

DIRECTOR OF SEARCH AND RESCUE TEAMS

Leads emergency-related operations by zeroing in on core challenges and bottom line objectives, requiring full engagement across departments. Always remains open to suggestions for shifting tactics in-the-moment and encourages cooperation at the highest levels. Resolves conflict swiftly and keeps others' professional dignity intact, while finding a productive way forward for all involved. *Builds teamwork through open dialog and action.*

EXPERIENCE

UNITED STATES NAVY   1993 - Present

Emergency Preparedness Management / *Captain* – Central Combined Forces, Anytown, FL
"Sol's style of collaborative leadership insures success when it comes to connecting together numerous public and private entities, as well as the military branches. No one has the ability to herd cats like Sol does. Sure, he has a high level of energy, but you'll find that Sol listens acutely and never tries to force the wrong solution. He gets results, but always at the highest level of integrity …" – Sid Sample, Rear Admiral, USN

- Created first combined forces framework to respond to level VI disasters. 16 month project involved full-time effort by staff of 245, in addition to collaborative efforts of 700+ individuals from 74 federal, state, and local entities; 4 branches of service; and 12 foreign governments. Project model currently being emulated in 3 other regions.
- Managed response to 240 emergency situations requiring close collaboration between 2 or more entities, including Maca-Wacul wave event in which 1,700+ individuals were rescued and 11 of 17 ships were salvaged over a 12 day period.
- Designed and implemented 1st-of-its-kind integrated catastrophic emergency planning IT solution, including double redundancy security. Involved from concept to bringing system online. Managed $11M capital budget and 23 member technical project staff.
- Co-created quarterly TAPM / Threat Analysis and Planning Meeting between emergency management leadership from 10 countries to promote ongoing dialog and cooperation.

SOLOMON S. SAMPLE

UNITED STATES NAVY *continued*

Emergency Operations Leadership / *Commander* – Northern Pacific Task Group, Anytown, AK
"If you want results, you want Sol. His approach involves all parties yet is laser-focused on getting the fastest and best response possible. He is driven, diligent, tactical, and thorough. His only fault is his unyielding work ethic – he must require little to no sleep. Without Sol's help, we wouldn't have been able to save as many lives or build the inter-service relationships to the level we did." – Simeon Sample, Deputy Director, FEMA

OPERATIONS

- Managed operations, $17M budget, and flight teams at 320+ staff base, with 8 helicopters and 32 pilots. Missions included emergency rescue and logistics, environmental response, and anti-terror, with USCG coordination and collaboration on 40%+ of all operations.
- Co-led and coordinated 3 Northern Pacific Rescue Cooperation Summits in Anytown, Russia, with planning meetings in Anytown, Japan. Summits involved 70-110 participants each from 4 countries and improved rescue/emergency planning and cooperation.

CONTINUOUS IMPROVEMENT PROJECTS

- Created, led, and completed six sigma project which used scatter plots to scrutinize monthly budget analysis and allowed 30%+ mission growth with flat funding over 4 years.
- Improved quality of "cockpit" relationships and crew communications by systematically identifying and removing cultural barriers. Created related technical mentoring program.
- Developed advanced safety checklists and procedures to remove 14 previously unknown causes of pilot and crew error. Efforts helped base rank #1 in safety for 3 years.

Flight Operations and Planning / *Lt. Commander* – Southern Pacific Rescue Base, Anytown, CA
"... Versatility defines Soloman. One morning, he's piloting one of those birds on a rescue mission in any sort of conditions and that afternoon he's concocting some Excel macro to improve our flight systems. Darn good pilot. Better manager. I'd like to order up another couple like him ..." – Sally Sample, Captain, USN

- Created algorithms to account for 50% more meteorological variables during rescues at sea, resulting in safety rating improvements from 3.7 to 3.95 out of 4 and improved planning.
- Utilized advanced Excel and SPSS skills to analyze flight accountability roster and missions, allowing improved pairings of pilot skills with mission requirements.
- Operated several types of rotary aircraft in rescue and supply missions for fleet task groups and in response to emergencies. Logged 1,306 flight hours, including 740 as instructor.

ADDITIONAL EXPERIENCE

Rescue Mission Instruction / *Lt. Commander* – CCB Service Academy, Anytown, MD
Intelligence Analysis / *Lieutenant* – Naval Operations HQ, Anytown, VA
Search and Rescue Piloting / *Lieutenant* – Disaster Resolution Pacific, Anytown, HI

EDUCATION

MPA, NHG University, Anytown, MA
BSME, CCB Service Academy, Anytown, MD

SELECT CERTIFICATIONS AND TRAINING

PMP Course - 50% complete
Six Sigma Black Belt
Motorola Invitational Process Improvement Series
Advanced Lean Emergency Preparedness Concepts I and II

SHARON S. SAMPLE
651 HIGHLANDER LANE, ANYTOWN, CO 00000
ssample@gmail.com | 000.000.0000 | linkedin.com/in/ssample

Delivers on-time logistics and operational results which exceed expectations.

Accomplished and visionary executive with high level of energy and motivation for solving complex problems to satisfy demanding internal customers. Detailed knowledge of government procurement processes and management philosophies. Reputation for resourcefulness and ability to leverage C-level contacts within DOD, government, and various defense contractors. Values-based and direct leadership style respects alternative points of view and seeks to turn natural conflict into collaboration. Requires results-driven environment in which integrity is uncompromised. *Top Secret clearance.* Core strengths:

LOGISTICS AND MATERIALS MANAGEMENT

Logistics, Warehousing, and Supply
Leads efforts to manage and exceed customer expectations within environments of increasingly limited resources. RESULTS: Improved 10 of 12 strategic metrics over 4 year period for logistics program involving 74 warehouses, 1,100 staff, and 21.4 million transactions per year.

Purchasing
Controls costs while ensuring decisions are aligned with longer-term strategic objectives and vendor relationships are prioritized. RESULTS: Saved $148M over 3 years via combination of improving ERP systems, bundling contracts, and introducing six sigma program.

OPERATIONAL LEADERSHIP

Leads continuous improvement and talent development initiatives focused on realizing better decisions at all levels of the organization. RESULTS: Achieved highest-ever levels of readiness and morale at 6 locations through 18 month "Top Flight" initiative.

STRATEGIC CONSULTATION

Advocates and models servant-leadership approach which prioritizes "going above and beyond" to build key relationships in which mutual sharing and advising is prized. RESULTS: Consulted to and served on numerous inter-service task forces, including the Joint Aircraft Engines Analysis Committee which streamlined $440M in combined purchasing contracts, realizing $22M in savings while increasing quality benchmarks.

EXPERIENCE

UNITED STATES AIR FORCE 1990 - present

Senior Executive - Logistics | *Major General*

Led reorganization of 2 programs representing 78% of all organizational traffic.
Advanced change in 3 logistics programs, including all purchasing and warehousing functions, to reduce costs, improve accountability, and create continuous improvement cultures. Senior leader with P&L responsibility at Anytown, CO; Anytown, TX; and Anytown, NB locations.

Strategic Reorganization of Anytown, CO Base Logistics

- Led development and implementation of 18 month plan to refocus logistics on meeting critical supply needs while reducing costs and increasing customer service ratings.
    - Improved metrics for customer service by 19%, cost-to-ship by 22%, and on-time delivery by 54% while measurably raising morale.
    - Led efforts which created 4 mobile quality task forces with 10-12 members each to develop new protocols, prevent bottlenecks, and instill culture of accountability.
    - Identified and increased resources to meet 17 new critical supply needs.
- Launched new six sigma program in 19 departments, resulting in 242 Kaizens and other initiatives over 15 months which reduced costs by a total of $12.4M, led cultural change to a continuous improvement philosophy, and developed 64 high potential managers.

Purchasing and Materials Management

- Saved $71M over 2 years by bundling contracts with trusted suppliers. Involved all levels of purchasing staff in project planning and execution, integrating efforts with launch of Six Sigma program and "Arm Our Airmen" campaign.
- Saved $11M+ in waste, processing time, and warehousing by introducing new ERP system for SAC supply parts. System currently being considered for organization-wide use.
    - *Researched* – Explored best options and developed 214 page proposal to HQ.
    - *Advocated* – Sponsored, presented, and defended proposal to initially hostile senior management committee. Won over committee members via extensive data analysis, pilot program results, and respectful but tenacious encouragement for green light.
    - *Implemented* – Led 21 member task force which managed 7 month conversion and retrained 550+ staff in 31 buildings. Completed project on-time and under budget.
    - *Customized* – Oversaw 3 separate efforts to customize, integrate, and adjust ERP, prioritizing open conversations, "no-excuses" problem resolution, and positive mutual support. CIO said conversion was "smoothest he had ever witnessed."
- Led culture change to prioritize relationship-building with top 100 vendors. Personally spoke with each vendor, visited 14 on "hot list," and personally led cultural change by base-wide visible actions and words. Efforts improved turnaround time for emergency orders from average of 8 to 2.5 days, set stage for cost reduction via bundling, and promoted teamwork at all levels.

Employee Engagement

- Co-developed comprehensive employee engagement strategy which keyed on breaking down cultural divisions between officer-managers and NCO-managers and promoting cross-functional collaboration at all levels. Productivity of 900+ employee operation increased by 14%+ over 2 year period and managers self-reported "collaboration" replacing "control" by 2-to-1 as most effective conflict management technique.
- Led introduction of enhanced health and wellness program which required each employee to meet more rigorous fitness and health standards through highly flexible personal action plans and coaching. Sick days down 40% and quarterly morale ratings up by 18%.
- Teamed with HQ analysts, consultants, and peer in charge of Enlisted Services to develop ongoing, custom employee engagement program, addressing unmet professional development and personal family needs at 2 locations. During year 3 of program, promotions increased by 54 or 61% and productivity at 1 location increased 15%.

Chief Operations Executive - Readiness | *Brigadier General*

Co-developed and led "Top Flight" program to cut costs and improve readiness.
Selected to reduce operations costs without impacting readiness, working out of Pentagon HQ. Took initiative to "raise the bar," making improvements to already high levels of readiness.

- Saved $8M in operations costs by reducing non-essential staff by 92 positions and negotiating intra-agency agreement to cover necessary tasks. Saved additional $3M+ by focusing only on level 1 and 2 readiness priorities.
- Improved readiness by 21%, resulting in highest level in 6 years
- Led transformation of culture to promote ongoing readiness and Six Sigma projects.
- Developed template from "Top Flight" program to be used across DOD operations. Presented program to Academy of Military Best Practices as keynote speaker.
- Trained and mentored 11 "Top Flight" senior leaders to continue program at their sites.

Senior Manager – Air Intelligence Liaison | *Colonel*

Selected to new role to increase collaboration between operations and intelligence.
Spearheaded initiative which increased communication and teamwork between operations at the Pentagon and the Air Intelligence Command in Anytown, OH. Took initiative to involve all levels of Air Intelligence group in both quantitative and qualitative needs assessment. Realized noticeable easing of tensions and increased sharing of data within 4 months.

Director – Quality of Operations | *Lt. Colonel*

Improved safety, readiness, and quality at Anytown, AL location.
Led continuous improvement efforts at 2,350+ staff base, turning around sub-par performance on 12 of 14 operations metrics over 22 month period to achieve all 14 metrics being rated at either excellent or outstanding. Overcame initial pushback by involving line supervisors / NCOs and leveraging high level of professional pride within support and maintenance staff.

EDUCATION

HBS BUSINESS SCHOOL, RGQ UNIVERSITY, Anytown, MA
Executive MBA with concentration in Logistics
MS Finance and Cost Accounting

GFH ACADEMY, Anytown, CO
BSEE

SELECT HONORS

Air Force Cross
Awarded for extraordinary heroism in combat just prior to Operation Python. During surprise enemy assault on diplomatic motorcade - directed Medevac rescue, called in close air support, and remained behind for 3 hours until reinforcements encircled enemy positions.

Distinguished Service Medal
Awarded for exceptionally meritorious service related to total overhaul and reorganization of logistics and purchasing at CO location and 8 other sites which saved $89M+, created ongoing efficiencies, cut waste, and created culture of continuous improvement.

4 Silver Stars
Awarded for various achievements during Gulf War, including two-time Ace, heroism in close combat support of supply task force, and participating in rescue of special operations forces.

PATENTS

Patent US#00000000: Modification to air intake on KKL jet propulsion systems.

Patent US#00000000: Enhancement to aerodynamic drag reduction device.

SPENCER S. SAMPLE

760 AGABRE STREET
ANYTOWN, CA 00000

000-000-0000
SSAMPLE@QQQSAMPLEWEBSITE.COM

Motivated to utilize high level of technical avionics expertise in private sector, following versatile career and extensive training related to maintaining public sector search and rescue aircraft. Takes initiative to go "above and beyond" in realizing highest readiness and safety levels. Completes tasks in timely fashion and achieves quality standards. Functions well in both lead and autonomous roles. Eager to learn new skills and methods. Demonstrated critical thinking ability. Core strengths:

Avionics Technical Troubleshooting

Proven expertise with various guidance and control systems, including the HG 171, FulWheel Pro 2, and NNG-21. Recognized for near-perfect readiness record and highest quality and safety ratings. Adapts easily to shifting priorities. *Efficiently and completely fixes root problems.*

Teamwork and Supervision

Experienced in relating to diverse individual motivators. Known for ability to bring together heterogeneous groups, build esprit-de-corps, and realize a high functioning team. Interacts easily and communicates effectively across functions. *Believes in success or failure as a team.*

EXPERIENCE

UNITED STATES COAST GUARD   2001 - present

Supervised team of 12 full-time service technicians and coordinated 25 part-time reserve staff to realize 99.4% readiness of 11 emergency and rescue aircraft. Consistently recognized for technical proficiency and best-practices leadership; promoted through various maintenance roles.

Senior Avionics Technician

- Authored 11 page training and technical orientation manual which established guidelines for onboarding new hires in 50% less time. Designed job shadowing approach to training as most efficient method to reach required competency levels. Guidelines adopted at 7 other facilities.
- Reorganized project workflow and introduced "accountability buddy" system, allowing engine and other overhaul project times to be reduced from an average of 17 days to 6 days.
- Managed $170K annual maintenance operations budget, including creation and use of Excel spreadsheets to accurately track and forecast 143 line items on monthly basis.
- Achieved highest quarterly safety ratings in all 7 ratings categories over 5 year period.
- Coached, developed, and trained 75+ staff over 6 year period at 3 facilities, including rapid deployment technicians. Mentored several staff who were promoted into management roles.

Aircraft Maintenance Lead

- Earned recognition for aircraft achieving 98% readiness under conditions often requiring nearly 18 of 24 hours daily use during certain months of the year. Performed technical troubleshooting related to mechanical and avionics issues with 3 different types of aircraft.
- Teamed with 3 co-workers to complete 2 month project involving extensive re-wire modifications to 42 aircraft at 6 locations. Efforts avoided $147K in contractor fees.
- Collaborated cross functionally to expedite parts and information flow.
- Analyzed and isolated problems, researched best solutions, and completed repairs.

EDUCATION

AS, Engineering and Avionics Technology, UBV Community College, Anytown, TX

TECHNICAL TRAINING

Flight Controls and Recorder	GPS and Compass	Turbine Overhaul
Electronics Troubleshooting	Control Calibration	JIT Inventory KL System
LN-9 Inertial Navigation	Digital Autopilot	Prevention of Collisions

SHAWN S. SAMPLE
4 COSGROVE STREET, ANYTOWN, FL 00000
SSAMPLE@WYUENGINEERING.EDU | 000.000.0000 | WWW.SSAMPLEDESIGNPORTFOLIO.COM

Motivated BSME with proven work ethic and ability to solve complex technical problems. Background includes software support, training, and design. Effective in team, individual contributor, and team lead roles. Appreciates need for cross-functional cooperation. Focused exceeding expectations of internal customers. Skilled at quantitative analysis. Core competencies include:

PROJECT ENGINEERING / PROTOTYPING

Training in development of new product features, prototyping, solid modeling / 3D and 2D CAD, managing RFP writing and vendor selection, collaborating with consultants, and writing reports.

SOFTWARE

Excel Macros, Pro Engineer Wildfire 4.0, SolidWorks, Dassault Compiler ADV, MatLab, MS Project and Access Math CAD, HTML, Visual Basic 2013, SafetyLink, C++ Vector, and ViscosityPlus 2.0.

EDUCATION

UNIVERSITY OF WQS, Anytown, IN

BS Mechanical Engineering *with minor in Project Engineering*, May 2014.

Engineers Beyond Our Borders – Completed 4 month irrigation equipment project in Haiti with team of 5 student engineers resulting in crop irrigation for 325 acres and 82 farms.

Environmental DAX Pumping Capstone Project – Designed and prototyped cost-effective pump and attachment platform for separating petroleum refinery waste.

Laboratory Assistant and Volunteer Physics Tutor.

Intramurals: Rugby 2010-2012, Squash 2011-2012, and Lacrosse 2013.

WQS-on-Radio 00.0 FM Station Manager and Disc Jockey.

EXPERIENCE

NBV ROBOTICS, Anytown, IN   2013-2014

Project Intern

- Assigned to 12 person consulting group which explored market potential for a robotic lawn maintenance system and reviewed 140+ related patents. Performed market research, took meeting notes, interviewed 3 government scientists, and organized 62 page final report.
- Developed and implemented 22 question survey to gauge market potential among 151 lawn care supply companies and large commercial landscapers in IL, IN, and OH.

TLL CONSULTING SOFTWARE, Anytown, IL   Summers 2012 and 2013

Assistant Project Engineer

- Assisted in the design of new features for TL-C Hyku Suite 3.0, contributing to 9 upgrades and designing improvements to synch with industry products. Completed 1,200+ code revisions.
- Co-led a kaizen for the R&D group which resulted in streamlining prototyping to improve process efficiencies by 17%, reduce scrap by 8%, and boost usability.

RDS CLIMATE CONTROL, Anytown, IL 2008-2012

HVAC Technician Apprentice

- Teamed with 3 technicians to perform repairs and installations of commercial heating and HVAC systems. Provided field support and troubleshooting on the phone and in the field.

SAM S. SAMPLE
10 HANSCOM LANE
ANYTOWN, CA 00000

000.000.0000
ssample@sampleuniversity.edu
LinkedIn.com/in/ssample

Entrepreneurial Microbiology major with proven research and marketing skill sets. Seeking research or startup opportunity which leverages new technologies and techniques. Takes initiative to realize creative and team solutions to complex problems. Competencies include:

- Laboratory Research
- Market Analysis
- Team Projects

Education

PLD RESEARCH UNIVERSITY, Anytown, CA

BS Microbiology, Minors in Entrepreneurship and Marketing. 3.62 GPA. May 2014.

Bio-Reactor Design Competition - GXC College, Cambridge, MA, 2012. Co-led student team which presented 3 designs, specification sheets, models, and marketing portfolio to panel of bio-engineering start-up executives and venture capitalists. 4th place out of 31 university teams.

Biology Student Start Ups Organization / BSSUO – 3 College Exchange, 2011-2014. Served on 5 person executive committee of newly formed student organization focused on vetting new bio-business ideas. Involved with monthly meetings and 4-5 field trips per semester for 35+ members.

Internships and Research Experience

HVQ COMPANY, Anytown, CA   2013-2014
Project Intern
- Explored feasibility and potential cultural impact of introducing six sigma principles into R&D, materials management, and marketing departments. Co-wrote 7 page implementation plan.

KLC FEDERAL NEW TECHNOLOGIES CENTER, Anytown, CA and Alexandria, VA   2012
New Technologies Marketing Intern
- Supported 2 teams in 3+ month reviews of potentially marketable technologies related to pharmaceuticals and vaccine applications. Developed marketing models, plans, usability indexes, ROI potential for commercial applications, and patent options.

PLD RESEARCH UNIVERSITY – *Professor Sippe Sample*, Anytown, CA   Summers 2012 and 2013
Researcher and Teaching Assistant
- Involved with research and summer institute teaching for leading PLD researcher, focusing on cell culture and passaging in the lab, as well as design of new cell transfer technologies.

Work Experience

KSZ LABORATORY EQUIPMENT SALES, Anytown, CA   Summer 2011
Customer Service Specialist
- Suggested changes to database and tracking system with 4,300+ customer accounts. Adopted improvements resulted in decreasing support wait times by 25%+ and easier notations.
- Received and placed new orders, invoiced, reviewed weekly orders, removed bottlenecks by teaming with warehouse staff, and resolved complaints. Completed 40-60+ calls per day.

SAMPLE FAMILY CATTLE RANCH, Anytown, WY   Summers 2008-2010
Ranch Laborer
- Performed variety of functions on family's ranch with 4,400+ head of cattle, including feeding, herding, vaccinating, repairing equipment and facilities, and transporting livestock.

SOPHIA S. SAMPLE, CMA   000.000.0000
133 HILBRAKE COURT   ssample@sampleschool.edu
ANYTOWN, CA 00000   LinkedIn.com/in/ssample

Certified Medical Assistant and Registered Phlebotomy Technician

Patient-centric and versatile CMA seeks to join family or pediatrics practice. Proven follow through and on-time completion of tasks in fast-paced environments. Takes appropriate initiative. Committed to continual professional learning. **Certifications: CMA / AAMA and RPT / AMT.**

Clinical Expertise - Trusted to provide error-free direct patient care, including clinical and diagnostic procedures, drawing blood, administering injections, performing EKGs, and assisting with preparation for exams and surgical procedures. *Provides clinical care with precision and efficiency.*

Administrative Experience - Experienced with medical billing and coding, scheduling, 82 wpm data entry, speaking to insurance companies, and resolving complaints. Extensive Excel and systems knowledge. Understanding of JCAHO and HIPPA. *Completes tasks quickly and accurately.*

Patient Satisfaction Focus - Recognized by medical and office staff for ability to relate to all patient personalities under all kinds of circumstances. *Diffuses tense situations with grace.*

EDUCATION

QQE COMMUNITY COLLEGE, Anytown, PA
Associates of Science, Medical Assisting – CAAHEP accredited. 3.94 GPA. May 2014.
Took initiative to complete additional 90 hours of direct patient care beyond required 185 hour practicum. Select Courses: Pharmacology, Medical Terminology, Ethics, Software Applications, and Medical Billing.

ZXZ COMMUNITY COLLEGE, Anytown, WV
Certificate, Phlebotomy Training Program – AMT approved. February 2010.
Completed 120 hour clinical externship and 10 week program. 2nd highest test score of 32 students in class.

HEALTH CARE EXPERIENCE

NCH MEDICAL OFFICE, Anytown, PA   2012 - 2013

Medical Assistant Intern - Clinical Practicum
- Created Excel macro, on own initiative, which streamlined billing process and freed up 5-6 staff hours per week while providing additional accountability check to improve accuracy.
- Served 15-25 patients per week in busy, 5 MD practice. Prepared patients for procedures and exams, drew blood, explained post-visit instructions, and compiled notes.
- Completed insurance reimbursements, billing, and medical coding during clinical breaks.

VRD COMMUNITY HEALTH CENTER *division of BXC Hospital*, Anytown, WV   2010 - 2011

Phlebotomy Technician
- Performed venipuncture, skin punctures, specimen processing, and lab liaison duties in multi-practice group encompassing urology, OB/GYN, and family medicine. Assisted 30+ patients during 20 hours per week part-time position. Prepared patients for urological procedures.

CUSTOMER SERVICE EXPERIENCE

GDS DEPARTMENT STORE, Anytown, WV   2006 - 2011

Customer Service Desk Specialist
Cashier
- Managed Customer Service Desk on weekend and evening shifts, in addition to cashier duties. Resolved all complaints and returns smoothly and de-escalated potentially significant conflicts.
- Recognized for accuracy and speed of transactions during peak check-out. Averaged processing 16+ customer purchases per hour. Award for being error-free 24 consecutive days.

STEVE S. SAMPLE

1355 COVENTREE DRIVE 000.000.0000
ANYTOWN, VA 00000 ssample@samplecollege.edu

Quality focused CNC programmer and machinist with versatile training, including milling machines, lathes, jigs and fixtures, tool room, CAD/CAM, engineering design, and ECOs. Completes tasks on time and to tight tolerance quality expectations. Keeps work area organized, clean, and setup for next shift. Highly motivated to learn new machining and manufacturing techniques. Collaborates and communicates easily with all personality types. Training and knowledge includes:

MACHINING	ENGINEERING	DESIGN
• CNC Programming	• Statistical Process Control	• SolidWorks
• ANSI Y 15.4 Certified	• Engineering Change Orders	• CADD Max 3.3
• Machine Operation	• Finite Element Analysis	• Axel Blueprinting
• Tolerances to .0001	• Mechanical Vibrations	• V-Prototyping

EDUCATION

GCX COMMUNITY COLLEGE, Anytown, VA
  AAS Precision Machining - *Engineering Design Concentration*. Expected December 2014.
   Robotic Carry-Cart Team Project – Machined 30+ parts, co-designed, and assisted 6 student team with assembly of 1:5 scale robotic transport device for use in cold storage facilities.

AFD STATE VOCATIONAL TECHNICAL CENTER, Anytown, VA
  Certificate – *ANSI Y 15.4*. May 2012.
  Certificate - *CNC Machine Operator*. November 2011.

EXPERIENCE

WRE MACHINE SHOP, Anytown, VA 2013-2014
  CNC Intern
  - Assisted machinists in 6 month project to overhaul 4 CNC modified Bridgeports.
  - Supported project engineer and machinists in building conveyor system for milling machine and convert 12 other machines to MQL.

FCS AEROSPACE ENGINES, Anytown, VA 2013
  Manufacturing Intern
  - Learned how to troubleshoot common challenges associated with Advanced Yoolies and Mazaks to optimize uptime. Helped toolroom supervisor re-assemble Yoolie feeder.
  - Setup tools and material for operators. Replaced coolant, removed scrap, cleaned and performed simple maintenance on 10+ CNC machines.

ORP SPECIALTY MACHINING JOB SHOP, Anytown, VA 2011-2014
  Lathe and Milling Machine Operator
  - Operated 7 different milling machines and lathes, including Cincinnati and Mori Seiki lathes, Hitachi mills, and Matsuura mills with both Yasnac and Fanuc controllers. Trained on watch lathe, toolroom support, cutting tools, and materials supply.
  - Wrote and proofed CNC programs, interpreting blueprints and instructions.
  - Assisted in 2 week move to new floor layout, while keeping production at 90%+.

Selected Sources

Most of these sources in this incomplete list are not connected directly to this book but have, instead, provided fuel for my thought and concept development over the years. A number of these books are available in a more recent version than the ones listed here. Each book can be found on my office shelf and I often recommend these titles to clients. This list is intended as much to serve as a resource starting point for the reader as it is to insure I give credit to those who helped inform my own professional development.

Alessandra, Anthony J., and Michael J. O'Connor. *The Platinum Rule: Discover the Four Basic Business Personalities--and How They Can Lead You to Success.* New York: Warner, 1996.

Beatty, Richard H. *The Five-minute Interview: A Job Hunter's Guide to a Successful Interview.* Hoboken, NJ: John Wiley, 2002.

Bregman, Peter. *18 Minutes: Find Your Focus, Master Distraction, and Get the Right Things Done.* New York: Business Plus, 2011.

Breitbarth, Wayne. *The Power Formula for LinkedIn Success: Kick-start Your Business, Brand, and Job Search.* Austin, TX: Greenleaf Book Group, 2011.

Burka, Jane B., and Lenora M. Yuen. *Procrastination: Why You Do It, What to Do about It.* Reading, MA: Addison Wesley Pub., 1983.

Chapman, Gary D., and Paul E. White. *The 5 Languages of Appreciation in the Workplace: Empowering Organizations by Encouraging People.* Chicago: Northfield Pub., 2011.

Clifton, Jim. *The Coming Jobs War: What Every Leader Must Know about the Future of Job Creation.* New York, NY: Gallup, 2011.

Dawson, Kenneth M., and Sheryl N. Dawson. *Job Search: The Total System*. Hoboken, NJ: Wiley, 1996.

Enelow, Wendy S., and Louise Kursmark. *Expert Resumes for Military-to-civilian Transitions*. Indianapolis, IN: JIST Works, 2010.

Ferrazzi, Keith. *Who's Got Your Back: The Breakthrough Program to Build Deep, Trusting Relationships That Create Success-- and Won't Let You Fail*. New York: Broadway, 2009.

Figler, Howard E., and Richard Nelson. Bolles. *The Career Counselor's Handbook*. Berkeley, CA: Ten Speed, 1999.

Fiore, Neil A. *The Now Habit: A Strategic Program for Overcoming Procrastination and Enjoying Guilt-free Play*. New York: Tarcher/Penguin, 2007.

Fisher, Roger, William Ury, and Bruce Patton. *Getting to Yes: Negotiating Agreement without Giving in*. New York, NY: Penguin, 1991.

Goleman, Daniel. *The Brain and Emotional Intelligence: New Insights*. Northampton, MA: More Than Sound, 2011.

Heath, Chip, and Dan Heath. *Made to Stick: Why Some Ideas Survive and Others Die*. New York: Random House, 2007.

Karrass, Chester Louis. *Give & Take: The Complete Guide to Negotiating Strategies and Tactics*. New York: Crowell, 1974.

Littler, Dale. *The Blackwell Encyclopedia of Management*. Malden, MA: Blackwell Pub., 2005.

Levinson, Jay Conrad., Jeannie Levinson, and Amy Levinson. *Guerrilla Marketing: Easy and Inexpensive Strategies for Making Big Profits from Your Small Business*. Boston, MA: Houghton Mifflin, 2007.

Lucht, John. *Rites of Passage at $100,000 to $1 Million: Your Insider's Lifetime Guide to Executive Job-changing and Faster Career Progress*. New York: Viceroy, 2007

Lynch, Liz. *Smart Networking: Attract a following in Person and Online*. New York: McGraw-Hill, 2009.

Myers, Isabel Briggs., and Peter B. Myers. *Gifts Differing*. Palo Alto, CA: Consulting Psychologists, 1980.

Patterson, Kerry. *Change Anything: The New Science of Personal Success*. New York: Business Plus, 2011.

Shatkin, Laurence. *150 Best Recession-proof Jobs*. Indianapolis, IN: JIST Works, 2009.

Schawbel, Dan. *Me 2.0: 4 Steps to Building Your Future*. New York: Kaplan Pub., 2010.

Sujansky, Joanne Genova., and Jan Ferri-Reed. *Keeping the Millennials: Why Companies Are Losing Billions in Turnover to This Generation--and What to Do about It*. Hoboken, NJ: John Wiley & Sons, 2009.

Tieger, Paul D., and Barbara Barron-Tieger. *Do What You Are: Discover the Perfect Career for You through the Secrets of Personality Type*. New York: Little, Brown, 2007.

Troutman, Kathryn K., and Laura Sachs. Hills. *Ten Steps to a Federal Job: Navigating the Federal Job System, Writing Federal Resumes, KSAs and Cover Letters with a Mission*. Baltimore, MD: Resume Place, 2002.

Watkins, Michael. *The First 90 Days: Proven Strategies for Getting up to Speed Faster and Smarter*. Boston, MA: Harvard Business Review, 2013.

Index

This serves as a quick reference and not a complete index. It is intended to rapidly connect the reader with the most useful information on a particular topic or area of subject matter.

A

Abbreviations, 77
Accomplishments in resume, 66
Acronyms, 106
Action verbs, 128-129
Addendums, 211-214
Adjectives, using, 77
Aligning with the market, 46
Anxiety, 9
Applicant Tracking, 229-230
Authenticity, 11-12
Availability of resume, 273

B

Back up your brand, 48
Barriers, 9
Barron, Barbara, 20
Behaviors, 20-23
"Before" and "after" example of resume 4-6
Bold, using, 75
Branding, 39-59
    Alternative approaches, 54
    Consistency, 57-58
    Customizing too much, 58-59
    Differentiators, 182
        Exercise, 49-51
    FAQ, 41-45
    Testing your brand, 55
Break the rules, 282-284

Bullets, 119-131
    Content, 120
    Guerilla tactics for writing, 130
    How to write, 126-131
    Samples, 121-124
    Accomplishments, 124-126
Business cards, 284-287

C

Capital letters, using, 75
Certifications, 150-151
Changes in your skill set, 16
Close the deal, x
Collaborate-competitors, 329-331
Combining sections, 156-158
Community activities, 154-155
Company title, 111-112
Contingency recruiters, 300-301
"Core Hiring Motives," 239-255
    Customizing, 243-248
    Identifying, 240-242
    In interviewing, 351-352
    In networking, 253
    Uncovering hidden, 252-255
"Core Strengths," 182-186
    Determining, 191-193
    Formatting, 190
Credibility, 11-12
Customizing, 219

D

Dates of employment, 75
Delivering alternatives, 278-280
Descriptions of companies, 115-116
Don't use a resume when, 280-281
DISC, 20
Do What You Are, 20

E

Education section, 133-145
    Importance-education, 133-135
        Abbreviating degree, 136-138
        Minors, 138-139
        Partially completed, 139-140
Elevator pitch, 324-328
Employment agencies, 170
Enlow, Wendy, xiv
Experience section, 109
    How far back to go, 70
Expert Resumes for Military, xiv

F

Failures, 19
Federal Resume Guidebook, xiv
Fear of/barriers to writing, 9
Federal resume, xiv
Finding job openings, 308-310
    Limiting online, 305-306, 311
Finding recruiting firms, 302-303
Fit, customizing to, 224
Font, 73
Formatting, 72-76

G

Gaps in Employment, 161-167
Get a resume noticed, 290-293
Get a resume noticed, 290-293
Get noticed, x
Getting organized, 10
Goals, 32-35
Good jobs, ix
GPA, 141-142
Great recession, ix

H

Hard skills, 171
Heading, 87
    Email, 89
    LinkedIn address, 90
    Small capital letters, 89
    Street address, 90-91
Hiring Manager, 282-284
How far back to go, 70, 110
How you will write, 76-77
Hyperlinks – remove, 90

I

Information bank, 85
Interviewing, 335-
    Core hiring motives, 351-352
    Example stories, 340; 353-357
    Interview-resume, 336-337
    In-person interview, 350
    Phone screen, 338-339
    Phone interview, 339
    Questions, types of, 348-350
    Thank you follow up, 356-357
Intimidating, 8-9
Involve others, 37
Italics, using, 75

J
Job ads, analyzing, 230-232

K
Key words and phrases, 233-236
Kursmark, Louise, xiv

L
Length of resume, 74
Letters of Reference, 202-204
LinkedIn, 294-296

M
Mailing a resume, 276-277
Market interest, 47
MBTI/Myers-Briggs, 20
Military service, 152-153

N
Negotiating, 359-369
    Post-negotiations, 368-369
    Pre-negotiations, 360-361
Networking, 313-333
    Daily goal, 316-317
    Elevator pitch, 324-328
    Email outreach, 322-323
    Follow up, 316-317
    Tracking contacts, 319-322
    Ranking contacts, 321
Number of pages, 74
Numbers in the resume, 66

O
Objective, 95
"One Resume," 181-193
Onboarding, 368-369
ONET, 173
Online applications, 68
Organize, 10

P
Paper, 253
Pareto's rule, 184
Pdf format, 78
Perception is reality, 82
Periods, using, 77
Personality, 20-23
Personality Inventory, 21-23
Portfolios, 199
Position title, 112-115
Posting to job boards, 275-276
Printed copies, 272
Professional Branding, 39-59
Profile, 93-101
Protect Your Brand, 40

R
Recruiters, 297-303
Reference List, 205-207
    "Targeted," 208-210
Reputation online, 306-308
Research, 225-229
Results, 222
Resume rules, 63-79
    Myths, 67-71
    No-nos, 71-72
    Phobia, 8
    Truths, 65-67
Resume writers, 175-179
Retained recruiters, 301-302
RIASEC, 20

S
Sections, 83
Self-assessment, 15-37
Self-assessment summary, 36

S

Shoebox office, 314-315
Staffing Firms, 299-300
Stories, interviewing, 353-356
Strengths, 18
Strong assessment, 20
Successes, 19
Summary, 93 *see Profile*
Sweet spot of the resume, 186

T

Take away their pain, 222
Technical Abilities/Skills, 28-29
    Writing skills, 103-107
    As core strengths, 187-189
Ten Steps to a Federal Job, xiv
Testing, 344-346
Tieger, Paul, 20
Title, 97-100
Training section, 148-149
Transferrable skills, 24-27
Troutman, Kathryn, xiv

U

Using your resume, 271-287

V

Verb tense, using, 77
Video resume, 172
Volunteer activities, 154-155

W

White space, 74
Word, use to write resume, 78
Work samples, 196-198, 200-201

Y

"You" in the resume, 13

About the Author

Greg has more than 15 years of experience in career coaching, resume-writing, outplacement and consulting for scores of companies. Previously an executive/retained recruiter, he has helped write thousands of resumes and has trained or coached more than 8,000 individuals in job-search techniques. Greg has also published *You, On Paper: Expert Help on How to Write a Resume*.

Greg has created unique career management concepts and has also done work related to authenticity and masks, capacity and resiliency, locus of control, self-efficacy, and the need for relationship. Greg is informed mainly by humanist thinking, including the work of Carl Rogers, Parker Palmer, and his mother, Marijane Fall.

When not working or traveling, you can find Greg at home in southern Maine with his wife, 2 children, 2 cats, and 1 dog. Greg and his family feel blessed to live near ocean and mountains where they can be active in the outdoors.

Every day Greg practices gratitude and unconditional positive regard. His energy is marked by positivity, genuine caring, forgiveness, and continuous learning.

Greg can be reached at greg@jobsearchrescue.com

www.ingramcontent.com/pod-product-compliance
Lightning Source LLC
Chambersburg PA
CBHW080453110426
42742CB00017B/2877